The Story of Napoleon

Harold Wheeler

Alpha Editions

This edition published in 2024

ISBN : 9789362923905

Design and Setting By
Alpha Editions
www.alphaedis.com
Email - info@alphaedis.com

As per information held with us this book is in Public Domain. This book is a reproduction of an important historical work. Alpha Editions uses the best technology to reproduce historical work in the same manner it was first published to preserve its original nature. Any marks or number seen are left intentionally to preserve its true form.

Contents

Foreword ....- 1 -

CHAPTER I Napoleon the Boy (1769–1778) ....- 6 -

CHAPTER II The Schooldays of Napoleon (1779–1784) ....- 11 -

CHAPTER III Napoleon as Officer and Author (1784–1791) ....- 18 -

CHAPTER IV Napoleon and the Corsican Volunteers (1791–1792) ....- 28 -

CHAPTER V The Eve of the Reign of Terror (1792–1793) ....- 33 -

CHAPTER VI Napoleon's First Fight with the English (1793) ....- 41 -

CHAPTER VII Napoleon the Soldier of Fortune (1794–1796) ....- 47 -

CHAPTER VIII "The Spark of Great Ambition" (1796) ....- 54 -

CHAPTER IX The Italian Campaign (1796–1797) ....- 60 -

CHAPTER X The Expedition to Egypt (1798) ....- 68 -

CHAPTER XI From Cairo to Fréjus (1798–1799) ....- 75 -

CHAPTER XII How Napoleon Seized the Reins of Government (1799) ....- 81 -

CHAPTER XIII The Passage of the Alps (1799–1801) ....- 85 -

CHAPTER XIV Blessings of Peace (1801–1803) ....- 96 -

CHAPTER XV The Dawn of the Empire (1803–1804) ....- 102 -

CHAPTER XVI The Threatened Invasion of England and its Sequel (1804–1805) ....- 108 -

CHAPTER XVII The War of the Third Coalition (1805–6) ....- 115 -

CHAPTER XVIII The Prussian Campaign (1806) ....- 123 -

CHAPTER XIX The Polish Campaign (1806–7) ....- 133 -

CHAPTER XX Friedland and Tilsit (1807) ....- 138 -

CHAPTER XXI Napoleon's Commercial War with Great Britain (1807) ....- 144 -

CHAPTER XXII The Genesis of the Peninsular War (1808) ....- 152 -

CHAPTER XXIII Glory at Erfurt and Humiliation in Spain (1808–1809) ....- 163 -

CHAPTER XXIV The Austrian Campaign (1809) .... - 173 -

CHAPTER XXV The Austrian Campaign—continued (1809) .... - 184 -

CHAPTER XXVI The War in Poland and Tyrol (1809) .... - 190 -

CHAPTER XXVII A Broken Friendship and what it Brought (1810–1812) .... - 199 -

CHAPTER XXVIII The Russian Campaign (1812) .... - 209 -

CHAPTER XXIX The Triumphal Entry into Moscow—and after (1812) .... - 218 -

CHAPTER XXX The March of Humiliation (1812) .... - 225 -

CHAPTER XXXI The Beginning of the End—The Leipzig Campaign (1813) .... - 231 -

CHAPTER XXXII The Conquest of the Conqueror (1814–1821) .... - 239 -

FOREWORD

THERE is no more marvellous story in human history than that of Napoleon I., Emperor of the French. His career is one long demonstration of the reality of the proverb, "Truth is stranger than fiction." So fascinating are the details of a life in which so much was attempted and accomplished that many thousands of volumes have been published dealing with its various phases. The demand is by no means exhausted, the supply continuous, as witness the present work. Busy pens are still employed in reviewing the almost superhuman activities of the once obscure Corsican, whose genius for war and conquest upset many a throne, secured for him the Overlordship of Europe, and eventually consigned him to an island prison. Indeed, there seems little likelihood of a lull in interest while the chief source of instruction and amusement of human nature is humanity—in other words itself. Most of us are content to be pupils in the school of experience, willing to sit at the feet of such a master as Napoleon, and learn the lessons he has to teach. The result cannot be other than profitable.

Napoleon has been dead nearly ninety years, but the dazzling brilliancy of his exploits has left a rich afterglow which enables us to get a much less distorted view of him than were our forefathers who were his contemporaries. A subdued light is more useful than one so strong that it almost blinds. With the former we can see details more distinctly, note faults and flaws if there be any, get a clearer idea of an object in every way. Within living memory the name of Napoleon, particularly in Great Britain, was associated with everything that was base and vile, now we know that he was neither the Borgia of his enemies nor the Arch-Patriot of his friends. Nevertheless it is easier for a sightless person to thread a needle than for the most conscientious historian to arrive at an absolutely just summing-up of the case. The "Memoirs" of those with whom the Emperor was intimately acquainted are seldom impartial; the majority of the writers are either definitely for or against him. Take those of Baron Méneval as a typical example. The author was one of Napoleon's secretaries, and every page of his work is a defence of his master. In the matter of the execution of the Duc d'Enghien, for instance, he takes up the cudgels on behalf of the man who was responsible for the tragedy at Vincennes, boldly stating that "One is forced to admit that Napoleon fulfilled a painful duty, as Head of the Government, and that instead of charging him with a crime, one should rather pity him for having been placed in the necessity of accepting all the odium of an act, the deplorable consequences of which, in the future, his foresight only too clearly pointed out to him."

Far from Napoleon being concerned as to probable political consequences, he asserted it would teach the Bourbons a lesson. On the other hand, the "Memoirs" of Barras, a prominent figure in the French Revolution, might have been of considerable service to us in gathering information as to Bonaparte's early career, had it not been proved beyond question that much he tells us is sheer bare-faced untruth, and he everywhere seeks to belittle the accomplishments of the young soldier.

"Bonaparte, on the 13th of Vendémiaire," he says, "performed no functions but those of an aide-de-camp of mine. I was on horseback, he was on foot; he could not follow my movements. The only order he received from me was to go to the Pont Royal, and to report to me what was taking place. He did not give, and had not to give, a single order, and was seen at only one point of the attack, at the Carrousel. He did not stir from thence; Brune was in command." The statements of Thiébault, Marmont, and many others prove beyond question that Napoleon, and he alone, saved the day.

Books which unduly eulogise or condemn should be read therefore with a certain amount of reserve. Of partisans such as Jung there are many, and they doubtless fulfil a useful purpose provided always that a representative of the other side is given a similar hearing. Lanfrey, whose vitriolic volumes may be perused in English, represents a school of thought which has no place in an age which refuses to listen or to read only of the evil in a man.

Special attention has been paid in the present work to the genesis of Napoleon's career, because it is in what is known as the formative period that we plant the seeds of future success. To-day and to-morrow are inextricably interblended, although we so often fail to appreciate what is assuredly one of the most vital facts of life. Periods of time are no more real boundaries than periods of history, which are merely make-believe divisions for purposes of clearness and reference. Of course, one reign may be more enlightened than another, one Statesman may confer more benefits on his country than his predecessor, but there is always a previous foundation on which to build. Napoleon did not create his vast Empire from nothing. A mosaic-worker who is given a pile of vari-coloured marble chips with which to glorify a cathedral pavement does not disdain the fragments because they are in confusion and appear of little worth. With infinite patience and skill he sorts them into their various grades, then combines them again, but giving each its proper order in the scheme. Presently from apparent chaos he produces a work of beauty. Napoleon came on the scene when the giant upheaval known as the French Revolution had thrown the whole nation out of gear. He brought the scattered masses together, recreated Government and the army, made laws, re-established religion—in a word, led the people back from anarchy and savagery to civilisation and order. Napoleon's true place in history is as an organiser. Conqueror he undoubtedly was, and his overgrown ambition in this direction was the cause of his downfall. Had he chosen to rule France solely all would have been well; neighbouring nations could not have raised legitimate objections. As it was they owe a debt of gratitude to him. Although no part of his scheme to awaken dormant ideals of nationality and of liberty, he unwittingly did so in the archaic Holy Roman Empire, Italy, Spain, and Tyrol, to mention the more important. A century ago, Europe hated the Man of Destiny, and not without cause; to-day, she has every reason, if not to revere his memory, to be thankful for having felt the iron grip of Napoleon. Surgical operations are extremely painful whether individual or national.

Napoleon cannot be called a "good" man in the usually accepted sense of so latitudinarian a word. He was the instigator of more than one political crime, yet he had a heart that could beat for the afflicted; he would say the most unkind and cruel things of Sir Hudson Lowe, to whose care he was committed at St Helena, and play at bears with little Betsy Balcombe during her stay in the same island. So complex a personality must necessarily defy to a great extent the set-square and compasses both of panegyrist and detractor. Guided by no standard code of morality, he created his own, that of expediency. "No name," says Lord Rosebery, "represents so completely and conspicuously dominion, splendour and catastrophe. He raised himself by the use, and ruined himself by the abuse, of superhuman faculties. He was wrecked by the extravagance of his own genius. No less powers than those which had effected his rise could have achieved his fall."

In a book limited to a certain number of pages many phases of a crowded life such as Napoleon's must necessarily receive somewhat scant treatment. It has been found impossible to treat military events in full, but the general outlines of the various campaigns have been given, and the narratives of first-hand authorities quoted whenever practicable. For general reading a description of a battle by a man who was present is always to be preferred to the minute details of the most painstaking student.

As regards authorities, special reference must be made to Volume IX. of the monumental "Cambridge Modern History," Dr J. Holland Rose's just and impartial "Life of Napoleon I.," Sir John Seeley's somewhat disparaging "Short History of Napoleon the First," Mr F. Loraine Petre's masterly studies of the Polish, Prussian, and Austrian campaigns, Sir Archibald Alison's "History of Europe," which has by no means lost its usefulness since more modern research has added to our knowledge of the epoch, Mr Oscar Browning's interesting "Boyhood and Youth of Napoleon, 1769–1793," and Mr Hereford B. George's "Napoleon's Invasion of Russia." A host of other volumes dealing with the same inexhaustible subject which line the shelves of my crowded library have also been utilised, I trust, to good purpose.

When the late Admiral Eden was a senior midshipman he was told by his Admiral that he should accompany him on a visit to the fallen Emperor at St Helena. "We waited for

Napoleon in an outer room," he afterwards told a friend, "and you must imagine how eagerly I expected his entrance. The door was thrown open at last, and in he came. He was short and fat, and nothing very attractive but for his eye! My word, sir, I had never seen anything like it.

"After speaking to the Admiral he turned to me, and then I understood for the first time in my life, what was the meaning of the phrase 'A born ruler of men.' I had been taught to hate the French as I hated the devil; but when Napoleon looked at me there was such power and majesty in his look that if he had bade me lie down that he might walk over me, I would have done it at once, Englishman although I was. The look on Napoleon's face was the revelation of the man and the explanation of his power. He was born to command."

And there you have part of the secret of Napoleon's career.

HAROLD F. B. WHEELER

CHAPTER I
NAPOLEON THE BOY (1769–1778)

WHENEVER we hear the name of Napoleon mentioned, or see it printed in a book, it is usually in connection with a hard-fought victory on the battlefield. He certainly spent most of his life in the camp, and enjoyed the society of soldiers more than that of courtiers. The thunder of guns, the charge of cavalry, and the flash of bayonets as they glittered in the sun, appealed to him with much the same force as music to more ordinary folk. Indeed, he himself tells us that "the cries of the dying, the tears of the hopeless, surrounded my cradle from the moment of my birth."

We are apt to forget that this mighty conqueror, whom Carlyle calls "our last great man," had a childhood at all. He was born nearly a century and a half ago, on the 15th August 1769 to be exact, in the little town of Ajaccio, the capital of picturesque Corsica. This miniature island rises a bold tree-covered rock in the blue waters of the Mediterranean, fifty miles west of the coast of Italy. It had been sold to France by the Republic of Genoa the previous year, but the inhabitants had fought for their independence with praiseworthy determination. Then civil war broke out, and the struggle finally ended three months before the birth of the boy who was to become the ruler of the conquering nation. The Corsicans had their revenge in time, although in a way very different from what they could have expected.

Letizia Bonaparte, Napoleon's mother, was as beautiful as she was energetic, and her famous son never allowed anyone to speak ill of her. "My excellent mother," said he, not long before his death, "is a woman of courage and of great talent ... she is capable of doing everything for me," and he added that the high position which he attained was due largely to the careful way in which she brought him up.

"It is to my mother, to her good precepts and upright example, that I owe my success and any great thing I have accomplished," he averred, while to a general he remarked, "My mother was a superb woman, a woman of ability and courage." A truly great man always speaks well of his mother.

Napoleon was Letizia's fourth child, two having died in infancy, while Joseph, the surviving son, was still unable to toddle when the latest addition to the family was in his cradle. His father was a happy-go-lucky kind of man of good ancestry, a lawyer by profession, who on the landing of the French had resigned the pen for the sword. He enlisted in the army raised by Pascal Paoli to defend the island, for the Corsicans were then a very warlike people and much sought after as soldiers, and it is supposed by some that he acted as Paoli's secretary. It is certain that the patriot showed him marked favour, which was never repaid.

When Paoli and his loyal band were forced to make their escape to the hospitable shores of England, Charles Bonaparte meekly accepted the pardon offered to those who would lay down their arms and acknowledge Louis XV. of France as their King. After events proved the wisdom of his choice, but scarcely justified his action.

The house in which the Bonaparte family lived at Ajaccio is still standing, but has been patched up and repaired so frequently that probably little of the original fabric remains. It now belongs to the ex-Empress Eugénie, the consort of Napoleon's ill-fated nephew who is known to history as Napoleon III. You would not call it a mansion, and yet it contains a spacious ballroom, a large square drawing-room, Charles Bonaparte's study, a dining-room, a nursery, several bedrooms, and a dressing-room. Some of the old furniture is left, namely the Chippendale sofa on which the future Emperor was born, his mother's spinet, and his father's desk. There is also a little etching of Napoleon on horseback by the late Prince Imperial, and one or two statuettes and portraits. In the Town Hall near by is a picture of Letizia which testifies to her good looks—she was known as "the beauty of Ajaccio!"

As a child Napoleon was impetuous, self-confident, and apt to be bad-tempered. If a playmate did something which displeased him the culprit was rewarded with kicks, bites and scratches. Letizia did her best to break him of this bad habit, with little success, for he resented interference to the end of his days. When he was Emperor he used to tell an anecdote of his early life which proves that his mother did more than scold him when he got into mischief.

There were some fig-trees in the garden attached to his home, and Napoleon was very fond of climbing them. Letizia, fearing an accident, forbade him to do so. "One day, however," he relates, "when I was idle, and at a loss for something to do, I took it in my head to long for some of those figs. They were ripe; no one saw me, or could know anything of the matter. I made my escape, ran to the tree, and gathered the whole. My appetite being satisfied, I was providing for the future by filling my pockets, when an unlucky gardener came in sight. I was half-dead with fear, and remained fixed on the branch of the tree, where he had surprised me. He wished to seize me and take me to my mother. Despair made me eloquent; I represented my distress, promised to keep away from the figs in future, and he seemed satisfied. I congratulated myself on having come off so well, and fancied that the adventure would never be known; but the traitor told all. The next day my mother wanted to go and gather some figs. I had not left any, there was none to be found: the gardener came, great reproaches followed, and an exposure." The result was a thrashing!

Probably the busy housewife taught Napoleon his letters, assisted by his uncle Joseph Fesch, who was but six years his senior, while from his great uncle, Archdeacon Lucien Bonaparte, he learned a little Bible history. The three "R.'s" were drilled into him by nuns, and as the establishment admitted girls as well as boys, Napoleon took a fancy to one of the former, thereby incurring the ridicule of some of his schoolfellows. They were never tired of jeering at him with a little rhyme, specially composed for the occasion, to the effect that "Napoleon with his stockings half off makes love to Giacommetta." The translation, of course, does not jingle as in the Corsican patois. It must not be inferred that he was a good-looking or attractive boy. On the contrary, he had a sallow complexion, was invariably untidy, and inclined to be moody.

Later, he went to a more advanced school, and from thence to the seminary of the Abbé Recco. If he was not a brilliant scholar he was certainly more interested in mathematics than is the modern boy in locomotives, and that is admitting a good deal. He also excelled in geography. Both studies proved useful *aides-de-camp* when Napoleon began to master the intricate arts of strategy and tactics. It is on record that when Napoleon was very young he rode on a high-spirited pony to a neighbouring windmill, and after persuading the miller to tell him how much corn it ground in an hour, quietly sat down and worked out the quantity used per day and week. The tyrant then returned to his panic-stricken mother, who had convinced herself that the boy had probably fallen off his fiery steed and been trampled to death.

When opportunity occurred, the youthful Napoleon scribbled sums on the nursery walls and drew crude outlines of soldiers marching in regimental order. A fondness for the open air early manifested itself, and the earnest student would remain out-of-doors for hours at a stretch, provided he was allowed to follow his favourite pursuits without being disturbed. Should his brother dare to interfere when he was working in the little wooden shanty which his thoughtful mother had caused to be erected for him, Napoleon's hasty temper would get the upper hand, and the intruder would be forced to beat a hasty retreat, perhaps in a shower of sticks and stones.

"My brother Joseph," he tells us, "was the one with whom I was oftenest in trouble: he was beaten, bitten, abused. I went to complain before he had time to recover from his confusion. I had need to be on the alert; our mother would have repressed my warlike humour, she would not have put up with my caprices. Her tenderness was allied with severity: she punished, rewarded all alike; the good, the bad, nothing escaped her. My father, a man of sense, but too fond of pleasure to pay much attention to our infancy, sometimes attempted to excuse our faults: 'Let them alone,' she replied, 'it is not your business, it is I who must look after them.' She did, indeed, watch over us with a solicitude unexampled. Every low sentiment, every ungenerous affection was discouraged: she suffered nothing but what was good and elevated to take root in our youthful understandings. She abhorred falsehood, was provoked by disobedience: she passed over none of our faults."

Napoleon's father had no difficulty in deciding what profession to choose for his second son. As for Joseph, he determined that he should enter the priesthood. Napoleon was positive his brother would make a good bishop, and said so.

In this matter of settling the life-work of his boys Charles Bonaparte was helped by the kindly-disposed Marbœuf, one of the two French commissioners appointed by the King to govern Corsica, who frequently visited the house in the Rue St Charles. Napoleon, although only nine years old was now about to enter a larger world, to have an opportunity to appreciate the benefits of education on sounder lines, and to tread the soil of the country which received him as a humble pensioner of the King, and elevated him twenty-five years later to the Imperial throne.

CHAPTER II
THE SCHOOLDAYS OF NAPOLEON
(1779–1784)

IN France there were twelve royal military schools to which a certain number of sons of the poor aristocracy were admitted without payment. Marbœuf was successful in securing this benefit for Napoleon, although his father had to prove to the satisfaction of the authorities that he was without fortune and to present a certificate to the effect that his family had belonged to the nobility for at least four generations. This done, the way was made clear for the boy to begin his first serious studies in the art of warfare. As the Corsicans spoke Italian and knew very little, if anything, of the French language, it was decided that Napoleon should stay for a time with his brother Joseph at the College of Autun so that he might acquire some knowledge of the language both were henceforth to speak. To the end of his days Napoleon never learnt to spell correctly, his pronunciation was oftentimes peculiar, and his writing invariably abominable.

Charles Marie de Bonaparte, duly accompanied by Joseph, Napoleon, Uncle Fesch, and a cousin named Aurelio Varese, set off for the land of their adoption in the middle of December 1778. The good Letizia sobbed bitterly when she parted with her two sons, but there were now several other children to be cared for, which must have consoled her to some extent. The travellers passed through Tuscany, where the beautiful city of Florence left an impression on the plastic mind of the embryo soldier, and a momentary sight of the Grand Duke afforded him intense pleasure. They were fragmentary foretastes of things to come, when Napoleon's troops would overrun the land of the Medici and the scions of royal houses would appreciate a nod or a glance from the now unknown lad whose eyes opened wide with astonishment at the sights and scenes of pre-Revolutionary Europe.

On the 1st January 1779, Autun was reached, and the boys had their first experience of what it means to be hundreds of miles from home and in a country where rugged little Corsica, if mentioned at all, was sneered at, and its inhabitants regarded as scarcely better than savages. Another separation came towards the end of the following April, when Napoleon left for Brienne, now inseparably associated with his name and fame. Tradition has it that Joseph wept copiously at the moment of departure, but down his brother's cheek there coursed a solitary tear. In the opinion of the Abbé Simon, who held the important post of sub-principal of the College, this was proof that Napoleon felt the wrench none the less keenly. Joseph allowed his emotions to govern him; Napoleon controlled his heart by his will, then as always.

It may be thought peculiar that Brienne, like the other military schools, was controlled by monks. The arrangement was really not so extraordinary as it would appear. Religion, up to the time of the Revolution, had always played an important part in the State, and that great epoch-making volcano had done nothing more than rumble at the period with which we are dealing. The Superior was, of course, the head of the establishment, the various Fathers having particular subjects to teach in which they more or less excelled. Occasionally a member of the laity assisted in a subordinate capacity. Pichegru, who was to become famous in the profession of Napoleon's choice, taught the elementary class at Brienne.

The pupils lived in almost monastic seclusion. They were not allowed to leave the precincts for the whole of the six years which were allotted to them for education, and during the holidays were never quite free from lessons. What seems a most exacting régime in some ways was, however, neutralised to some extent by rules judiciously forgotten.

St Germain, the energetic Minister of War who had advised the King to found the military schools, had spent much time and thought in drawing up elaborate regulations for their government. The studies included geography, history, grammar, mathematics, Latin, French poetry, German, drawing, music, and eventually English. Special attention was paid, as was only natural, to the art of war, "the trade of barbarians," as Napoleon once termed it in a capricious moment. Although rich in promise the colleges fell far short of the high ideals which St Germain had hoped for them, as do so many plans for the improvement of the existing order of things.

Notwithstanding all that has been written of Napoleon's morose and sullen disposition during his student days, it must not be forgotten that the young cadet was at a decided disadvantage in making friends. The matter of language alone was a sufficient barrier to intimate intercourse at this stage of his scholastic career, and his habit of diligent study ill-accorded with the frivolous frittering away of time indulged in by so many of the King's scholars. Napoleon was a hard worker, but only in subjects which most appealed to him, such as history, geography, and mathematics, all of which had a special bearing on his future career. Latin he despised as being of no practical value to a soldier; translations he positively loathed. He early learned to eliminate the non-essential and trivial, and the easy mastery of details became almost second nature to him.

Napoleon at Brienne

By Réalier Dumas

Photo Neurdein

His patriotism for his own country burned like a consuming fire. It is related that one day Napoleon came across a portrait of Choiseul, the hated Minister of Foreign Affairs under Louis XV. who had been the main instigator of the seizure of Corsica by the French. The most insulting remarks were hurled at the painted presentment of the man he so detested. On another occasion it is said that he averred he would do the French as much harm as he possibly could. If the story is not legendary, the statement was doubtless made in a moment of anger; perhaps after some thoughtless fellow student had taunted him about the poverty of his family, or the downfall of Paoli, the Corsican patriot whom he so much admired. His hot Southern blood boiled with indignation when anything was said which gave offence, and he scarcely, if ever, endeavoured to curb his hasty temper. He went so far as to challenge a cadet to a duel. To Bourrienne alone, a lad of his own age, did he show a marked attachment, and a warm friendship was cemented between them. Napoleon did not forget his school-chum in later years, and when a General appointed him to the important position of his private secretary. In his "Memoirs" Bourrienne gives us several intimate glimpses of the obscure lad who was to make Europe his footstool. He tells us that Napoleon frequently meditated on the conquest of his native island; that the unworthy part played by his father was never forgiven; that he spent much of his time in solitude. Bourrienne also confesses that in exchange for assistance in Latin the future Emperor would lend him a helping hand with his mathematics, the calculations being made with extraordinary clearness and rapidity.

"At Brienne," his school-fellow adds, "Bonaparte was remarkable for the dark colour of his complexion, which the climate of France afterwards very much changed, as well as for his piercing and scrutinising glance, and for the style of his conversation, both with his masters and companions. His conversation almost always gave one the idea of ill-humour, and he was certainly not very sociable. This I think may be attributed to the misfortunes of his family during his childhood, and the impressions made on his mind by the subjugation of his country."

In these trying days Napoleon's reticent disposition served him in good stead. He preferred the library of the school to the playground. While the other boys were enjoying a game Napoleon was usually poring over the pages of

Plutarch, and deriving inspiration and encouragement from the deeds of old-time heroes who figure in the "Lives of Illustrious Men." Greek poetry had a fascination for him not evident in many lads of his tender age. "With my sword by my side," he writes to his mother, "and Homer in my pocket, I hope to carve my way through the world." Cæsar's "Gallic War" was also a favourite. Although Napoleon was by no means generally popular, and certainly never inclined to be genial, the majority of the students gradually began to respect him. It is on record that he was never a sneak, preferring to bear punishment himself rather than to divulge the name of a miscreant.

The love of monks for the soil is proverbial; this may have been the reason why a small portion of ground was allotted to each student at Brienne. Whatever healthy exercise Napoleon was supposed to derive from his garden was speedily discounted. He set to work with feverish activity, transformed the desert into an oasis, planted trees and shrubs, and surrounded the whole by a palisade in true military fashion. This done, he troubled no more about agricultural pursuits but was content to sit in his bower and read with little fear of disturbance.

In the winter of 1783–4, an abnormally severe season, the anchorite had an opportunity to show his military powers. Napoleon suggested to the students that they should build a fort of snow complete in every detail. The school was then divided into two armies, Napoleon sometimes directing the assault, at others defending the fortifications. It was rough play, and several serious accidents befel the cadets, who entered into the spirit of the thing with more alacrity than the peace-loving monks approved. Day after day this mock warfare was kept up, and Napoleon was usually the hero of each encounter.

You can imagine him standing there in his picturesque costume: blue coat with red facings and white metal buttons, blue breeches, and a waistcoat of the same colour faced with white. Horace Vernet has depicted the scene in one of his many Napoleonic paintings. The young commander, erect and defiant, is directing the storming of the fort by cadets who, for the most part, have taken off their coats in order to secure a better aim. An attacking party is climbing the ramparts, some of the units with success, others with disaster. The picture has been reproduced many times, and is one of the few dealing with the early period of the Conqueror's career.

Without question these were the happiest days of Napoleon's youth. He was not a brilliant scholar, and there are no records to show that he won particular distinction beyond sharing a first prize for mathematics with Bourrienne, which goes to prove that the latter profited by the teaching of his chum. Napoleon however, was made commander of a company of cadets which amply atoned, from his own point of view, for all the "ploughing" he underwent at examinations. The opinion of M. de Keralio, one of the inspectors of the military schools, as to Napoleon's efficiency is as follows:

"SCHOOL OF BRIENNE: State of the King's scholars eligible from their age to enter into the service or to pass to the school at Paris; to wit, M. de Buonaparte (Napoleon) born the 15th August, 1769, in height 4 feet 10 inches 10 lines, has finished his fourth season; of good constitution, health excellent; character submissive, honest and grateful; conduct very regular; has always distinguished himself by his application to mathematics; understands history and geography tolerably well; is indifferently skilled in merely ornamental studies and in Latin, in which he has only finished his fourth course; would make an excellent sailor; deserves to be passed on to the school at Paris."

In the light of after events this diagnosis of his character is peculiar; it may be added that he had a deep-rooted affection for those at home in the far-off little island in the Mediterranean. He took upon himself the burden of thinking for the family, and provided them with plenty of gratuitous advice not altogether without wisdom.

A few months before Napoleon placed his foot on the next stepping-stone to fame and fortune he was joined at Brienne by his brother Lucien, who had been at Autun. In a note to one of his uncles Napoleon expresses his satisfaction with the newcomer, "for a beginning," but pours out a fierce diatribe against Joseph's wish to give up his idea of becoming a priest and entering the army. In reality there were more difficulties in the way than those mentioned by the writer, and eventually the eldest son was taken home to Corsica by his father. Neither was it destined that Napoleon should become a sailor. Another inspector named Reynaud de Monts visited the school in 1784, and decided that the promising cadet should enter the Military School of Paris, for which institution he left on the 30th October. To the certificate which was forwarded, a brief but sufficiently comprehensive note was added: "Character masterful, impetuous and headstrong." A complete contradiction of M. de Keralio's statement.

No one seeing the dwarfed figure of the lad of fifteen, as he passed through the entrance of the École Militaire, would have cared to prophecy that in a few years the King's scholar would be sitting as Emperor of the French on the throne of his benefactor. Time reveals its own secrets.

CHAPTER III
NAPOLEON AS OFFICER AND AUTHOR (1784–1791)

WITHOUT waiting to see if he would like the school and the tutors at Paris, or making the hundred and one excuses which usually crowd a schoolboy's brain before definitely settling down to work, Napoleon applied himself to the various subjects necessary to enable him to enter the artillery. This branch of the service held out most possibilities from the point of view of sheer merit, and he chose wisely. At the examination held in September 1785, his name appears as forty-second on the list of candidates, which is neither particularly good nor particularly bad, and would suggest that a certain portion of his time was devoted to studies outside the immediate radius of the official course.

Napoleon had the good fortune to find a friend in Alexandre Desmazis, who shared his room with him and became Administrator of the Crown Buildings during the Consulate. Many other instances might be given of Napoleon's kindness of heart to those who were not so successful in the race of life as was their benefactor. It is a point, and an important one, lost sight of by many of his biographers. There was certainly a better side of the mighty Corsican—he was not all blood and iron.

Apparently the studies of the chums at the École Militaire were successful, for they were appointed in the succeeding October, to the regiment of La Fere, stationed at Valence, Napoleon as second lieutenant. The two newly-fledged officers had so little money that they were forced to tramp a considerable distance on foot. It was very ignominious and humiliating, but pride is best swallowed quickly and forgotten, like a blue pill. Napoleon was now fatherless, and he felt his responsible position very keenly. Although not the head of the family in reality, he was nominally, for Joseph was far behind his brother in every material respect.

Besides his ordinary military duties Napoleon had to attend lectures on many subjects connected with his profession, including fortifications, chemistry, and mathematics. He seems to have worn off some of the rugged corners of his character. We find him with many friends, including one or two members of the fair sex. Upon one lady in particular, namely Mme. Grégoire de Colombier, he made a most favourable impression, and he received many invitations to her country house at Basseaux. She flattered him, but also tendered much practical advice. Napoleon was too young to fall in love seriously, but he passed many bright hours with Caroline, the daughter of his hostess, and a warm attachment sprang up between them. He ate fruit with her in the garden, and afterwards remarked that those days were some of the happiest in his triumphant but pathetic life. "We were the most innocent creatures imaginable," he says, "we contrived little meetings together; I well remember one which took place on a midsummer morning, just as daylight was beginning to dawn. It will scarcely be believed that all our happiness consisted in eating cherries together."

Bonaparte also visited the Permons; and Madame Junot, afterwards Duchess of Abrantès, has left us a witty pen-picture of him as he appeared in full regimentals at the age of sixteen.

"There was one part of his dress," she writes, "which had a very droll appearance—that was his boots. They were so high and wide that his thin little legs seemed buried in their amplitude. Young people are always ready to observe anything ridiculous, and as soon as my sister and I saw Napoleon enter the drawing-room, we burst into a loud fit of laughter. Buonaparte could not relish a joke; and when he found himself the object of merriment he grew angry. My sister, who was some years older than I, told him that since he wore a sword he ought to be gallant to ladies, and, instead of being angry, should be happy that they joked with him. 'You are nothing but a child, a little school-girl,' said Napoleon, in a tone of contempt. Cécile, who was twelve or thirteen years of age, was highly indignant at being called a child, and she hastily resented the affront by replying to Bonaparte, 'And you are nothing but a Puss in Boots!' This excited a general laugh among all present except Napoleon, whose rage I will not attempt to describe." A few days later the young officer went to a bookseller's shop, purchased a dainty edition of "Puss in Boots," and presented it to the culprit. This was his way of apologising.

For a time he relaxed his close application to study without neglecting his books altogether, and turned author. There is a pessimistic strain in all his literary efforts at this period, due no doubt to home-sickness, overwork, and perhaps lack of means, his income certainly never totalling more than twenty shillings a week. He even contemplated suicide, evidence of which is found in a manuscript dated the 3rd May, 1786.

"Always alone in the midst of men," he complains, "I come back to my rooms to dream with myself, and to surrender myself to all the vivacity of my melancholy. Towards which side is it turned to-day? To the side of death. In the dawn of my days I can still hope to live a long time, but I have been away from my country for about six or seven years. What pleasures shall I not enjoy when in four months' time I see once more my compatriots and my relations? From the tender sensations with which the recollections of the pleasures of my childhood now fill me, may I not infer that my happiness will be complete? What madness leads me, then, to wish my death? Doubtless the thought: What is there to do in this world?"

This makes strange reading, but it shows that even the greatest men have periods of depression like ordinary folk. He continues in this strain, passes sentence on France for having humiliated his beloved Corsica, and says scarcely less hard things of his own countrymen: "They are no longer those Corsicans, whom a hero inspired with his virtues, enemies of tyrants, of luxury, of demoralized towns." Towards the end he shows a tinge of enthusiasm; his fighting instinct gets the better of him: "A good patriot ought to die when his Fatherland has ceased to exist. If the deliverance of my fellow-countrymen depended upon the death of a single man, I would go immediately and plunge the sword which would avenge my country and its violated laws into the breast of tyrants." He again lapses into melancholy, concluding with a disgust for everything.

The second lieutenant did not take his own life; he lived down his troubles instead. Indeed his favourite motto, and one well worthy of note by every reader of this volume, was "The truest wisdom is a resolute determination." In August 1786, a rift in the cloud showed the proverbial silver lining, and the chance of a little excitement, which was bread and meat to him, came along. A miniature rebellion had broken out at Lyons, and it was deemed necessary to call out the military. The company at Valence to which Napoleon belonged was marched to the seat of the trouble. Before it arrived the insurrection had blown over, thereby shattering the officer's hope of distinguishing himself.

From Lyons he proceeded northward to Douay, in Flanders, where he contracted malarial fever which tended to undermine his constitution for several years afterwards. Bad news also reached him from Corsica. His mother appealed to him to come home and give her the benefits of his advice and assistance. Archdeacon Lucien—Napoleon's great-uncle, who had hitherto acted as head of the family—was daily growing more feeble: the good Letizia feared the worst. Her means were distressingly small, her family inordinately large for the scanty resources at her disposal. On the 1st of September 1786, he set out for his beloved island. Passing through Aix, he was cheered by a visit to his uncle Fesch and his brother Lucien, both of whom were studying at the Seminary with a view to entering the priesthood. Exactly a fortnight afterwards, Napoleon landed at Ajaccio with a small trunk of clothes and a larger one of books. The works of Plutarch, Plato, Cicero, Nepos, Livy, Tacitus, Montaigne, Montesquieu, Raynal, Corneille, Racine, Voltaire, and the poems of Ossian were all represented.

Napoleon applied himself with his usual industry to straightening out the tangled skein of family troubles. He found it by no means an easy matter, especially as the French Government was involved. The latter had been anxious to introduce the silk industry in their new dependency, and Charles Bonaparte had been one of the first to seize upon the idea because he thought there was "money in it." In 1782 he had made a plantation of young mulberry trees for the purpose of rearing silkworms, but instead of handing over the whole of the money which had been agreed upon in advance, 2700 livres still remained to be paid by the State. On the strength of a certificate of ill-health, Napoleon's leave was extended from the end of March 1787, to the beginning of December, and later until the 1st June 1788. He wandered about the island, visiting his old haunts and companions, but more often finding his greatest consolation in lonely communion with Nature. Sometimes he would turn to his literary pursuits, adding a few paragraphs to a "History of Corsica," which was occupying some of his leisure moments. He also composed a short story dealing with English history, entitled "The Count of Essex." A novel having its setting in Corsica followed, and another attempt at fiction, which he called "The Masked Prophet," perhaps the best of the three as regards literary style.

On the 12th September 1787, he left Corsica for Paris, in order to clear up the matter of the mulberry trees. He found it impossible to exact money from a bankrupt exchequer, and although he pressed the claim no success attended his efforts. Napoleon accordingly returned to Ajaccio, where he spent part of his spare time drawing up plans for the defence of places round the coast, and postponed his departure until the day he was due to join his regiment at Auxonne. Ever of a calculating nature, the young officer rightly surmised that in those days of lax discipline his absence would not be noticed, or if it were that the insubordination would be passed over.

In the following August (1788) it became evident that the serious work he had put in while his companions were lounging about or frittering away their time was beginning to have its due effect. He became a member of a commission appointed to inquire into the merits or demerits of certain pieces of artillery, and one of the duties—no slight one—which fell to his share was the drawing up of the report. Misfortune, however, had not altogether ceased paying him unwelcome attentions, and, for some reason or other, probably a matter connected with some work on the fortifications of which he had the oversight, Napoleon was placed under arrest for a day.

His own scheme of education went on apace, as his manuscript note-books, now in the Lorenzo Medici Library at Florence, abundantly testify. One of the works singled out by him for attention was a French translation of Barrow's "History of England, from the Times of Julius Cæsar to the Peace of 1762." His remarks show that he had a special admiration for such men as Hereward the Wake, familiar to all of us in the pages of Kingsley, or in the more recently published historical romance, "The Story of Hereward," by Mr Douglas C. Stedman; Simon de Montfort, whom Napoleon terms "one of the greatest Englishmen"; and the Earl of Arundel, who "died a martyr for the liberty of his country." Cromwell, he says, "was in his early days a libertine. Religion took possession of him, and he became a prophet. Courageous, clever, deceitful, dissimulating, his early principles of republican exaltation yielded to the devouring flame of his ambition, and, after having tasted the sweets of power, he aspired to the pleasure of reigning alone. He had a strong constitution, and had a manly but brusque manner. From the most austere religious functions he passed to the most frivolous amusements, and made himself ridiculous by his buffoonery. He was naturally just and even-tempered." Many of these remarks might be applied not inaptly to Napoleon himself, and if he is not absolutely just to Cromwell, they show that he had a very good understanding of the Protector's general character, and that he read to learn and not simply to "kill time," or for amusement.

In April 1789 was heard the distant rumble which heralded the French Revolution, before it broke out in all its hideous extravagancies. Riots had taken place at Seurre, but as in the case of the affair at Lyons, they were quelled before Napoleon or his colleagues put foot in the place. Two months of enforced idleness were spent in the former town before the company was marched back to its headquarters at Auxonne without having had the slightest chance to distinguish itself. When it could have proved useful it broke into open mutiny. This was in July 1789, when a riot took place and the soldiers joined the rebels.

Napoleon had now completed his "History of Corsica," and on the disgrace of Marbeuf, Bishop of Sens, to whom he had hoped to dedicate it, he decided to ask Paoli to become his patron. He sent him his precious manuscript feeling assured that it would be well received, but the acknowledgment was a rebuff couched in courteous terms. Moreover, the original was mislaid by Paoli, and this unfortunate happening went far to shake the faith of its writer in the great Corsican leader at a later date.

It is now necessary for us to try to understand in some measure the aims and objects of the vast disturbance known to history as the French Revolution. For generations the monarchy and aristocracy of France had refused to listen to the cry of the oppressed people whom they governed. The State was grossly mismanaged; money which should have remained in the pockets of the distressed people was exacted from them and given to unworthy Court favourites, who spent it in a variety of ways which did not benefit the nation. The nobles and titled clergy paid no taxes, the burden thus fell with undue weight on the middle classes—even now the milch-cow of the State—and the peasants, who toiled day and night for bread. Serious reform was always postponed, although it had been attempted by King Louis XVI. in a feeble and half-hearted way.

A bitter hatred of the persons, institutions, and traditions which contributed to this undesirable state of things was the inevitable consequence; as so often happens, those who desired the righting of wrongs carried their measures too far. "Liberty, equality, and fraternity" were the passwords of the leaders of the new order, but obviously the ideal could not be brought about when nearly everybody held a different theory as to how the abuses were to be rectified. The writings of such philosophers as Montesquieu, Voltaire, and Rousseau, all of which had been diligently perused by Napoleon, had done much to fan the smouldering embers into flames. Soon the whole land was ablaze, massacres became of daily occurrence, the King and Queen paid the price with their heads, the monarchies of Europe were shaken to their very foundations. And what did the people get in exchange for this giant upheaval? The iron despotism of one man, who continued the Revolution in his own person; made the Continent one vast battlefield; drew from France her best manhood and her treasure, and left her territory smaller than when he first put foot on her soil.

At the moment it was impossible for Napoleon to realise the true meaning of the dreadful events which were approaching with such unrestrained rapidity. He foresaw the end of the old state of affairs, and rightly conjectured that they would be swept away never to return; but Corsica was the centre of his interests rather than France. Rent asunder by conflicting ambitions and civil war, his native island might yet tear herself from her hated conquerors. So at least he told himself in his moments of reflection.

In September 1789, Bonaparte again obtained leave of absence until the 1st June 1790. His health was by no means good when he embarked at Marseilles; a mutiny had occurred in his regiment, and altogether his outlook was as gloomy as ever. Freedom from his irksome military duties, however, and the bracing effect of the sea-air rapidly revived his drooping spirits and failing energy.

The echo of the Revolution had been heard in far-off Corsica; there were disturbances, and serious trouble seemed likely, as soldiers were on the move intent upon restoring the sway of the hated royalist authorities. Napoleon called a meeting of patriots, harangued them, and headed a petition to the democratic National Assembly to restore independence to Corsica. He began to organise a National Guard, which was almost immediately dissolved by Vicomte de Barrin, the French Governor. The ardent young man of twenty thereupon set out for Bastia, the official capital of the island, where a passage of arms took place between the soldiers and the people. The latter won the day, and Barrin was forced to order the arming of the Civic Guard as they wished.

Shortly afterwards news arrived that the National Assembly had decided that Corsica should become a part of the Kingdom of France and enjoy the same constitution. All thought of independence seems to have instantly vanished from Napoleon's mind. He laid down the cudgels without further ado, saying that France "has opened her bosom to us, henceforth we have the same interests and the same solicitudes; it is the sea alone which separates us." Joseph being elected a member of the Municipal Council, the Bonaparte family was able to lift up its head again. Further leave of absence on the score of ill-health was again requested by Napoleon and granted. In reality he was taking an active part in affairs, and enjoying it, for Corsica was more or less in a state of anarchy. At Ajaccio he joined a Radical Club called the Patriotic Society, and wrote and printed a "Letter" to Buttafuoco, one of the most hated men in Corsica, who, since the death of Napoleon's father, had represented the nobility of the island at Versailles. It is full of abuse, the writer in his passionate ardour going so far as to say that, having burnt Buttafuoco in effigy, most of the Corsicans would like to burn him in person. Moreover, Paoli was returning, and he foresaw an opportunity of serving him. Paoli received a magnificent reception at Bastia when he arrived on the 17th July. The time for aiding the General of the Corsicans had not yet come, however, and Napoleon again set sail for France, reaching Auxonne, a picturesque little town on the river Saône, in February 1791.

Several years afterwards, in 1803 to be precise, when he was planning the invasion of our own fair land, Napoleon thus summed up his youthful days to Madame de Rémusat: "I was educated at a military school, and I showed no aptitude for anything but the exact sciences. Every one said of me, 'That child will never be good for anything but geometry.' I kept aloof from my schoolfellows. I had chosen a little corner in the school grounds, where I would sit and dream at my ease; for I have always liked reverie. When my companions tried to usurp possession of this corner, I defended it with all my might. I already knew by instinct that my will was to override that of others, and that what pleased me was to belong to me. I was not liked at school. It takes time to make oneself liked; and, even when I had nothing to do, I always felt vaguely that I had no time to lose.

"I entered the service, and soon grew tired of garrison work. I began to read novels, and they interested me deeply. I even tried to write some. This occupation brought out something of my imagination, which mingled itself with the positive knowledge I had acquired, and I often let myself dream in order that I might afterwards measure my dreams by the compass of my reason. I threw myself into an ideal world, and I endeavoured to find out in what precise points it differed from the actual world in which I lived. I have always liked analysis, and, if I were to be seriously in love, I should analyse my love bit by bit. *Why?* and *How?* are questions so useful that they cannot be too often asked. I conquered, rather than studied, history; that is to say, I did not care to retain and did not retain anything that could not give me a new idea; I disdained all that was useless, but took possession of certain results which pleased me."

It was this skilful combining of the practical and the imaginative which enabled Napoleon to project his vast schemes for the reformation of Europe; it was the elimination of the former and the substitution of an overweening self-confidence which deprived the mighty conqueror of "the throne o' the world."

CHAPTER IV
NAPOLEON AND THE CORSICAN VOLUNTEERS (1791–1792)

NAPOLEON again had a companion on his return voyage to France in the person of his brother Louis, a bright little fellow twelve and a half years old. If the latter could not be expected to take any intelligent interest in the many schemes for advancement which were now coursing through Napoleon's super-active brain, he was at least a living link with the family in Ajaccio. The young lieutenant's political ambitions which had received so marked an incentive in Corsica were not allowed to sink to zero, as is so frequently the case when one is away from the whirl and excitement of their practical influence. Rather were they nourished and fed by the sights and scenes Napoleon beheld as the two made their way to Auxonne after they had landed. The fact that he had exceeded his leave of absence worried him not at all, the penalty of six months' imprisonment, should his excuse be deemed invalid, being dismissed from his mind as an unlikely sequel. In his pocket were certificates from the Directory of the district of Ajaccio setting forth in glowing terms the services Napoleon had rendered to Corsica, and stating that his had been an enforced absence from duty owing to the unfavourable weather precluding the vessel from leaving. These credentials proved sufficient; he did not so much as lose a sou of his pay.

Napoleon quickly returned to his old habits of hard work, and his democratic opinions were voiced with greater vehemence to his fellow-officers, many of whom failed to agree with him and were not afraid to say so. Polite discussions frequently led to less gentlemanly arguments.

The room which the two Bonapartes occupied was almost as poorly furnished as was Chatterton's garret. Facing the window was a table loaded with books, papers, and writing utensils. There was a chair apiece: should a visitor come, either Napoleon or Louis had to sit on the edge of the bed, the younger brother being accommodated at night on a mattress in an adjoining apartment, which was in reality a part of the room and scarcely larger than a cupboard. If at a later period of his career Napoleon showed a desire for lavish display, he certainly was not able to indulge in luxury at Auxonne. He paid for everything required by Louis, clothed him, educated him, and thrashed him when he was disobedient or particularly dense in the matter of lessons. The younger Bonaparte soon became a general favourite, both in and outside the regiment. Napoleon writes with a certain amount of satisfaction that "all the women are in love with him." His faults seem to be summed up in the comprehensive but cynical phrase, "All he needs is knowledge."

In the middle of June 1791, Napoleon bade farewell to Auxonne and set out for Valence, where the Fourth Regiment was in garrison, he having been made first lieutenant of the first company of the second battalion. His brother accompanied him, lodging elsewhere, as it was not found convenient for Louis to remain in the same house. By way of recreation, frequent visits were paid to Madame de Colombier, but politics more and more absorbed Napoleon. He entered with great zest into the doings of the Society of the Friends of the Constitution, an avowedly revolutionary and republican gathering, and soon became so popular with its members that he was elected secretary and librarian.

The Academy of Lyons having offered a handsome prize, amounting to about £50, for the best essay on "What Truths and what Sentiments is it most Important to impress upon Men for their Happiness?" Napoleon found further scope for his literary gifts. "By sentiment," he assures us in his competitive composition, "we enjoy ourselves, nature, our country, and the men who surround us," and in support of the statement he draws on his own experience. "You return to your country," he writes; "after four years of absence, you visit the spots where you played in your earliest age, where you first experienced the knowledge of men and the awakening of the passions. In a moment you live the life of your childhood, you enjoy its pleasures, you are fired with the love of your country, you have a father and a tender mother, sisters still innocent, brothers who are like friends; too happy man, run, fly, do not lose a moment. If death stop you on your way you will never have known the delights of life, of sweet gratitude, of tender respect, of sincere friendship. These are the real pleasures of life, and they are greater if you have a wife and children." He says hard things of immoderate ambition, the very disease which was to prove his own ruin, and calls it "a violent unreflecting madness, which only ceases with life—a conflagration, fanned by a pitiless wind, which does not end till it has consumed everything." We wonder whether the Emperor, in his hours of introspection on the island of St Helena, when he was proving the truth of the above statement, ever thought of his essay. It did not gain the prize— Napoleon's name was last but one on the list of competitors.

Yet another leave of absence was requested and granted. It seems little short of extraordinary that, when France was at white heat, holidays should have been granted to soldiers, but such was the case. Napoleon and Louis saw the blue mountains of Corsica and their family in September 1791, a few weeks before the death of Archdeacon Lucien. It almost seemed, from Napoleon's point of view, as though Fate invariably had an unpleasant surprise for him when he visited Ajaccio, but Letizia always regarded her second son's homecoming as an act of Providence. Fortunately, his venerable relative left a handsome sum of money to the Bonapartes, a certain amount of which was invested by Napoleon in the purchase of a house in Ajaccio and two properties some little distance away.

It looked for a time as though the tide of fortune was beginning to turn in their favour. Joseph was elected a member of the Directory, the executive committee of the island, and on the 22nd February 1792, Napoleon was appointed Adjutant-Major of the Corsican Volunteers at Ajaccio. Some six weeks later, he was elected second lieutenant-colonel, a position which allowed him to absent himself from his French regiment but made for him an enemy in Pozzo di Borgo, a man who afterwards rose to distinction at the Russian Court, and had much to do with his successful rival's fall in after years.

Napoleon's opportunity for action soon came. Revolutionary principles regarded religion as of little consequence, and it was decided that the convents in the four most important towns of Corsica should be suppressed. This was not to be achieved without difficulty, and as strife and possibly bloodshed were thought highly probable, it was decided that a number of volunteers should be on hand at Ajaccio. On Easter Day 1792, a disturbance occurred in one of the streets. A dozen volunteers marched out to end it, only to make the disorder more general. Napoleon felt it his duty to interfere, but was obliged to take refuge after one of the men had been killed. The action of the volunteers was, of course, illegal, as they had acted on their own responsibility. Napoleon defended them, and in company with Quenza, his senior in command, endeavoured to persuade Colonel Maillard, the commander of the fortress, to deliver it into their hands. The Colonel, however, would have nothing to do with them beyond giving food for their men.

Early the following morning another band of volunteers entered the Seminary, fired indiscriminately, and angered the inhabitants. Disorder increased to such an extent as the day began to wane that it became necessary to proclaim martial law—in other words, the regular military were given absolute control until order should be restored. Various outrages on the part of the volunteers, of which Napoleon was by no means innocent, followed during the night. He endeavoured to corrupt the regular soldiers without success, and thus began that scheme of lying and plotting which he was to pursue even after he had been elected Emperor of the French. He was absolutely unscrupulous when, as always, he had his own ends to serve. In the case under consideration, he undertook that his men should be kept under restraint, the authorities promising that they would see that the people did not interfere with the volunteers. Napoleon's intention may have been good, but his men certainly continued to behave in a most disgraceful manner.

Eventually order was restored, and a rebuke administered to Napoleon by his battalion being ordered to retire to Corte.

The part he had played did not increase his popularity, and he thought it well to return to the French capital a month after war had been declared against Austria. As he himself said, "The beginning of a revolution was a fine time for an enterprising young man!"

CHAPTER V
THE EVE OF THE REIGN OF TERROR (1792–1793)

PARIS was in a ferment. The King had to be guarded by a double cordon of soldiers, so bitter was the animosity against the Royal Family and all that it stood for. With his usual shrewdness and faculty for penetrating into the probabilities of the future, Napoleon correctly anticipated events, and wrote to his brother Joseph that "everything tends to a revolution." On the 20th June 1792, a wild procession of insurrectionists, accompanied by cannon, made its way to the Tuileries, and intimidated the Guard. The latter opened the gates of the courtyard and the motley mob crowded into the beautiful palace, openly insulting King Louis and Queen Marie Antoinette. A republican Assembly had been forced upon the monarch, who was duly reaping the first-fruits of the harvest. Bourrienne gives a graphic account of what happened and how it affected the ardent politician of twenty-three. Napoleon's remarks clearly show that he had no belief in the aspirations of the rebels, notwithstanding his own ardent republicanism. Throughout his life he always held the *canaille* in profound contempt.

"We met," Bourrienne tells us, "by appointment, at a *restaurateur's* in the Rue St Honoré, near the Palais Royal. On going out we saw a mob approaching in the direction of the market-place, which Bonaparte estimated at from five to six thousand men. They were a parcel of blackguards, armed with weapons of every description, and shouting the grossest abuse, whilst they proceeded at a rapid rate towards the Tuileries. This mob appeared to consist of the vilest and most profligate of the population of the suburbs. 'Let us follow the rabble,' said Bonaparte. We got the start of them, and took up our station on the terrace bordering the river. It was there that he was an eye-witness of the scandalous scenes that ensued; and it would be difficult to describe the surprise and indignation which they excited in him. 'Such weakness and forbearance,' he said, 'could not be excused'; but when the

King showed himself at a window which looked out upon the garden, with the red cap, which one of the mob had just placed upon his head, he could no longer repress his indignation: 'What madness!' he loudly exclaimed, 'how could they allow that rabble to enter? Why do they not sweep away four or five hundred of them with the cannon? and then the rest would take themselves off very quickly.' When we sat down to dinner, he discussed with great good sense the causes and consequences of this unrepressed insurrection. He foresaw, and developed with sagacity, all that would follow; and in this he was not mistaken."

In a letter to Joseph written on the 3rd July, Napoleon again reveals himself as a philosopher. "Every one seeks his own interest," he says, "and wishes to rise by means of lying and calumny; men intrigue more contemptibly than ever. All that destroys ambition. One pities those who have the misfortune to play a part, especially when they can do without it. To live quietly, to enjoy the love of one's family surroundings—that, my dear fellow, if one had 4000 or 5000 francs a year, would be the wise thing to do. One should also be between the ages of twenty-five and forty, when one's imagination has calmed down, and is no longer troublesome. I embrace you, and recommend to you moderation in everything—in everything, do you understand?—if you wish to live happily."

A week later Napoleon received a welcome letter from the Minister of War appointing him Captain of the 4th regiment of artillery, and his arrears of pay were also sent. Life seemed to be worth living once more. Promotion is a fine antidote against depression.

It soon became evident that nothing short of civil warfare would satisfy the rioters, and on the 10th August 1792, the long pent-up storm burst with awful fury. The King, Queen, and other members of the royal family made their way to the Assembly, or Parliament, where they sat in a reporter's box listening to a debate as to whether Louis should be deposed or suspended, and which ended in a unanimous vote for the latter course. Meanwhile the mob was quickly gathering, a dozen pieces of artillery were drawn up, and the insurgents assumed a threatening attitude. Many of the Swiss and National Guards, whose duty it was to defend the Tuileries, found it necessary in the face of such overwhelming numbers to withdraw into the palace. Firing commenced, and for a time the royalists triumphed. Probably the crowd would have thinned away had not a foolish message arrived from Louis to the effect that the Swiss were to withdraw to their barracks. While this was being done the rioters rushed into the palace and in their mad frenzy slaughtered indiscriminately nearly every male attendant to be found, shooting wildly at the body-guard as they retreated. Another order came from the King that the Swiss were to lay down their arms. This the brave fellows did, although they knew what might happen. Those who were not killed by the mob were taken prisoners and put in the Church of the *Feuillants*, and on the following day many of them were mercilessly massacred. Those of my readers who have been to Lucerne have doubtless seen the noble monument in bas-relief of a dying lion erected to the memory of the brave Swiss. Napoleon himself saved one of the body-guard, and asserted that "If Louis XVI. had mounted his horse, the victory would have been his—so I judge from the spirit which prevailed in the morning." He always believed in a bold front; the King's action was an unmistakable sign of weakness.

Years after at St Helena Napoleon related the events of the fatal day as he watched them from a furniture shop belonging to Bourrienne's brother, Fauvelet. "Before I arrived at the Carrousel," he says, "I had been met in the Rue des Petits Champs by a group of hideous men carrying a head on the end of a pike. Seeing me well dressed, and looking like a gentleman, they came to me to make me cry, '*Vive la Nation!*' which I did without difficulty, as you may believe. The *château* was attacked by the violent mob. The King had for his defence at least as many troops as the Convention had on Vendémiaire 13th, when they had to fight against a better-disciplined and more formidable enemy.1 The greater part of the National Guard was on the side of the King—one must do them this justice. When the palace had been fired, and the King had taken refuge in the bosom of the Assembly, I ventured to penetrate into the garden. Never since have any of my battle-fields given me such an idea of death as the mass of the Swiss corpses then presented to me, whether the smallness of the space made the number appear larger, or whether it was because I was to undergo this experience for the first time.... I visited all the *cafés* in the neighbourhood of the Assembly; everywhere the irritation was extreme, rage was in every heart, it showed itself in all faces, although the people present were not by any means of the lower class, and all these places must have been daily frequented by the same customers, for although I had nothing peculiar in my dress—but perhaps my countenance was more calm—it was easy to see that I excited many looks of hostility and defiance as being unknown and a suspect."

---

1 5th October, 1795.—See *post*, chapter vii. p. 71.

August 1792 was indeed a month of events fraught with far-reaching consequences. The decree went forth that all religious houses should be confiscated and sold. Along with the death-knell of royalty was sounded that of religion. Élise, the most determined and resolute of Napoleon's three sisters, was then at the College of St Cyr, and he felt it would not be safe for her to stay in France a single moment longer than was absolutely necessary. He still put family ties before patriotism; in reality each is part and parcel of the other. His position was difficult, for it would have been foolish to have jeopardised his captaincy, but he thought he saw a way out, and applied for a commission which would insure his going to Corsica, which was not granted. A petition to the Directory of the district of Versailles, requesting that he be allowed to accompany Élise, met with a more favourable response. On the 1st September, the day before the revolutionary Commune of Paris began the massacre of hundreds of citizens because they did not happen to sympathise fully with the Revolution, Napoleon conducted his sister from St Cyr. In October they were in their native town once more, Napoleon resuming his duties as second lieutenant-colonel of the volunteers.

The island of Sardinia, which is separated from Corsica by the Strait of Bonifacio and now belongs to Italy, had cherished dreams of declaring her independence. It was therefore determined that Admiral Truguet and a number of troops and volunteers should sail from Marseilles, call at Ajaccio for additional men, and under the command of Raffaelle Casabianca, endeavour to assist the rebellious islanders. Almost as soon as they had landed in Corsica there was trouble between the sailors and the unruly volunteers, three of the latter being hanged in consequence. Paoli, now President of the Administration and Commander-in-Chief of the National Guards, felt that this was indeed a sorry prelude to an expedition in which loyal co-operation was an absolute essential. The aged patriot therefore wisely decided that only regular troops should be sent. Cagliari, the capital of the island, was deemed the most important point of attack; San Stefano was to be occupied by a second division under the command of Colonel Cesari-Colonna, Paoli's nephew, and accompanied by Napoleon. The attempt on the first place failed miserably owing to a want of confidence on the part of the besiegers, and the troops at San Stefano accomplished little. They certainly effected a landing, and on the night of the 23rd February, 1793, Napoleon and his men hastily erected a battery, from which point of vantage they proceeded to bombard Maddalena. On the following evening, however, the troops showed that they had no more heart for warfare than their compatriots at Cagliari, and a retreat became absolutely necessary. For this Napoleon is in no way to be blamed. There is more than a suspicion of treachery, and it has been suggested that either Paoli or some of his followers had arranged that the expedition should fail in order to humble the too enterprising and over-confident Bonaparte, who was nearly left behind in a disgraceful struggle to get into the boats.

Napoleon's dream of a free Corsica had long since passed away; he was convinced that without France she might fall a prey to any Power or bold maritime adventurer who cared to risk the attempt upon her. Relations between him and Paoli became more and more strained. Probably he felt in his own mind that the dictator's cause was hopeless, and consequently offered no advantages. France on the other hand, appeared likely to become all-powerful. She seemingly stopped at nothing, and was as bent on "setting Europe to rights" in her fashion as was Pitt in his. But what was of more immediate importance was the startling and unexpected intelligence that the Convention had ordered Paoli's arrest, as well as that of Pozzo, his right-hand man. The author of this ill-service was none other than Lucien Bonaparte, who had acted as Paoli's secretary for several months and was now in France occupying his leisure moments in securing the downfall of the patriot by denouncing him to the authorities at Toulon. This conduct can only be described as infamous, and goes to prove that a keen sense of morality was not a conspicuous trait of the Bonaparte family. Lucien had not taken his brother into his confidence, and no one was more astonished than Napoleon when the truth of the matter was revealed to him. The net result was to embroil more deeply the island in a civil war which had been carried on in a desultory kind of way for some time, breaking out into flame here and there, and dying down almost as speedily.

We now catch a glimpse of Napoleon as a diplomatist. He sent a communication to the Convention glowing with fulsome flattery and pleading that "the patriarch of liberty, and the precursor of the French Republic," might be spared this last ignominy. The young officer was playing a double part. With Salicetti he planned to secure the citadel of Ajaccio by artifice, but without success. He then decided to tramp to Bastia, where the French Commissioners were investigating the condition of affairs and making preparations for resistance against the islanders. Here he hoped to meet Joseph, who had also attached himself to the French cause. One cannot but admire the dogged determination which prompted such a proceeding. His precept that "It is only by perseverance and tenaciousness that any object can be obtained," was not a mere moral maxim, a passing thought to be dismissed as casually as it had entered the brain.

Napoleon's journey across the island was quite an adventurous one. Accompanied only by a poor but sagacious shepherd he traversed rugged ravines and valleys, every recess of which was dangerous and might shelter a band of Paolists. In passing through the village of Bocognano he fell into the hands of the enemy and was locked up in what was considered a safe place. But under cover of night, and by the aid of friends, he effected his escape through a window, and the whole of the following day he was forced to conceal himself in a garden. From this unhappy and insecure hiding-place he made his way to the house of a cousin, but on the evening of his third day there a Nationalist brigadier entered and demanded to search the place. Good fortune again attended the fugitive. The unwelcome visitor was cajoled into a belief that Napoleon, against whom an order for arrest had now been issued, had neither been seen nor heard of in that quarter, and he did not persist in his demand. Shortly after he had left the house he was followed by the refugee, who had been sitting in another room with the servants, all of whom were sufficiently well armed to offer a desperate resistance if necessary.

A ship was riding at anchor awaiting him, and, stealthily finding his way to the dinghy on the beach, Napoleon was quickly on board. It was a case of touch and go, for the Nationalists would not have allowed him to escape from their hands a second time.

Eventually he reached Bastia, and made such a good impression on the Commissioners that a naval expedition against Ajaccio was fitted out and he was given command of the artillery. A week later the little band of some four hundred men sighted the harbour. The attempt to make the patriotic citizens surrender was a complete fiasco, for while Lacombe Saint Michel, Salicetti, Napoleon, and Joseph were joined by a few dozen soldiers and citizens, Paoli was being reinforced by people from all over the island. The men were disembarked, captured a fortress known as the Torre di Capitello, which they soon evacuated, and returned. Another failure had been added to Napoleon's record. The Bonaparte family paid dearly for the part they played at this time. Their enemies, and they were many, wrecked Madame Letizia's house. Fortunately her resourceful son had foreseen such an event, and not only warned his mother but arranged for her escape. She and her children were thus enabled to leave the place before the angry Paolists set about their work of destruction, and after a long tramp were taken to Calvi by sea. Eight days after their arrival a small merchant vessel was chartered for a voyage to Toulon, and late on the night of the 11th June 1793, the dispossessed family, including Napoleon, sailed in the direction of France and of Fortune.

CHAPTER VI
NAPOLEON'S FIRST FIGHT WITH THE ENGLISH (1793)

THE first six months of the year 1793 were notable ones in France. No more fortunate than many others who did not wear the imperial purple, the King paid for his incompetency with his head. Louis XVI. was one of those weak persons who mean well but carry their good intentions to no practical issue. His execution on the 21st January brought more important and far-reaching results than his thirty-eight years of life. Republican France, proclaimed on the 22nd September 1792, was no longer a mere dream of enthusiasts, but a reality, although the foundations were insecure and the superstructure top-heavy. The seed of liberty had been planted, and it was fondly hoped that it would bring forth an increase which would blossom in every country.

In the previous April the luckless Louis had been reluctantly compelled to declare war on Austria, the latter Power receiving the support of Prussia. The attempt on the part of the half-disciplined French troops under General Dumouriez to invade the Austrian Netherlands signally failed. This poor beginning was amply retrieved at Valmy and by the seizure of the Netherlands after the battle of Jemappes on the 6th of the following November. Savoy and the Rhine Valley were also occupied, and promises of assistance made to all countries that cared to raise the standard of revolt.

With the execution of Louis XVI. monarchical Europe assumed a more threatening aspect. The Convention had already stated that its business was to drive out "tyrants" who occupied thrones, and such a proclamation was not pleasant reading for those whom it most concerned. Owing to an "attachment to the coalition of crowned heads" on the part of George III., France declared war against England on the 1st February 1793, and as the latter had allied herself to Holland, that country also received the same unwelcome challenge. The two Powers shortly afterwards joined hands with Russia, Spain and the Holy Roman Empire for the purpose of mutual support. France had more than her hands full, especially as she was in an unsettled state within her own borders. The momentary triumphs of the Revolutionary troops did not last. The Convention supported the war in the Netherlands half-heartedly, and so enraged Dumouriez that he deserted to Austria and subsequently retired to England, where he spent his remaining days. Government passed into the hands of a select few known as the Committee of Public Safety. In the Convention were two parties, the Girondists or moderate republicans, and the Mountain, whose views were considerably more advanced and far less reasonable. They could not rule themselves much less the nation. The Mountain prevailed, and the cause of the Girondists was taken up with enthusiasm by the people of La Vendée, a department of Brittany, which had no sympathy with the extreme measures advocated by the Mountain. In company with several other populous centres Marseilles revolted, and it was to this city that the Bonapartes proceeded in September, 1793, after having led a dreary existence on the outskirts of Toulon. By this time affairs had quieted down again. Napoleon's sympathy was with the policy of the Mountain. Having been promoted to the position of *capitaine commandant* he had joined his regiment at Nice in the previous June. He sent his family every sou he could spare from his meagre pay, but this did not suffice to keep its members from actual want, and the proud Letizia and her children were obliged to eat the bread of charity. Gradually things took on a rosier complexion, and Joseph, Lucien, and Joseph Fesch, who was of the party, obtained positions which presumably left a small margin for the benefit of their sorely-stricken relations. It seemed as though Dame Fortune were indeed smiling when small pensions from a fund which had been voted for Corsican refugees were granted to the mother and each child under the age of fifteen.

Being unable to get an appointment on active service, for which he ardently longed, Napoleon sought solace in literature. Had he failed in the army it is not at all improbable that he would have become a literary man; although it is doubtful if his achievements in this field would have made his name famous. For the moment he sheathed his sword and took up his pen, producing a pamphlet written in the form of a dialogue, entitled "The Supper at Beaucaire." To quote the opinion of Sir John Seeley: "It is highly characteristic, full of keen and sarcastic sagacity, and of clear military views; but the temperature of its author's mind has evidently fallen suddenly; it has no warmth, but a remarkable cynical coldness." It was published at Avignon in August 1793. Like his previous publications it attracted little or no attention in the days when printing presses were turning out pamphlets by the thousand, but as if to counterbalance the failure, Napoleon was about to have an opportunity to show his talents along the line they were slowly but surely developing.

The inhabitants of the great southern seaport and arsenal of Toulon, the majority of them royalists to the core, had openly rebelled. Unlike those of Marseilles, who had raised an army against the Convention, they had gone so far as to call in the assistance of the enemy. English and Spanish fleets under Hood and Langara respectively, blockaded the harbour; in other words prevented or attempted to prevent the entry and exit of vessels; and troops which had been hastily landed were in command of the town. It soon became evident that the Convention would have to re-take the place by force.

The commander of the artillery having been wounded, Napoleon, now *chef de bataillon*, was called upon to take his place. The army which he joined consisted of a motley crowd hastily gathered together. Trained officers were in the minority, for the simple reason that until the fall of Louis XVI. none but the nobility had been allowed to hold a command. Their plebeian successors endeavoured to make up for a lack of military education by a zeal which was not infrequently manifested in the wrong place and at the wrong moment. For instance, Carteaux, originally an artist, having been invested with the command of the army marching on Toulon and failing miserably, his place was taken by Doppet, a retired doctor who succeeded no better. Not until the amateurs had been tried and found wanting was the position given to Dugommier, a veteran who had served with the colours for half a century, and who was to meet his death by a Spanish bullet in the following year.

Modern authorities regard with suspicion the oft-repeated assertion that Napoleon persuaded the Council of War to adopt the plan he had drawn up for the purpose of capturing the well-nigh impregnable town. There is no doubt that he behaved with consummate bravery throughout the siege. He seemed to know instinctively what to do in a case of emergency. Examples could be multiplied, but one must suffice. A soldier who was serving a big gun was struck lifeless while Napoleon was standing near. Without hesitation he took the dead man's place and proceeded to ram home the ammunition until another artilleryman stepped forward. He did not expect others to do what he feared to undertake himself, and he was never backward in appreciating bravery and resource in others.

One day he was directing the construction of a battery when it became necessary for him to dictate a despatch. He called for some one to write it for him, and a young man named Junot offered to do so. A heavy shot came to earth within such a short distance of them that Junot was literally covered with dust. "Good," he exclaimed, "we shall not want sand this time," referring, of course, to the old method of blotting wet ink. Napoleon never forgot the incident, and Junot received his reward when Napoleon came into his own. Victor Perrin also came under the notice of Napoleon at the siege of Toulon. He was twice wounded, but stuck to his guns, which he fired with much skill.

Having ordered a battery to be erected in an exposed position in the near vicinity of Fort Mulgrave, one of the most important of the English strongholds, Napoleon named this "the battery of the fearless." His keen sense of the dramatic told him that henceforth it would be deemed an honour to be there, either dead or alive. Doppet says that "whenever he visited the outposts of the army, he was always sure to find the Commandant of Artillery at his post; he slept little, and that little he took on the ground, wrapped in his mantle: he hardly ever quitted his batteries." Napoleon developed extraordinary initiative. He sent for the guns not in use by the Army of Italy, procured horses by requisition, established a repair shop, ordered five thousand sand-bags to be made every day at Marseilles to be used for purposes of defence, and had a small army of smiths, wheelwrights, and carpenters at his command. "Nothing was done but by Bonaparte's orders or under his influence; everything was submitted to him," Marmont assures us. "He made tables of what was required; indicated how this was to be obtained; put everything in motion, and, in a week, gained an ascendancy over the Commissioners almost impossible to be concealed."

Fort Mulgrave, called by its besiegers "the little Gibraltar," was the key of the position, for it commanded the inner harbour. Before dawn on the morning of the 17th December, three columns of soldiers set out to reduce it, a previous attack having failed largely owing to the premature sounding of the retreat. Twice the attacking party was all but successful, and as a last resource the reserves under Napoleon were called up. Although his battalion was not the first to scale the walls, young Bonaparte and his men did magnificent work, and soon the guns which had been trained on the French were firing in the direction of the enemy. On the same day the Tricolour waved over two more forts which had been evacuated, the enemy finding Toulon untenable and resistance impossible in the face of the 37,000 men who were confronting them; the English, Spanish, Piedmontese and Neapolitan forces not numbering more than 17,200. Napoleon began to bombard the now doomed city and the fleet which still lay in the roadstead. That night Sidney Smith, a gallant young English captain, with a little body of men equally brave, set fire to a dozen French ships in the harbour. The naval stores were soon well alight, the flames spreading with bewildering rapidity, and the Spaniards exploded two powder-ships. On the 19th, Lord Hood in the *Victory* weighed anchor, and the British fleet left the scene of disaster with over 14,000 of the terror-stricken inhabitants on board, and four ships-of-the-line, three frigates and several smaller vessels as spoil.

The luckless Toulonese paid heavily for their defection. For hours the city was given up to pillage, the Republican troops losing all restraint and refusing to listen to the humane pleadings of Dugommier. Nor was this all, for about 1800 persons perished by the guillotine or were shot. The Reign of Terror was not confined to Paris.

"Who is that little bit of an officer, and where did you pick him up?" some one is reported to have asked Dugommier. "That officer's name," was the reply, "is Napoleon Bonaparte. I picked him up at the Siege of Toulon, to the successful termination of which he eminently contributed, and you will probably one day see that this little bit of an officer is a greater man than any of us."

It is certain that Dugommier was highly pleased with the conduct of his able lieutenant, indeed he "mentioned him in despatches," an honour for which every soldier longs. "Among those who distinguished themselves most," he writes, "and who most aided me to rally the troops and push them forward, are citizens Buona Parte, commanding the artillery, Arena and Cervoni, Adjutants-General." Generals Du Teil and Salicetti also said kind things of the Corsican. "Words fail me to describe Bonaparte's merit"; says the former, "to a mind well stored with science, he brings great intelligence and unlimited courage. Such is a weak sketch of the qualities of this incomparable officer."

For the services thus rendered Napoleon received another step in rank, and on the 1st February 1794, he became General of Brigade. His duties were to inspect the defences of the southern coast and to supervise the artillery and stores of the Army of Italy, commanded by General Schérer, whose headquarters were at Nice. Napoleon arrived at that town in the following March, and a month later was appointed General in Command of the Artillery.

CHAPTER VII
NAPOLEON THE SOLDIER OF FORTUNE (1794–1796)

FRANCE resounded with the tramp of armed men. No fewer than five armies, largely made up of volunteers and probably numbering nearly 700,000, in addition to those on garrison duty, were facing the enemies of the Republic. There was the Army of the North, of the Moselle, of the Rhine, of the West, and of Italy. It is interesting to note that many of those who held important positions in these forces were men who, like Carteaux and Doppet, had followed other trades or professions previous to the Revolution. By adapting themselves to circumstances, exercising ingenuity when their slight knowledge of tactics failed them, and proving their ability in the field, they had risen to positions of power and influence. Jourdan, with the Army of the North, had been a dealer in cloth; with the Army of the Moselle were Hoche and Moreau, the former the son of an ostler, the latter once a lawyer in beautiful Brittany; Kléber, of the Army of the West, had been educated as an architect, while Masséna, who was with the Army of Italy, had started life as a sailor. The promise of the Revolution to every son of France, "A career open to talent," was not a mere boast, but was realised in many cases. Napoleon himself studied to make his soldiers feel that no rank was beyond their aspiration. There was a marshal's baton in every knapsack.

Although Napoleon received an appointment in the Army of Italy in the dual capacity of General of Artillery and Inspector-General, the opportunity of showing his now recognised abilities as an executant was denied him in this campaign. The chance came from another and an unexpected direction, namely that of diplomacy. It cannot be said that his diplomatic attempts in Corsica had been particularly brilliant; this, however, did not preclude Augustin Robespierre, a Commissioner of the Convention with whom Napoleon had struck up an intimate acquaintance, from placing a difficult problem requiring the greatest political skill and tact in his hands for solution. Genoa, once a great Sea Power, but now in the evening of her decline and decay, was supposed to be neutral, in other words, taking sides with none of the warring nations. But she had allowed enemies of France to pass through her territory, and by so doing had incurred the wrath of the mighty Republic, notwithstanding her excuse that she was not powerful enough to prevent them.

To Genoa, the city of palatial buildings and gorgeous churches, Napoleon accordingly proceeded in July 1794, and so well did he manage his cause that his mission was completely successful. On the 28th of the same month he returned to the headquarters of the Army of Italy in the full expectation of an ample recognition. His hopes were shattered by the astounding news that his friend and patron had been executed in company with his brother Maximilien Robespierre, the cruel chief of the Jacobins.

During the reign of the "Incorruptible," as the latter was named by his friends and supporters, the streets of Paris ran with blood. By his orders, and those of his satellites, scores of prisoners were dragged daily from gaol and put to death. The flower of the Nobility of France suffered in company with the lowest of the low, for the guillotine was no respecter of persons.

Napoleon found that his diplomatic triumph did not avail to prevent his arrest on account of what was held to be his suspicious conduct in connection with the Army of Italy, his recent mission to Genoa, and his intimacy with the younger Robespierre, whose admiration had gone so far as to prompt a reference to Napoleon in a despatch to Government as "a man of transcendent merit." For a time his destiny hung in the balance. Had Salicetti, Albitte and Laporte, the Commissioners of the Convention who examined his papers, cared to condemn him, the General in all probability would have met the same terrible fate as his friend. There is more than a suspicion that Salicetti now viewed Napoleon with jealousy, but, according to Marmont, he used his influence to procure his release. It is difficult to arrive at the truth in a matter such as this, when contemporary narrators do not agree. In history one must not take too much for granted, and perhaps it may be a reasonable conclusion to assume that Salicetti was not ignorant of the potential powers of his countryman, and that he recognised that no good could be done by condemning such a man, while much advantage might accrue to himself if he supported him.

Meanwhile the enterprising General was deprived of his rank. Instead of bemoaning his fate, Napoleon penned an energetic letter to his judges in which he defended his case on the grounds of his patriotism, his hatred of all tyrants, and his public services. On the 20th August a counter-order was issued in which mention was made of the "advantages which might be derived from his military information and knowledge of localities, for the service of the Republic," and recommending that Citizen Bonaparte be "restored provisionally to liberty, and that he should remain at headquarters pending further instructions from the Committee of Public Safety."

Napoleon spent fourteen days in suspense at Fort Carré, near Antibes, but he was mercifully allowed a supply of books and maps which helped to pass the time. On the last day of his imprisonment an officer came at two o'clock in the morning to announce the pleasing intelligence that his release was ordered.

"What! Are you not in bed yet?" he cried in astonishment as he entered the cell and saw Napoleon poring over the litter of papers on the little table.

"In bed!" was the contemptuous retort. "I have had my sleep, and am already risen."

"What, so early?" the officer replied, amazed beyond measure at so unusual a statement.

"Yes," continued the prisoner, "so early. Two or three hours of sleep are enough for any man."

To use a familiar and expressive simile, Napoleon had now "jumped from the frying-pan into the fire." Although he was restored to his former rank he was not sent back to the army, but remained for a time unemployed, living with his family at Marseilles. While there he fell in love with Mademoiselle Désirée Clary, the daughter of a wealthy soap merchant, whose sister Julie had married Joseph Bonaparte. The enraptured lover went so far as to arrange for the wedding to take place in the following autumn. "Perhaps I am doomed to shine like a meteor," he told the object of his affection, "but I will ensure you a brilliant existence." Love's young dream was soon shattered by the disturbing spirit of ambition, and vowing eternal faithfulness Napoleon left his sorrowful sweetheart and promptly forgot his pledge. An expedition against Corsica, which had passed into the hands of the British, had been decided upon. In company with his brother Louis, now a sub-lieutenant of artillery, he set sail on the 3rd March 1795, and came near to being captured, two of the ships carrying the soldiers falling prey to the "ravening wolves of the sea," as Napoleon called English sailors. The defeat sustained on this occasion added one more to his long list of disasters in connection with Corsican affairs.

At the beginning of May he went to Paris to anticipate or await future events. He now resumed his friendship with Bourrienne, who had been in Germany. Offered an appointment as Brigadier-General of Infantry in the Army of the West, then engaged in putting down the civil war in La Vendée, he refused it on his usual plea of ill-health. In reality he considered it beneath his dignity to accept the command. The Central Committee retaliated by having his name struck off the active list.

This displeasure was not to be of considerable duration. Napoleon turned his attention to the drawing up of a definite scheme of campaign for the Army of Italy, now meeting with rebuffs at the hands of the Austrians. The documents were sent to the Committee of Public Safety in July, and helped him to secure a staff appointment in the topographical department of the War Office, where he worked at plans and operations for the benefit of the various French armies in the field. Incidentally he made the acquaintance of various people likely to be of use to him in the furtherance of his career, and renewing that with Barras whom he had first met at Toulon.

Meantime Paris, well named the Gay City, had assumed something of its former aspect. There was marriage and giving in marriage, the theatres and other places of amusement opened anew, and the infallible barometer of business began to rise. Almost everywhere the half-trained armies had been victorious. Apparently "better times" had begun. The change in the political weather, although clearer, was not so noticeable. To be sure a constitution had been framed by the National Convention and was given to the world on the 22nd September 1795, but it did not give the universal satisfaction hoped for by the more enthusiastic of its supporters. In certain minor respects the Legislative Body upon which they had decided was not unlike our own Parliament, in so far as it consisted of two Houses, the lower chamber being called the Council of Five Hundred and the upper chamber the Council of Ancients. The former drew up the laws, the latter passed, adjusted, or rejected them. From the two Councils a Directory of five men vested with the executive power was to be chosen, one of whom was to retire for re-election every year.

Having decreed that one-third of the members of both Councils should also retire in the same way, either to be re-elected or to surrender their places to others, the Convention stirred up a hornet's nest for itself by deciding that two-thirds of its members should be retained in the new Legislature, whereas it had originally assembled for the purpose of drawing up a constitution and not to govern. Girondists and supporters of the Mountain alike clung tenaciously to office, anxious to retain the spoils of victory. The members of the Convention soon found that public opinion was against them. "This measure," says Baron de Frénilly, "aroused general indignation, for nobody, apart from its accomplices, wished that it should possess either power or impunity."

Paris was again in a ferment as serious as it was unexpected. The old battle cry of "Down with the aristocrats!" gave place to that of "Down with the two-thirds!" A rival government called the Central Committee was set up and almost as speedily suppressed by the regular troops, acting on the authority of the Convention. They met with more difficulty in attempting to disperse the insurgent electors of Paris, who had 30,000 National Guards on their side. General Menou, the commander of the troops, was taken prisoner, only to be put under arrest on his release by the party whom he had attempted to defend. The command was then given to Paul Barras, who among others chose Napoleon as a lieutenant. He could not have selected a better man, as subsequent events proved. Barras ordered cannon from the Sablons camp, and the trained eye of his colleague enabled him to place them in the best possible positions to command the various thoroughfares and bridges which led to the Tuileries, the building against which the National Guard and the citizens were marching. Napoleon had certainly not more than 7,000 armed men at his disposal, but his troops were victorious on the ever-memorable 13th Vendémiaire (5th October 1795), and the "whiff of grape shot," as he termed it, helped materially to pave the way to the throne. For the present his skill was rewarded by the rank of second in command of the Army of the Interior, and later, when his friend Barras vacated the senior position, Napoleon received the appointment.

The National Convention could afford to be generous to the beardless young General who had saved the situation. It forthwith settled down to elect five Directors, namely, La Réveillière-Lépeaux, Letourneur, Rewbell, Carnot, and Barras.

Napoleon now began to take an interest in Society. He frequented the *Salons* where wit and beauty gathered for mutual admiration and intellectual entertainment. It is doubtful whether he cared for either to any considerable extent. Certainly he had no mock modesty, and realising more than ever the value of being on speaking terms with those likely to be of service to him, he regarded the precious hours thus apparently wasted as a future asset. He preferred the *Salon* of Barras to any other. This led to his introduction to his future first wife, the fascinating Josephine de Beauharnais, whose courtier husband had suffered the same fate as Robespierre during the Reign of Terror. Addison, the famous essayist, tells us that "a marriage of love is pleasant; a marriage of interest—easy; and a marriage where both meet—happy." Napoleon's matrimonial venture may be regarded as a judicious combination of the two, and to a certain extent it was happy. The marriage, which was not blessed by the Church, it being a Civil contract, took place on the 9th March 1796. The bridegroom was twenty-six years of age, his bride thirty-four.

Ten days before Napoleon had been given command of the Army of Italy at the instigation of Carnot. Barras, in his *Mémoires*, insinuates that his influence led the Directory to this decision. In reality the General had largely won his own case. His pen had not lost its cunning, and further plans which he had brought forward for a decisive campaign by the now moribund Army of Italy had attracted considerable attention, although when sent to Schérer, who had succeeded Kellermann in the command, they met with a rebuff at the hands of that worthy. As a direct consequence he was superseded by the soldier who had dared to interfere.

During his exile, when the glamour of his second marriage with the daughter of the Cæsars had passed and the memory of better times was the bitter-sweet consolation of his turbulent mind, Napoleon frequently reflected on his affection for the vivacious woman who shared his first triumphs and his throne. "Josephine was devoted to me," he tells Montholon, one of the little band of faithful followers who refused to desert him in the hour of failure. "She loved me tenderly; no one ever had a preference over me in her heart. I occupied the first place in it; her children the next; and she was right in thus loving me; for she is the being whom I have most loved, and the remembrance of her is still all-powerful in my mind."

CHAPTER VIII
"THE SPARK OF GREAT AMBITION"
(1796)

"SOLDIERS! you are ill-fed and almost naked; the Government owes you much, but can do nothing for you. Your patience, your courage, do you honour, but bring you neither advantage nor glory. I am about to lead you into the most fertile plains of the world. Rich provinces, great cities will be in your power. There you will find honour, and fame, and wealth. Soldiers of the Army of Italy, will you be found wanting in courage?"

Thus Napoleon addressed the half-starved and dejected legions who had been struggling for two years on the Maritime Alps against the Austrians and Sardinians in an apparently impossible attempt to gain a footing in Northern Italy. The army was little more than a mob of malcontents, lacking even the common necessaries of life. Forty thousand outcasts, if you will, undisciplined, many of them without boots, more of them in tatters, all of them with scarcely a ray of hope; soldiers in name rather than in reality. Brave men and heroes there were, order and subordination there were not. To introduce cohesion and discipline into these unruly forces was the almost superhuman task Napoleon had undertaken.

He arrived at Nice, the headquarters of the Army of Italy, on the 26th March 1796; he began to investigate the conditions of his problem the same day, issuing the above General Orders twenty-four hours afterwards. His allies were the mountains which separated him from his enemies; the Mediterranean which faced him was the highroad of the English squadron. A concerted effort on the part of the land and the maritime forces would most assuredly catch him like a rat in a trap. Fortunately the Austrians and Sardinians were suspicious of each other, their dispositions were faulty and not always in concert, and their forces were scattered over a long line of territory, defending the passes across the mountains. The officers viewed the Directory's choice of a commander with suspicion. If Schérer, a veteran over seventy years of age, had not been able to lead them to victory, what could be expected of this fledgling? They reckoned without their host. Genius knows no age and takes no count of birthdays. Napoleon's amazing fertility of resource, his astounding energy and thorough grip of the situation, gradually overcame their opposition whether acknowledged or only felt. Masséna, Augereau, Sérurier, Cervoni, La Harpe, and Rampon, to mention some of the more important, joined loyal hands with Napoleon's own chosen men, Murat, Berthier, Duroc, Marmont, and the fear-nothing Junot. We shall find many of these names occurring again and again, as the story develops and the career of the Master General expands. Few, if any, individuals succeed unaided, least of all the soldier and the statesman. Napoleon early recognised that the so-called self-made man is very rarely entitled to the credit implied in the name. He fostered the ambitions of his colleagues, but saw to it that he was the chief gainer by them.

After having provided so far as was possible for the creature comforts of the troops and raised their drooping spirits by his enthusiasm and the promise of good things to come, the commander prepared to strike a quick and decisive blow at his enemies. The armies of the King of Sardinia and Piedmont and of the Emperor of the Holy Roman Empire were not united in one large body, but separated by more than thirty miles. The central idea of this arrangement was that in case of necessity each could fall back on the capital of the country they were defending, the Austrians on Milan and the Sardinians on Turin. The wiser way, as Viscount Wolseley points out, would have been to concentrate at a place commanding both cities, in the valley of the Eastern Bormida, for instance. Napoleon saw the folly of the plan, and determined to force his way between the two armies and fight them separately. "United," as he said, "the two forces would have been superior to the French army: separated, they were lost." Napoleon hurried troops along the rut-wrinkled road to Voltri, within easy march of Genoa, to give the impression that the latter place was about to be attacked. Meantime, however, he and the main body encamped at the foot of the mountains, above Savona. After strongly fortifying the pass of Montenotte, the Austrians occupying a ridge above the village of that name, he prepared to attack, and on the 12th April took the enemy completely by surprise. The onset was deadly, the result certain. Masséna bore the brunt of the fight, the commander contenting himself with the highly important duty of preventing the enemy from reaching their Sardinian allies. The Imperialists were driven from the field with a loss of 700 dead and wounded. "My title of nobility," said Napoleon, "dates from the battle of Montenotte." Another Austrian defeat took place at Millesimo on the following day, and they were also ousted from the village of Dego, upon which they had fallen back, on the 14th.

Early on the morning of the 15th, an Austrian division, unaware of the disaster which had overtaken their comrades, seized Dego. Had not Napoleon acted with great promptitude, they might possibly have retrieved the defeat of the previous day. While Masséna and La Harpe bravely disputed the ground, Napoleon brought up reinforcements with an energy which alone saved the occasion. Having shattered this army, the Commander-in-chief turned his attention to the Sardinians at Ceva, under Colli, and at first met with a rebuff. Hoping to catch Napoleon in a trap, the enemy's camp was hastily broken up and the army marched off to occupy what the General fondly imagined were stronger positions. Defeat awaited them, however, at the hands of Sérurier and Dommartin, who came up with the Sardinians and forced them to fly towards Turin, their base of supplies. The town of Mondovi fell to the French, Marmont captured Cherasco. As a result of these operations, Savoy and Nice were ceded to France and the Austro-Sardinian alliance came to an abrupt end. The important fortresses of Coni, Tortona, and Alessandria were surrendered to the French and others were demolished. These strategic positions have been called "the keys of the Alps," and were necessary to the success of Napoleon's next operations. The Commissioners who represented Sardinia would not willingly grant demands which they held to be extortionate and which left but two fortified places worthy of consideration to the dismembered State. Napoleon told them that it was for him to make conditions. "Listen to the laws which I impose upon you in the name of the Government of my country," he added, "or to-morrow my batteries are erected, and Turin is in flames." Arguments which can be backed by deeds are unanswerable. Parma, also on the losing side, likewise sued for peace, the arrangement being that she should furnish specie and supplies for the French army. Napoleon during the course of his negotiations made use of a striking phrase which explains another of the secrets of his success. "It may happen to me to lose battles," he remarked, "but no one shall ever see me lose minutes either by over-confidence or by sloth."

Having concluded his diplomatic measures, the General was now ready to turn his attention to his remaining enemy. Before doing so he thought it well to make a further appeal to the patriotic instincts of his troops. Triumphant as never before, they were nevertheless beginning to weary of the ceaseless marching and fighting:

"Soldiers! you have gained in fifteen days six victories, taken twenty-one standards, fifty-five pieces of cannon, many strong places, and conquered the richest part of Piedmont. You have made fifteen thousand prisoners, and killed or wounded ten thousand men. Hitherto you have fought on barren rocks, illustrious, indeed, by your courage, but of no avail to your country. Now you rival by your services the Armies of Holland and of the Rhine. You were utterly destitute; you have supplied all your wants. You have gained battles without cannon; passed rivers without bridges; made forced marches without shoes; bivouacked without bread! The phalanxes of the Republic—the soldiers of liberty—were alone capable of such sacrifices. But, soldiers, you have accomplished nothing while anything remains to be done. Neither Turin nor Milan is in your hands; the ashes of the conqueror of Tarquin are still trampled on by the assassins of Basseville! I am told that there are some among you whose courage is failing, who would rather return to the summits of the Alps and the Appenines. No—I cannot believe it. The conquerors of Montenotte, of Millesimo, of Dego, of Mondovi burn to carry still further the glories of the French name! But, ere I lead you to conquest, there is one condition you must promise to fulfil; that is, to protect the people whom you liberate, and to repress all acts of lawless violence. Without this, you would not be the deliverers, but the scourge of nations. Invested with the national authority, strong in justice and law, I shall not hesitate to enforce the requisitions of humanity and of honour. I will not suffer robbers to sully your laurels. Pillagers shall be shot without mercy.

"People of Italy! the French army advances to break your chains. The French people are the friends of all nations. In them you may confide. Your property, your religion, your customs shall be respected. We will only make war as generous foes. Our sole quarrel is with the tyrants who enslave you!"

Without losing unnecessary time, Napoleon entered Piacenza, crossed the river Po on a hastily-constructed bridge of boats in face of a hostile force, and prepared to take the village of Fombio. Here some 5,000 Austrian infantry and cavalry were prepared to make a stand. The place literally bristled with artillery, even the churches were fortified; but the French routed the enemy, and the Imperialists were forced to retire.

Behind the swiftly-flowing Adda a strong rear-guard was posted, and on the 10th May Napoleon appeared at Lodi, on the opposite bank. A narrow bridge, some 200 yards in length and thirty feet wide, was the only means of crossing the turbulent stream. At first the Austrians tried to hold the structure, then attempted to break it down, but the steady fire of the French prevented them from doing so. To cross to the opposite bank was absolutely essential for a decisive action, and Napoleon gave orders that a column of picked men should be sent to seize the bridge. He was told that such an attempt could not possibly succeed. "Impossible!" he is asserted to have cried, "that word is not French!" He started the column. It meant certain death to many, but in warfare men are simply fighting machines controlled by the human dynamo at their head. The troops pressed forward. Those in front fell like leaves in autumn, as the shots from the opposite shore ploughed their ranks. Some of the most daring reached the middle of the bridge only to sink in a lifeless heap under the murderous hail. A retreat seemed inevitable, the bravest wavered.

Napoleon, quick to notice the slightest sign of weakness, again urged his troops forward. Lannes, Masséna, and Berthier, threw themselves into the thick of the fight, and shortly afterwards the bridge was carried. The rest was comparatively easy. The Austrian cannon were taken, the infantry which covered them was forced to give way, and the Imperialists again retreated, leaving 300 dead and wounded. It was in very truth a hard-fought field, for the victors lost a greater number of men. Had they been able to follow the retreating army, the triumph would have been complete. Napoleon declared that "it was not till after the terrible passage of the Bridge of Lodi that the idea flashed across my mind that I might become a decisive actor in the political arena. Then arose, for the first time, the spark of great ambition." It was after this battle that the soldiers nicknamed Napoleon "the little corporal." Sebottendorf, who commanded the defeated troops, bent his steps towards Mantua, to which Beaulieu, his superior officer, was also making his way.

CHAPTER IX
THE ITALIAN CAMPAIGN (1796–1797)

ON the 15th May 1796, the conqueror and his troops entered Milan, the Austrians retiring behind the banks of the Mincio, a river inseparably associated with the history of the Roman Empire. He encouraged the soldiers by telling them that they had overwhelmed and dispersed everything which had opposed their progress, that the Republic had ordered *fêtes* to be given in honour of the victories, and that on their return home "fellow citizens will say of each of you in passing: 'He was a soldier in the Army of Italy!'" He did not minimise the task before them, however, and bluntly asserted that much still remained to be done. "To restore the Capitol (at Rome); to replace there the statues of the heroes who have rendered it immortal; to rouse the Romans from centuries of slavery—such will be the fruit of our victories: they will form an era in history; to you will belong the glory of having changed the face of the most beautiful part of Europe." Such a proclamation was well calculated to inspire the inhabitants with ideas of liberty as well as to encourage soldiers still flushed with victory. The satisfaction of the people at these honied words, however, gave way to consternation when the news was noised abroad that 20,000,000 francs was the price of peace, to say nothing of free supplies for the troops. A futile flicker of resistance was shown by some of the more patriotic folk of Lombardy, who backed their opinions by force and came to blows with the pretended "liberators" at Milan and at Pavia. The retribution which followed swiftly, did not encourage other towns to rise; the Italian national spirit was but a weak thing then. The village of Brescia, although on Venetian and therefore neutral territory, was razed to the ground by fire. Napoleon himself marched on Pavia, which was carried by assault and sacked. Again Beaulieu attempted to check Napoleon, but he might as well have tried to prevent the sun from rising. The Austrians were defeated at Valeggio, Verona was entered by Masséna, and Napoleon prepared to lay siege to the well-fortified town of Mantua, the key to

Austria and Italy. Fifteen thousand troops were detailed for the purpose in addition to those who were to guard their communications. After compelling the insurrectionists at Milan to surrender, he entered Modena and Bologna, and sent Murat to Leghorn, thus violating the neutral territory of Tuscany.

But Napoleon was not to have it all his own way. The Austrians having revived their drooping spirits, were bent on making a last desperate resistance, and for a time it looked very much as though success would attend their efforts. They discomfited the French on more than one occasion, but instead of concentrating they fell into the fatal error of distributing their forces over a large area, and were thus precluded from striking decisive blows and following up their victories. Napoleon, equally determined, and much more wary, decided on a bold stroke. In order to secure the greatest possible number of troops, he raised the blockade of Mantua, which fortress was entered by Würmser, Beaulieu's successor, on the 1st August. After having gained a victory at Lonato Napoleon barely escaped capture. He and a garrison of some 1200 men were summoned to surrender by a corps of 4000 Austrians. The envoy, bearing a flag of truce, was led to Napoleon blindfolded, as is the custom. When the bandage was removed the Commander coolly asked him, "What means this insolence?" and added that he was in the middle of the French Army! The envoy was so overcome with fright that he told his superior officer more fiction than fact. Lonato was occupied by French troops, he assured him, and if the corps did not lay down their arms in ten minutes they would be shot. They preferred the less unpleasant expedient. Their feelings, when they discovered the clever trick which had been played on them, can be better imagined than described. On the same day Augereau, after considerable difficulty and much hard fighting, secured the important strategic position of Castiglione.

On the 5th August 1796, Würmser and Napoleon fought the battle of Médola. A lull followed the retreat of the Imperialists after this action, both sides utilising the time in repairing or attempting to repair the injuries sustained by them. Napoleon advanced to Verona, and Mantua was relieved by Würmser. Davidovich, the Austrian commander's colleague, met with defeat near Calliano, and Napoleon was thereby enabled to enter Trent, the capital of the Italian Tyrol. Shortly afterwards Würmser himself was defeated by Masséna near Bassano, Napoleon again having a narrow escape from capture as the Austrians retreated upon Mantua.

The Imperialists had now been reinforced and numbered some 60,000 troops. The force at Napoleon's disposal did not exceed 42,000, including the 8000 engaged in watching Mantua, who were therefore not available for more active co-operation at the front. On the 8th October 1796, he confided to the Directory that the situation was critical, that everything was going wrong in Italy, and appealed for further soldiers and more skilful diplomatic measures. The seriousness of his position became particularly evident in the following month, when Napoleon was forced to retreat owing to Vaubois' defeat in Tyrol. He told the soldiers without reserve that he was displeased with them, and even went so far as to say that he would have the standards of two of their regiments emblazoned with the words, "They are no longer of the Army of Italy." At Arcola on the 15th November, the Imperialist and Republican forces contested the ground with feverish and amazing energy, and as at Lodi, Napoleon behaved with conspicuous bravery. He carried a standard half way across the bridge, and was only prevented from proceeding further, amidst a hail of shot, by some grenadiers. Fearing for his life, they compelled him to return to a safer position. As it was, the brave fellows and their commander were pushed into the marsh by a body of the enemy who, taking advantage of the confusion, were crossing from the Austrian side. Napoleon was dragged out of the marsh by his brother Louis and Marmont.

When night closed in upon the armies victory rested with the Austrians. The battle was renewed, however, on the following day, and on the third the tide turned in Napoleon's favour. The repulse had robbed him of some of the sweets of conquest, but his worn-out soldiers knew that they had regained the confidence of their commander, and slept the sleep of the contented as they lay around their bivouac fires.

There is an oft-told story of this period which illustrates the alertness of Napoleon and shows how he could make allowances for human nature on occasions. One of the French sentries was discovered by Napoleon fast asleep at his post. The poor fellow had been harassed by frequent duty, and luckily Napoleon was in a sympathetic mood. He took the soldier's musket and stood patiently by, with tireless eyes, until he awoke. The man's consternation may be imagined when he saw who had been keeping watch in his place. He prepared for the worst, but, to his immense relief, Napoleon forgave him.

"It is the Emperor!"

By H. de T. Glazebrook

By permission of Messrs. Goupil & Co.

For two months affairs were at a standstill. Negotiations were begun and ended in a fierce war of words which settled nothing. Meantime fresh troops joined both forces, and when Napoleon became aware that the Austrians were concentrated not far from Rivoli, he was ready to throw the full force of his army upon them, although it was the weaker by nearly 10,000 men. On the 14th January 1797, the awful battle of Rivoli was fought. At the commencement some of the French regiments wavered under the Austrian attack, Masséna losing his temper so far as to strike several of the officers with the flat of his sword. While the fate of the day still hung in the balance a division of his troops was brought up, and the enemy found themselves engaged in a very determined manner. But try as they might to overthrow the white-coats, the French could not do so. The position became so desperate at last, that Napoleon had recourse to a stratagem which alone saved his army from disaster. It was all but surrounded by the Imperialists when, pretending that important despatches had just arrived from the seat of Government with reference to proposed negotiations between the conflicting parties, Napoleon sent a flag of truce to General Alvintzy. While Junot talked to the Austrian commander, Napoleon quietly re-arranged his forces. The conference broke up, as Napoleon intended, without result, and soon the combatants were again in action. The day ended in the triumph of the French.

Much remained to be done. Under Napoleon's command many of the weary soldiers were forced to march towards Mantua, in the direction of which Provera was hastening to raise the siege. The keen eyes of a sergeant who was engaged in the homely occupation of chopping wood at Fort George saved that French stronghold, in the early morning of the 15th January 1797. A regiment of the enemy's hussars, dressed somewhat like the French, misled the garrison of Fort George into the belief that they were friends come to their relief. The veteran gave the alarm before the Austrian hussars could make good their entry, and the drawbridge was hauled up and the enemy held in check while reinforcements were approaching. On the following day Napoleon drew near Mantua, and at La Favorita brought the Austrians to battle. Aided by the superb daring of Victor, whose achievements at Toulon have been noticed earlier, he forced Provera and some 6000 men to lay down their arms. It was one of the most brilliant achievements in the whole of this terrible campaign, and a fitting conclusion to the siege of Mantua, which capitulated on the 2nd February. For many a long day the regiment commanded by Victor was known as "The Terrible," a name it richly deserved.

Napoleon, aided by Joubert and Masséna, followed rapidly on the heels of the residue of the defeated army and gave it no rest. Pope Pius VI. having made himself objectionable by stirring up strife, the Commander-in-chief turned towards Florence preparatory to marching on Rome. The latter, however, became unnecessary, as a humiliating peace was signed at Tolentino on the 19th February 1797, by the terms of which the Pope was compelled to pay 30,000,000 francs, and to cede a considerable portion of territory, and various valuable works of art. The French, moreover, gained certain military and maritime advantages.

The contest with Austria continued to occupy the French, the Imperialists now being under the command of the Archduke Charles, the Emperor's brother. Finding himself in an awkward situation, Napoleon agreed to a suspension of hostilities, and preliminaries of peace were signed at Leoben on the 18th April, 1797, preparatory to the Treaty of Campo Formio on the 17th October. Dr J. Holland Rose thus summarizes the terms of the latter: "Austria ceded to the French Republic her Belgic provinces. Of the once extensive Venetian possessions France gained the Ionian Isles, while Austria acquired Istria, Dalmatia, the districts at the mouth of the Cattaro, the city of Venice, and the mainland of Venetia as far west as Lake Garda, the Adige, and the lower part of the River Po. The Hapsburgs recognised the independence of the now enlarged Cisalpine Republic.... The Emperor ceded to the dispossessed Duke of Modena the territory of Breisgau on the east of the Rhine."

Having so successfully played the parts of conqueror and diplomatist Napoleon went to Rastatt. One might have imagined that the journey was the triumphal progress of an Emperor. Feted by townsfolk and cheered by peasants as he went, the enthusiasm expressed might well have turned his head but that Napoleon had learnt his lessons in the hard school of experience. Bourrienne remarked on the admiration shown, that it must be delightful to be so greeted. "Bah!" Napoleon replied with disgust, "this same unthinking crowd, under a slight change of circumstances, would follow me just as eagerly to the scaffold." The Reign of Terror and his intimacy with the younger

Robespierre were too recent for their moral to be forgotten. From Rastatt he proceeded to Paris.

It is fortunate that a contemporary, who saw Napoleon at this time, has committed his observations to paper. "I beheld with deep interest and extreme attention that extraordinary man," he writes, "who has performed such great deeds, and about whom there is something which seems to indicate that his career is not yet terminated. I found him much like his portraits, small in stature, thin, pale, with an air of fatigue, but not, as has been reported, in ill-health. He appeared to me to listen with more abstraction than interest, as if occupied rather with what he was thinking of, than with what was said to him. There is great intelligence in his countenance, along with an expression of habitual meditation, which reveals nothing of what is passing within. In that thinking head, in that daring mind, it is impossible not to suppose that some designs are engendering which will have their influence on the destinies of Europe."

The magnificent reception accorded to Napoleon by the Directory in the Luxembourg on the 10th December 1797 surpassed all others. Madame de Staël, that witty woman whom Napoleon detested because of her meddling in politics, tells us that "Bonaparte arrived, dressed very simply, followed by his aides-de-camp, all taller than himself, but nearly bent by the respect which they displayed to him. M. de Talleyrand, in presenting Bonaparte to the Directory, called him 'the Liberator of Italy, and the Pacificator of the Continent.' He assured them that 'General Bonaparte detested luxury and splendour, the miserable ambition of vulgar souls, and he loved the poems of Ossian particularly, because they detach us from the earth.'" Napoleon, who had a keen sense of the dramatic, knew very well that the plainer he dressed on such an occasion the more conspicuous he would be in a crowd of such magnificence. One sentence of his short but telling speech is worthy of notice: "From the peace you have just concluded," he said, "dates the era of representative governments." In a certain sense this was true, notwithstanding that his own despotism was destined to have its day.

Napoleon was now given command of the so-called Army of England, which the Government fondly hoped would plant its standards on the banks of the Thames. The general soon dispelled this delusion. The time was not yet come for his gigantic preparations to subdue "perfidious Albion." The glamour of the East beckoned him. "All great fame comes from that quarter," he told Bourrienne. An expedition to Egypt and the restoration of French rule in India were more to his liking at the moment and offered more possibilities of enhanced fame. Not slow to read the signs of the times, and knowing the Directors were jealous of his reputation, Napoleon felt that an absence from France might have the desired effect of showing how very useful he was to the Republic.

CHAPTER X
THE EXPEDITION TO EGYPT (1798)

THERE is no more romantic phase of Napoleon's career than that of his expedition to the sunny land of the Pharaohs. He has himself told us that "Imagination rules the world," and although he was essentially practical by nature, a man who invariably worked out his plans to almost fractional details, whenever practicable, his ardent Southern temperament readily responded to the glow and glamour of the Orient. There history had been made, there history was to be made. He saw vast possibilities in the slumbering East, perhaps an awakening into prodigious activity under the rule of a military dictator with liberal ideas. He might revitalise Asia as he had revivified some of the moribund States of worn-out Europe. Briefly his object was to conquer Egypt, oust the British from India, where their rule was by no means consolidated, and on his return, crush the power of the Sultan. Everything seemed to favour him in engineering the machinery of this vast project. The scientists of France took up the scheme with avidity, and learned members of the Institute, to which he had been admitted in the place of Carnot, gave him the benefit of their researches.

The notion of the expedition was not a sudden inspiration, acted upon on the spur of the moment. So far back as the 10th August 1797, when affairs in Italy were still far from settled, Napoleon had mentioned the subject to the Directory, following it up by a lengthy letter a month later. He now reasoned it out, read travel books, examined maps, interrogated men of accurate knowledge, brooded over it in the solitude of the study, and mentally weighed the chances of success and failure. The scales turned in its favour, and Napoleon determined to rival the doings of Alexander.

Before long, extensive preparations were going on apace at Toulon, Genoa, Ajaccio, and Civita Vecchia. It was eminently necessary that Great Britain, which was still at war with France and had commanded the sea since the

Tudor Navy had broken the giant power of Spain, should be deceived as to the destination of the fleets. As a subterfuge the so-called Army of England solemnly paraded, marched, and counter-marched. Those who were not in the secret thought the soldiers were awaiting the signal to embark for England, but it became evident as time passed that offensive operations against the English were not intended, some of the smartest battalions being gradually drafted into a newly-formed Army of Egypt. Everything was done with as much secrecy and celerity as possible; the meetings of the Directory, when the project was under discussion, were held with closed doors. It is significant that the cost was largely defrayed by plunder and forced contributions from the long-suffering Swiss.

A magnificent fleet was fitted out at Toulon, and when all the convoys at the various ports already mentioned had been concentrated, it reached a total of thirteen battle-ships, fourteen frigates, seventy-two corvettes, and nearly four hundred smaller craft, chiefly merchant vessels. Even with this great armament there was overcrowding, for quarters had to be found for no fewer than 35,000 troops. In addition there were over a hundred members of the Commission of the Arts and Sciences, all of whom were liberally provided with instruments and books likely to be of service in the warfare against ignorance and the intellectual conquest of the East. The admiral in command was Brueys, who had weathered the battle and the breeze for many a long year, the generals were the pick of the French Army, doughty champions of the Republic and reliable upholders of Napoleon's supreme command; Kléber, Desaix, Berthier, Murat, Menou, Lannes, Andréossi, to mention a few of the more prominent.

Good fortune attended the expedition at the outset, and it was regarded as of good augury that Nelson's reconnoitring squadron had been forced to retire by a gale and obliged to make for Sardinia, and that the morning of departure was sunny and cloudless. The Fates were surely with the French! For good or evil, the armada left Toulon on the 19th May 1798, picking up the vessels lying in other ports, as it proceeded eastward. Napoleon, accompanied by the *savants*, sailed on *l'Orient*, reputed to be the finest three-decker afloat. Malta was the first object of conquest, or rather of aggression. The Knights of St John, to whom the island belonged, surrendered quietly and without opposition. A Judas had been found willing to sell the once great Order which had fought the infidel and the Turk in the Holy Land, before Napoleon had put his foot on shore. Having garrisoned the island, planned an incredible number of reforms within a week, and replenished his coffers, Napoleon gave orders for the anchors to be weighed. The monotonous voyage was continued; monotonous because the lust of conquest coursed through the veins of commander and men alike, and they were impatient to be in action, so long as it was not action against Nelson, who was to be avoided at any cost.

Napoleon was not a good sailor, and passed most of the time in his cabin reading, one of the works in his travelling library being "Cook's Voyages." Sometimes he would talk over nautical matters with Brueys, or discuss abstruse subjects with one or other of the scientists. One fine night on deck he pointed to the stars, and said: "You may talk as long as you please, gentlemen, but who made all that?" He lost no time, availed himself of every opportunity of adding to his already extensive knowledge of the East, and was as energetic mentally as an athlete is physically.

On the 1st July the sandy shore of Alexandria was sighted, and in the evening disembarkation began. It was a long and trying task to hoist the horses from the holds and land the heavy artillery, ammunition wagons, supplies, and the thousand and one impedimenta of warfare, but by the following morning the task was accomplished. Napoleon had already counselled moderation in his soldiers, telling them to respect the Mohammedan religion and those who represented it as well as the national customs. The conquest they were about to undertake was to be "fraught with incalculable effect upon the commerce and civilization of the world." Having secured the city after a short fight, in which the Mohammedans behaved with traditional daring, Napoleon issued a proclamation to the people to the effect that he had come to restore their rights and their religion, and to punish the usurpers, namely the Mamelukes. He said harsh things of the savage hordes who held the country in terror, threatening dire results to those who should join their marauding forces against the French. "For them there will be no hope; they shall perish!"

He infused new life into the sleepy civic institutions of Alexandria, gave orders for the repair of the age-worn fortifications, and for the erection of new batteries as well as for building factories and schools. In less than a week he was ready to make a move in the direction of Cairo, leaving 3000 men at Alexandria under Kléber, who had been wounded in the preliminary brush with the Mamelukes.

A march across sixty miles of burning sand was but the beginning of the hardships these tried soldiers of fortune were to endure in a land which neither provided water nor flowed with milk and honey. It seemed more like the abomination of desolation. Parched, footsore, dispirited, soldiers and officers alike drew invidious comparisons between the barren deserts of Egypt and the fertile plains of Lombardy. The die was cast; there was nothing to do but to follow the leader who frequently walked at the head of the columns supporting the same discomforts with cheerful fortitude. Attacks by bands of Mamelukes occasionally created a diversion and thinned the ranks. A cloud of dust in the distance would put the army on the defensive. Presently little specks would emerge which ultimately would resolve themselves into horses and riders. A short, sharp tussle and again the wild warriors would be flying over the sand on their swift Arab steeds. The troops soon became inured to this kind of warfare and learnt to meet it by forming into squares which the native cavalry, however swift their onslaught, could not pierce. When the army reached the banks of the Nile the whole aspect of the country changed and the soldiers took fresh courage.

At last the minarets of Cairo glimmered through the haze. The city boasted a population of many thousands, and their task-masters were prepared to sell their lives dearly in its defence. Near the Pyramids, those monuments of ancient greatness, the army halted. "Soldiers!" Napoleon cried, "from those summits forty centuries contemplate your actions." A more pregnant sentence cannot be conceived; it acted on the soldiers like a stimulant. There was difficult work to do, for the city was intrenched and defended by artillery, musketry, and cavalry under the command of Murad Bey, one of the chiefs of the Mamelukes.

A flotilla with supplies had met the French previously, so there was no question of lack of ammunition, but the enemy, probably numbering 18,000 men, looked as though they would make a brave fight of it. They did not belie their appearance. The Mamelukes charged the dense squares with amazing recklessness but were driven back. Presently Napoleon gave the word, his troops surged forward, and Frenchman and Arab met in a death-struggle in the trenches. Those of the enemy who could make good their escape did so, others were mown down as they made the attempt. Some expired on the wind-swept sand, others perished in the turgid waters of the Nile. Thus ended the Battle of the Pyramids. At nightfall the Egyptian camp presented a very different spectacle from its appearance in the morning. Soldiers were ransacking the scarcely cold bodies of those who had fallen in the rout, searching the camp for booty, for jewels, for ornaments of silver and of gold. Never was there richer plunder. Napoleon, now master of Cairo, made his headquarters in a palace formerly occupied by the defeated Murad. As at Malta, Napoleon at once began his scheme of reform, only on a necessarily larger scale. A general Congress was established for the government of the country. A scientific institute was founded, its chief object being to collect facts and figures likely to be of use in the development of Egypt. Many of the indispensable accessories of modern civilisation, from windmills to printing presses, were introduced. Romantic fancies were becoming realities, when Napoleon heard of the irreparable loss of his fleet, news which burst upon him with almost stunning force. Think for a moment what the disaster meant. The fleet was his sole means of communication with France. Brueys had signally neglected to carry out his master's orders that he was either to enter the harbour of Alexandria or to return to Corfu, and he had thereby given Nelson the opportunity which he had long been seeking and which had eluded him again and again. Some excuse is afforded Brueys by reason of his bad health, and it is certain that he found it next to impossible to control his insubordinate crews. On the 1st August 1798 the little one-eyed, one-armed British seaman not only shattered a French fleet considerably superior in strength, but dealt a crushing blow at the supremacy of the Republic in Egypt, although the full effects were not to be felt at once. The French, who fought with conspicuous bravery, were aided by the batteries which they had erected on shore, whereas the British had only their naval armament to rely upon. Within a short time five French ships were put out of action; when fighting finished, but two of Napoleon's men-of-war and two frigates remained to make good their escape. The magnificent *l'Orient* caught fire, and "by the prodigious light of this conflagration," Southey tells us in his "Life of Nelson," "the situation of the two fleets could now be perceived, the colours of both being plainly distinguishable. About ten the ship blew up, with a shock that was felt to the very bottom of every vessel. Many of the officers and men jumped overboard, some clinging to the spars and pieces of wreck with which the sea was strewn, others swimming to escape the destruction which they momentarily dreaded. Some were picked up by our boats; and some, even in the heat and fury of the action, were dragged into the lower ports of the nearest British vessel by the British sailors. The greater part of the crew, however, stood the danger to the last, and continued to fire from the lower deck. This tremendous explosion was followed by a silence not less awful. The firing immediately ceased on both sides; and the first sound that broke the silence was the dash of her shattered masts and yards falling into the water from the vast height to which they had been exploded.... About seventy of the *l'Orient's* crew were saved by the English boats. Among the many hundreds who perished were the Commodore, Casa-Bianca, and his son, a brave boy, only ten years old. They were seen floating on a shattered mast when the ship blew up."

Brueys paid for his carelessness with his life, and his victorious antagonist was severely wounded. The French admiral fought with superb daring, and his dying words: "Fight to the last!" muttered on the quarter-deck as he bore the most excruciating agony, are a fitting parallel to those of Nelson when he was struck down. "I will take my turn with my brave fellows," he said, as the surgeons came to attend to his wounds. They were both worthy sons of their countries, and if the gods had denied Brueys the genius they had so lavishly bestowed on Nelson, he proved himself to be every inch a man.

CHAPTER XI
FROM CAIRO TO FRÉJUS (1798–1799)

NAPOLEON was not the type of man who meets troubles half way and quietly accepts what some might consider to be the inevitable. He certainly believed, or pretended to believe, in his star, which was only another word for Fate, with a persistency worthy of an astrologer. At the beginning of his career this did not preclude him from taking the utmost precautions that his destiny should not be averted by any want of energy or forethought on his part. Such a policy is by no means the paradox it would appear. A soldier must pull the sword from its scabbard if it is to be of service; faith must be supported by works. Therefore, while the General recognised the seriousness of his position in Egypt, he was no less determined to fight to the end.

As Murad Bey was still at large, Desaix was sent with a detachment to Upper Egypt, where he was known to be, Napoleon setting off for Suez for the purpose of seeing at first hand whether the cutting of a canal was a practicable proposition. While he was engaged in this peaceful occupation, Europe, encouraged by Nelson's victory, was preparing to resist him in the field. England, Russia and Turkey were determined to overthrow French influence in Egypt. At Rhodes 20,000 Turks were ready to sail for the seat of war, in Syria a second army assembled to assist the other, while a third army was preparing in India to land on the shores of the Red Sea and attack the French in their rear. There seemed, indeed, a possibility that Napoleon might be caught between the upper and the nether millstones.

With the craft of the Oriental, Murad Bey, defeated but not crushed, still plotted and planned to rid Egypt of her conquerors. At his instigation Cairo revolted, but was taught a severe lesson by Napoleon; other conspiracies were dealt with in the same stern way. Presently came the startling news that the vanguard of the Syrian army was not only in the field, but had actually taken El Arish. With one of those swift movements inseparably associated with his science of war, Napoleon started with 10,000 troops on a five-days' march across the treacherous desert, the sun blazing down upon the men, scorching their faces, baking their feet, and parching their tongues. At last the dreary march came to an end, and at midnight the French bombarded El Arish and captured the town. But there was to be no rest for the tired troops; they resumed their march to Gaza, where another division of the Turkish army was routed. On the 4th March 1799, Jaffa was reached. It was more a massacre than a battle which ensued, and the Turks were compelled to retreat in disorder before the iron hail which decimated their ranks.

After this battle Napoleon ordered many prisoners to be shot. Warfare never has been child's play, and it must be remembered that Napoleon could ill afford to have his army hindered by the care of captives. At the same time it is difficult to extenuate the act, although some of the victims had been captured before and broken their promise not to fight again.

To reduce Acre, where a strong army was gathered, was the next item on the French military programme. The Turks were fortunate in having the assistance of so able an officer as Commodore Sir Sidney Smith, who commanded a small fleet with which he captured a French flotilla conveying a large number of guns and a considerable quantity of ammunition for Napoleon from Damietta. The task of reducing Acre soon began to look as difficult as that of Mantua in the last campaign. The French General had also to fight an unseen enemy in the plague which broke out in the army and caused serious mortality. To crown all, news was received of the approach of some 30,000 Turks and Mamelukes. Kléber, with an advance guard of 3,000 troops, was pushed forward in the direction of the enemy, followed by Napoleon with an equal number. Two thousand men were left at Acre to maintain the siege as best they could. "The fate of the East depends upon the capture of Acre," he told Bourrienne. "That is the key of Constantinople or of India." He counted on being able to raise and arm the whole population of Syria on the fall of the town. "My armed masses will penetrate to Constantinople, and the Mussulman dominion will be overturned. I shall found in the East a new and mighty Empire, which will fix my position with posterity." Vain and empty dream, but perhaps not so vain or so empty as a casual reader might suppose.

On the 16th April, Kléber came up with the enemy near Mount Tabor, and notwithstanding the disparity in numbers, held out for hours against the Turkish host. Napoleon and his troops arrived on the scene not a minute too soon; another half an hour in all probability would have decided the issue in favour of the Turks. The new detachments helped to stem the tide, but the Mussulmans continued their valiant attacks upon the French squares. The sterling courage of Murat was never seen to greater advantage. Apparently throwing prudence to the winds he charged with his troops into the enemy's ranks regardless of consequences. It may have been foolhardy, it was certainly dramatic, and turned the scales in favour of the French. The issue of the battle of Mount Tabor was an annihilation rather than a victory.

By the 19th Napoleon had returned to his work at Acre. Three French frigates brought him six cannon of large calibre and intelligence of a rapidly-approaching Turkish fleet, two vessels of which they had been fortunate enough to capture.

Almost every conceivable method of concluding the siege was now tried by both parties, and the place was literally honeycombed with mines. When the vanguard of the Turkish fleet was sighted, Napoleon knew that if he were to triumph it was to be now or never. With additional forces, both naval and military, the enemy would outnumber him in an alarming proportion, while his own ranks were diminishing hourly. Three columns were hurled to the attack; one was driven back, the others seized a tower which occupied an important strategic position. On the following day it became evident that without assistance the defenders would be forced to surrender. Sir Sidney Smith landed parties of sailors and marines, and was afterwards joined by reinforcements from the Turkish ships. By a subtle stratagem the French were prompted to make a false move which led them into the palace garden, where they were literally mown down. For ten days afterwards Napoleon struggled against the inevitable, and then, during the night of the 20th May, he began his first retreat to Cairo, via Jaffa and El Arish, a distance of some 300 miles, harassed by many a sharp skirmish with the enemy on the way.

After defeating Murad Bey and restoring some sort of order in Upper Egypt, Napoleon found it necessary to order Desaix to evacuate the province, an immediate concentration of troops having become imperative owing to the approach of yet another Turkish fleet at Alexandria and the landing of 10,000 Turks at Aboukir. Two battles were fought at Alexandria within a few hours, and many of the enemy were literally driven into the sea, but it was a close shave and Napoleon was within an ace of losing the second battle. Of the 10,000 Mussulmans who had landed to annihilate the French and restore Turkish rule in Egypt, 2,000 prisoners alone remained to tell the tale. It was one of the most marvellous of Napoleon's many extraordinary achievements in that country.

When arranging for an exchange of prisoners Sir Sidney Smith took the opportunity to send a little packet of newspapers containing news of vital importance to the French commander. He read of French reverses, of the great armies of the Second Coalition coming into being against the Republic, of despair and discontent in official and public circles. Indeed, the Directory had gone so far as to negotiate for Napoleon's return, so inextricable was the muddle they were in, but the General did not hear of this until later. He determined upon a policy which has been discussed in and out of season by historians for over a century; he would go back to France. Modern philosophers would have us believe that his decision was "perfectly justifiable on political grounds," but many Frenchmen at the time thought otherwise. To them it seemed a flagrant injustice to the army he commanded. "Bonaparte had fled from Egypt, as he fled from Russia and from Waterloo," says Baron de Frénilly. "A general does not flee—he retreats. But Bonaparte was ever the general of Fortune, and every time that she abandoned him he fled like a soldier, leaving the others to get out of the difficulty as best they could. This man, then, crept out of Egypt by night, glided between the English frigates and entered Paris. There he had to stoop and take what he wanted. France—after passing, during eight years, from the anarchy of revolutionaries to the anarchy of political comedians—was eager for the despotism of a single man."

There is much truth in the Baron's irony. For Napoleon the Orient had lost much of its charms; his political horizon was bounded again by the west solely because he had an eye for the main chance. His thoughts frequently wandered to the east at later periods of his career, the appeal becoming at times almost irresistible, so completely had the spell enchanted him. For the time being, however, it had lost its hold.

On the night of the 22nd August 1799, Napoleon left the inhospitable land of the Pharaohs never to return. There were grumbles and desertions on the part of the troops, which vague promises of relief from France did little to compensate. Kléber remained in command. On board the two frigates, alone available for Napoleon's use, he found accommodation for many of the best officers, including Lannes, Berthier, Murat, Marmont, and Duroc, useful men to have at any time. Few ships have ever had a more distinguished passenger list. God may be on the side of the biggest battalions, as Napoleon said, but assuredly Providence was with the little band which set out on so hazardous a voyage on that still summer night. The undertaking was fraught with perils, for many British ships were sighted, but having once more gazed on his beloved Ajaccio, where he was greeted with every sign of respect and admiration, Napoleon landed safely at St Raphael, near Fréjus, on the 9th October 1799, after an absence from France of nearly fifteen months. He had not accomplished all he had set out to do, but he had added considerably to his military prestige, and that was everything in the position in which *la belle France* was now placed.

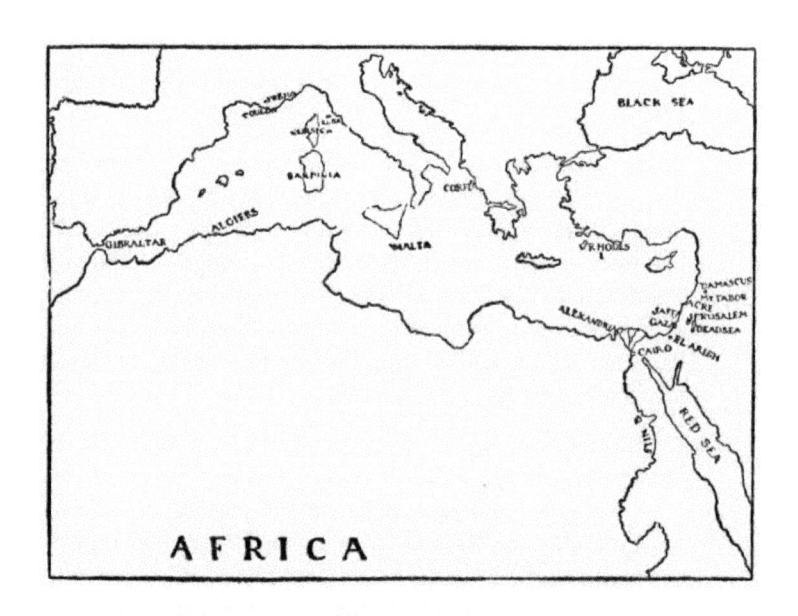

AFRICA

CHAPTER XII
HOW NAPOLEON SEIZED THE REINS OF GOVERNMENT (1799)

"WE were plunging under full sail back to the abyss of the Terror, without a gleam of consolation or of hope. The glory of our arms was tarnished, our conquests lost, our territory threatened with invasion.... All the efforts made by honest statesmen to secure the legal enjoyment of their rights had been crushed by violence. There seemed to be nothing before us but to return to a bloodthirsty anarchy, the duration of which it was as impossible to foresee as it was to find any remedy."

Thus writes the Duke de Broglie of this period, and his picture is none too black for reality. The attempt to establish a Constitutional Republic had failed; the Directors had proved their inability to hold the reins of government or to check the disaster which almost everyone felt must inevitably come. One gleam of sunshine alone brightened the horizon of the bankrupt nation, namely the news of Napoleon's landing. From the point of view of the general public this was worth more than Masséna's victory at Zurich over the Austrians and Russians in the previous month, which had alone saved the unhappy country from invasion.

Clearly the Republic needed a strong man at the head of affairs; and in Napoleon it soon recognised its master. He arrived in Paris on the 16th October 1799, and as on the occasion of his return from Italy he was feasted and fêted. Again he showed the same taciturnity and seeming absence of interest. Perhaps to unbend would have been to unmask himself; a haughty demeanour often hides a fluttering heart. He lived quietly, affecting the unobtrusive dress of the National Institute, seeming to take more delight in the company of philosophers than of politicians. In reality he was waiting the turn of events, weighing his chances of securing the reins of government, and carefully considering the possible policies of Moreau and Bernadotte, the rival generals who shared public sympathy with him. Either of the two great parties in the government, the Moderates and the Democrats, the former under the leadership of Director Sieyès, the latter under Director Barras, would have been glad for Napoleon to throw in his lot with them; indeed, so keen was popular enthusiasm that his glory, reflected in his brother Lucien, carried the election of the latter as President of the Five Hundred. Without undue haste Napoleon decided in favour of the less aggressive and semi-monarchical policy represented by Sieyès and supported by the majority of Ancients. Between them they determined to overthrow the Directory, their immediate accomplices being Lucien Bonaparte, Talleyrand, and Roederer. Later the conspirators received the support of many of the leading generals, including Lannes, Lefebvre, Murat, Berthier and Marmont, as well as of many influential legislators.

Meantime accomplices in the Council of Ancients had been skilfully at work, and had induced their colleagues to decide to transfer the meetings of the two legislative bodies from the too-accessible Tuileries to the less-frequented St Cloud, ostensibly because of a Jacobin conspiracy, in reality that the Parisian mob might not interfere, for it was hoped that the coming *coup d'état*, or "stroke of state," might fall with as little disturbance as possible. Régnier de la Meurthe, who was in the General's confidence, proposed that Napoleon be called upon to see that the decrees of removal were executed, which was duly carried, a large number of troops thus being placed under his command for that purpose, which was exactly what he required for the complete success of the plot. Proceeding to the Tuileries on the 18th Brumaire (November 9), Napoleon addressed the assembled Ancients in a short flattering speech, assuring them that they were the collected wisdom of the nation, and offering the support of his generals and of himself. When the Council of Five Hundred heard the decree which removed them to St Cloud, there were wild scenes which they soon found could serve no useful purpose. Military under the command of Lannes, Murat, Mureau, Serrurier, and others had been so disposed as to be ready for any emergency either within or without the building, and no amount of argument could have swayed Napoleon from his purpose. If the Directors were not actually deposed they were practically forced to resign; Gohier and Moulins, offering opposition, were put under arrest.

Installation of Napoleon as First Consul, December 25, 1799

By L. Couder

By permission of Braun, Clément & Co., Dornach (Alsace)

On the following day Napoleon appeared before the Ancients at St Cloud and made a short speech, then proceeded to an apartment known as the Orangery in which the Five Hundred were sitting. The building itself was surrounded by troops, and accompanied by a guard he made his entrance, the soldiers remaining within call in case their presence should be required. Immediately cries of "Down with the tyrant! No Cromwell! Down with the Dictator! Outlaw him!" arose from different parts of the hall. Attempts were made to lay violent hands on the General, who was bodily removed in a half-fainting condition by a couple of grenadiers acting under the orders of his supporter Lefebvre. Lucien Bonaparte endeavoured to make himself heard, but without effect; the utmost disorder reigned. General Augereau attempted to put the question of outlawry to the vote, whereupon the former renounced his office of President, flung off his official robes, left the building, and joined his brother. He made a rousing speech to the troops, declaring that the majority of the Council of the Five Hundred "is enthralled by a faction armed with daggers who besiege the tribune and interdict all freedom of deliberation. General, and you soldiers, and you citizens, you can no longer recognise any as legislators but those who are around me. Let force expel those who remained in the Orangery; they are not the representatives of the people, but the representatives of the dagger," and so on. "Soldiers," cried Napoleon, "can I rely on you?" There seemed some hesitation, and Lucien swore to plunge his sword in his brother's breast should he make an attempt on the liberty of France. This aroused the troops from their apathy, and they at once threw in their lot with Napoleon. Bayonets were fixed and the order given to march into the Orangery. Not a few of the politicians jumped from the windows in their alarm. The Ancients were then informed by Lucien that daggers had been used by their fellow politicians—probably a figment of his imagination—and the Council of the Five Hundred dissolved. Within an hour of midnight a little group of legislators who sided with Napoleon passed a decree which abolished the Directory, adjourned meetings of the Councils for three months, and created Napoleon, Sieyès and Ducos provisional Consuls.

"The 18 Brumaire," to again quote the Duke de Broglie, "was the salvation of France, and the four years that followed it were a series of triumphs, alike over our external enemies, and over the principles of disaster and anarchy at home. These four years are, with the ten years of the reign of Henry IV., the noblest period of French history."

"The little Corporal" had won the day. Henceforth until his fall he was to dominate France.

CHAPTER XIII
THE PASSAGE OF THE ALPS (1799–1801)

IT must be conceded that Napoleon signalised this phase of his career by measures which promised exceedingly well for the future. He showed the velvet glove, but it was obvious that he, and he alone, was the controlling power in France. The Republic was in chaotic disorder; his first task was to unravel the tangled skein. Under the careful nursing of Gaudin, subsequently Duke of Gaëta, aided by the energy of Napoleon, some kind of business stability was ensured. The claims of religion were recognised and re-established; the horrible law of hostages, which visited the presumed sins of the fathers upon the heads of their children, and made the latter responsible for the actions of the former, was revoked; such eminent exiles as Lafayette and Latour-Maubourg were allowed to return. Civil war was almost, if not entirely, stamped out by the introduction of strong measures, and several of the more untractable leaders were shot.

Under Berthier, who became Minister of War, the army was speedily rejuvenated. Sieyès produced a new constitution, a not too practicable one be it said. It was obviously designed to limit the power of Napoleon as much as possible, the actual reins of government being in the hands of his two colleagues. Sieyès reckoned without his host, who was not prepared to play second fiddle to anyone, and Napoleon soon had everything in his grip. Eventually the Government, according to the Constitution of the year VIII. of the Republican Calendar, was established as follows: After the Consuls and Ministers came the Council of State, consisting of not more than forty Members, all of whom were appointed by the First Consul. They were divided into five sections—Legislation, the Interior, War, Marine and Colonies, Finance. The Consuls or their seven Ministers of State placed all proposed Bills before the section to which they belonged, who reported upon them to the Council as a whole. If they were deemed worthy they were passed on to the Tribunat, who debated on them, and the Corps Législatif, who adopted or rejected them, the Council carrying out those which were accepted. Then there was the Conservative Senate, the members of which held office for life. They discussed and decided whether acts or laws submitted to them by the Government or the Tribunat were constitutional or otherwise. A list of National Notability was to be formed from which the Conservative Senate was to select the Consuls, members of the Tribunat and Corps Législatif, and various other officials.

The Sovereignty of the People was doomed; their power was strictly limited. As to Napoleon's own aim at the time perhaps Sir Walter Scott is not far wrong when he suggests that "his motives were a mixture of patriotism and the desire of self-advancement."

Before long Sieyès and Ducos resigned. Their places were filled by Cambacérès, a lawyer who had been a member of the Convention, and Lebrun, who had royalist sympathies—men eminently fitted for the positions of Second and Third Consuls respectively. Neither was too clever nor too dull to exercise the strictly limited power they enjoyed, both were moderate in their views, and possessed a fair stock of common sense. Of other persons whom Napoleon attached to himself and his now rapidly-increasing prospects we need only mention Talleyrand, who combined the wisdom of the serpent with its cunning, and who was reinstated Minister of Foreign Affairs, and Fouché, of even more easy conscience, who became Minister of Police, a department with which he likewise had made acquaintance previously.

Napoleon, now officially styled First Consul and having a salary of half a million francs a year, speedily removed to the magnificent palace of the Tuileries, where he had a Court worthy of a reigning monarch. The levelling process of the Revolution gave place to the observance of formal rules and the stateliest ceremonies. Napoleon was monarch in all but name, which was to come.

So much for home affairs; the outlook abroad was not so bright. A second coalition had been formed by Russia Austria, England, Turkey, Naples, and Portugal against

France during Napoleon's absence in Egypt, and the Republic was still at war with Great Britain and Austria. In order to make it appear that he was sincere in his expressions of a desire for peace, Napoleon wrote personal letters to the heads of the belligerent States. It is extremely unlikely that he meant what he said. Neither the means by which he had obtained power nor his previous career were calculated to give confidence in his sincerity. Nothing practical came of the overtures. Austria and Russia had defeated such tried generals as Schérer, Moreau, Macdonald, and Joubert, and as "nothing succeeds like success," the Emperor Francis was unusually optimistic. In Northern Italy, Genoa alone remained to the French, and although the Republicans had gained splendid victories in Holland and Switzerland, Austria was determined to bring the war to the very doors of the French. In order to make the succeeding operations clear the movements of the various armies will be detailed separately.

The French army of Italy, on the Riviera and at Genoa, which was in a most distressing condition, was under Masséna, their opponents being commanded by Melas, whose actual fighting strength was more than double that of the Republicans. The Imperialists succeeded in dividing the French army, whereby Suchet was cut off from the main force, but he defended himself with conspicuous energy. Masséna retreated to Genoa, the British under Lord Keith preventing exit and ingress at sea, the Austrians besieging the city. The French general held out until the 4th June, when he was allowed to evacuate the place by the Allies.

The Republican army of the Rhine, commanded by Moreau, was distributed between Strassburg and Constance, and was also in smaller numerical strength than the Austrian forces under Kray, whose total forces reached 150,000, or some 40,000 more than the French. The Imperialists had also the additional advantage of occupying a magnificent strategic position at Donaueschingen. Moreau crossed the Rhine, fought several victorious battles, and prevented the enemy from keeping in touch with Melas. Napoleon had wished him to strike a decisive blow at Donaueschingen, but the more cautious Moreau, lacking the military genius of the First Consul, regarded so drastic an operation as extremely hazardous and exposing his force to annihilation. He was successful, however, in enticing the Austrian general from his commanding position, and Kray's subsequent movements were so disastrous that he was forced to take shelter in Ulm, a town so strongly fortified as to be almost impregnable.

There was much hard fighting before the city capitulated. Subsequently Munich was entered, and it seemed as though nothing could stop Moreau's progress save only his want of faith in himself, for even a brave soldier does not always realise his own strength. The Armistice of Parsdorf, signed on the 15th July 1800, suspended hostilities in Germany for a short period.

Meantime Napoleon, with a reserve army numbering from 40,000 to 50,000 troops, decided to cross the Alps and so manœuvre that the "white coats" would be placed between Masséna's forces and his own. In addition he was determined that Austria should surrender what he doubtless considered her ill-gotten gains, namely those parts of Italy which the French had lost. It was a bold plan, for the ranges were in very truth "mountains of difficult." The greatest secrecy was observed, a corps being assembled at Dijon to deceive the enemy, the troops intended for the expedition being quietly concentrated at Geneva and Lausanne. It was a deep-laid plot and worked wonderfully well. While Austria was poking fun in caricature and print at the nondescript troops which were to be seen lounging about or parading in the streets of the old capital of Burgundy, Napoleon and Berthier, the latter of whom had been appointed Commander-in-Chief, were working all day and oftentimes far into the night perfecting arrangements for the great surprise. The means of transport for the heavy artillery alone presented considerable difficulty, and this was but one of many difficulties unknown in previous campaigns. It was finally decided that the cannon should be placed in hollowed-out tree-trunks sawn in half after the manner of primitive boats. When on the march these were to be hauled by gangs of peasants or soldiers, for it was soon found that sufficient mules were not procurable.

In May 1800, Napoleon was at Geneva. After consultations with the engineers it was determined that the main army should cross into Lombardy by the Great St Bernard, smaller divisions travelling by the St Gothard, Mount Cenis, and Little St Bernard routes, the better to mislead the enemy. A start was made on the 15th. Column after column began the weary tramp along the desolate, snow-covered tracks, feeling their way across narrow ledges over precipices, cheered again and again by a sight of the First Consul as, wrapped in a grey overcoat and seated on a mule led by a guide, he traversed the rugged route of the Great St Bernard. The twenty miles of soldiers crossed in less than a week, and considering the treacherous nature of the march, or rather scramble, very few lost their lives.

The post of Bard, on the banks of the Aosta in the valley of that name, garrisoned by the Austrians, had been attacked by the advance guard under Lannes without success. It was the most serious opposition they had yet encountered, and it was necessary to pass almost under the shadow of the guns. Marmont conceived a happy device which proved entirely successful. At night the streets through the village were liberally strewn with straw and other stubble by the French soldiers. The wheels of the gun-carriages were then carefully covered to avoid rattling, and the passage was successfully achieved, although the alarm was sounded and there was some desultory firing.

On the 2nd June Napoleon, marching with the utmost rapidity, entered Milan. A week later, and almost at the same time as the First Consul was withdrawing his troops from the old city for further offensive operations, Lannes with the advance guard won the important victory of Montebello. The nature of the battle was such that the French general said he could hear the bones crash in his division like hail falling on a skylight. Cremona, Piacenza, and other places fell, but on the 14th, at a specially inopportune time, because Napoleon had thought it necessary to divide his forces owing to his uncertainty as to the precise whereabouts of the enemy, Melas and 31,000 Austrians appeared in the plain of the Bormida. The skill of Lannes and Victor proved of no avail; the reinforcements which the First Consul brought up could not shake the determination of the Imperialists. The wounded Austrian commander, foreseeing no further engagement and complimenting himself on his success, left the field. In this he committed an irretrievable blunder. Desaix, but recently returned from Egypt, was in command of 6000 men some miles away, and having heard the dull roar of cannon, was hurrying to Napoleon's assistance. He arrived late in the afternoon, and is said to have assured the First Consul that "the battle is lost, but there is time to gain another."

There must be no retreat on the part of the French. This was the decision arrived at after a short council of war. New dispositions were made; Desaix was to stop the Austrian columns, the main forces were to fall upon the enemy's flank. Thiers tells us what happened during the second battle of Marengo.

"General Marmont suddenly unmasked a battery of twelve pieces of cannon; a thick shower of grape-shot fell upon the head of the surprised Austrian column, not expecting any fresh resistance, for they fully believed the French were decidedly retreating. It had scarcely recovered from this sudden shock, when Desaix drove down the Ninth Light Infantry. 'Go tell the First Consul,' said he to his aide-de-camp Savary, 'that I am charging, and want some cavalry to support me.' Desaix, on horseback, led this half-brigade. At its head he ascended the gentle elevation which concealed him from the Austrians, and abruptly disclosed himself to them by a volley of musketry from his leading column, at point blank distance. The Austrians replied to this, and Desaix fell, struck by a bullet in the chest. 'Conceal my death,' said he to General Boudet, who was his chief of division; 'it may dispirit the troops.'

The Death of General Desaix

By A. Le Dru

Photo Neurdein

"Useless precaution of this hero! They saw him fall, and his soldiers, like those of Turenne, with a terrific shout, insisted on avenging their leader. The Ninth Light Infantry—which on that day earned the title of 'Incomparable,' a name which it bore to the termination of our war—having poured forth their fire, formed in column, and fell upon the dense mass of the Austrians. At the sight of it, these two first regiments which headed the line of march, taken by surprise, fell back in disorder upon the second line, and disappeared in its ranks. The column of grenadiers of Latterman then found itself alone at the head, and stood this charge like troops inured to fight. It stood firm. The conflict extended on both sides of the road; the Ninth was supported on the right by Victor's rallied troops, on the left by the Thirtieth and Fifty-ninth half-brigades of the division of Boudet, which had followed the movement. The grenadiers of Latterman were with difficulty defending themselves, when suddenly an unlooked-for storm now burst upon them. General Kellerman, who, on the application of Desaix, had received the order to charge, galloped forward, and passing Lannes and Desaix, posted part of his squadrons, to make head against the Austrian cavalry which he saw before him, then with the remainder charged the flank of the column of grenadiers, already attacked in front by the infantry of Boudet. This charge, executed in brilliant style, divided the column in two. The dragoons of Kellerman sabred the Austrians right and left, until, pressed on all sides, the unfortunate grenadiers laid down their arms. Two thousand surrendered prisoners of war. At their head, General Zach himself was obliged to surrender."

The fight continued, Kellerman charged again and again, while Lannes and Saint Cyr showed that they had lost none of their prowess. The Austrian cavalry was driven back by Bessières and Eugene Beauharnais. "The confusion at the bridges of the Bormida," adds Thiers, "became every moment still more irremediable. Infantry, cavalry, and artillery crowded together in disorder, the bridges could not afford a passage for the entire army, then *en masse*; multitudes threw themselves into the Bormida for the purpose of fording it. An artilleryman attempted to cross it with his gun, and succeeded. The entire artillery then followed his example, but without success, as several of the carriages stuck fast in the bed of the river. The French, now hotly pursuing, took men, horses, guns, and baggage. The unfortunate Baron Melas, who, but two hours before, had left his army in possession of victory, galloped up on report of this disaster, and could scarcely credit what he saw; he gave himself up to despair."

"Tell the First Consul," gasped the dying Desaix, "that my only regret in dying is to have perished before having done enough to live in the recollection of posterity." His fame, however, will always be recorded in connection with the battle of Marengo. "A glorious day's work," said Napoleon. "If only I could have embraced Desaix upon the battlefield! I should have made him Minister of War, and a prince, too, had it been in my power." During his weary exile Napoleon also spoke lovingly of the fallen general, as he did of Kléber, who perished on the same day in Egypt, the victim of an assassin's dagger.

"Of all the generals I ever had under my command," said the fallen Emperor, "Desaix and Kléber possessed the greatest talent—Desaix pre-eminently, as Kléber loved glory only as the means of acquiring wealth and pleasure. Desaix loved glory for itself, and despised every other consideration. To him riches and pleasure were of no value, nor did he ever give them a moment's thought. He was a little, black-looking man, about an inch shorter than myself, always badly dressed, sometimes even ragged, and despising alike comfort and convenience. Enveloped in a cloak, Desaix would throw himself under a gun and sleep as contentedly as if reposing in a palace. Luxury had for him no charms. Frank and honest in all his proceedings, he was called by the Arabs, 'Sultan the Just.' Nature intended him to figure as a consummate general. Kléber and Desaix were irreparable losses to France."

Melas, broken in spirit and wounded, requested an armistice. After considerable dallying on the part of the Court of Vienna and ruthless determination to have his own way on that of Napoleon, hostilities were resumed in November, 1800.

The First Consul had now returned to Paris, and the interest of the campaign centres around the armies led by Moreau and Brune, who had succeeded Masséna. It will be remembered that the former had agreed to a truce in the previous July, and when the sword was again unsheathed owing to the causes briefly mentioned in the previous paragraph his opponent was no longer Kray, but the Archduke John, a brother of the Emperor. At first the Archduke enjoyed a temporary triumph, but Moreau wreaked a terrible vengeance at the battle of Hohenlinden, fought on the 2nd December. No fewer than 20,000 Austrians were captured or left dead or wounded on the snow-clad plain and in the under-growth of the forest.

The poet Campbell has painted a vivid picture of the tragic scene:

On Linden, when the sun was low,
All bloodless lay th' untrodden snow;
And dark as winter was the flow
Of Iser, rolling rapidly.

But Linden saw another sight,
When the drum beat, at dead of night,

Commanding fires of death to light
The darkness of her scenery.

By torch and trumpet fast arrayed,
Each warrior drew his battle-blade,
And furious every charger neighed,
To join the dreadful revelry.

Then shook the hills with thunder riven;
Then rushed the steed to battle driven,
And louder than the bolts of Heaven,
Far flashed the red artillery.

But redder yet that light shall glow
On Linden's hills of stainèd snow;
And bloodier yet the torrent flow
Of Iser, rolling rapidly.

'Tis morn, but scarce yon level sun
Can pierce the war-clouds, rolling dun,
Where furious Frank, and fiery Hun,
Shout in their sulph'rous canopy.

The combat deepens. On, ye brave
Who rush to glory, or the grave!
Wave, Munich! all thy banners wave!
And charge with all thy chivalry!

Few, few shall part, where many meet!
The snow shall be their winding-sheet,
And every turf beneath their feet
Shall be a soldier's sepulchre.

Moreau gave the enemy no time to recover from the disaster, and brought them to action again and again with the most favourable results. Indeed, he was within easy distance of Vienna itself when he agreed to sign an armistice at Steyer on Christmas Day 1800, the terms of which were particularly advantageous to his own country.

Macdonald hastened to the assistance of Brune. He crossed the Splügen from Switzerland to Italy in the face of colossal difficulties, difficulties far greater than those when Napoleon turned the Alps. The passage was made in winter, snow beating in the faces of the soldiers, some of whom were whirled to destruction by an avalanche. Eventually the junction was effected, Brune having bravely forced his way to Macdonald by overcoming the opposition of the Imperialists whenever he had an opportunity. Finding that he could make no progress, Bellegarde, the Austrian commander, proposed a truce, and the armistice of Treviso was signed on the 16th January 1801.

Peace, a "peace at any price" let it be said, was secured by the signature of the Treaty of Lunéville on the 9th February 1801, by which France added considerably to her greatness and Napoleon to his fame, both in the Republic and abroad. Foreign admiration of the First Consul's genius, however, was not unmixed with disgust at the exacting nature of his demands. Belgium and the left bank of the Rhine again became French territory; the Batavian (Dutch), Helvetic (Swiss), Ligurian, and Cisalpine republics were recognised, and various changes effected in Tuscany and elsewhere. The River Adige became Austria's boundary in Italy, and she retained Venice.

Brief mention must be made of an alliance arranged by the Czar and the First Consul which almost certainly would have had far-reaching results but for the assassination of the former and the British naval victory off Copenhagen in which Nelson played so conspicuous a part. Alexander I., who succeeded his father, refused to play into the hands of Napoleon, and friendly relations between his Court and that of St James was definitely re-established by the Treaty of St Petersburg, the 17th June 1801. The Maritime Confederacy was dissolved, the Czar's example being followed by Sweden and Denmark.

The First Consul felt Paul's death very keenly, but more from a political than a friendly point of view. "In concert with the Czar," he told Bourrienne, "I was sure of striking a mortal blow at the English power in India. A palace revolution has overturned all my projects." One can imagine how the vexation caused by the complete abandonment of such a scheme was intensified by the knowledge that Great Britain continued to hold command of the sea.

CHAPTER XIV
BLESSINGS OF PEACE (1801–1803)

IT now became eminently desirable that Napoleon should pay some attention to the domestic affairs of France and of the countries dominated by her. He determined to infuse a little of his own inexhaustible energy into the departments of State, and to restore public confidence generally. That some kind of mutual understanding should be arrived at with the Powers who were not under his thumb was a prime necessity. Affairs on the Continent were by no means without possibilities of danger to the Republic. Russia and Great Britain had become allies, the hitherto neutral scales of Prussia might at any moment lean towards the latter, and Austria had not become reconciled to the loss of her territories.

When England set on foot proposals for a cessation of hostilities which had continued since 1793, Napoleon was busily preparing a flotilla for the invasion of that island, to which project he had devoted considerable thought. Although he did not betray his eagerness, he certainly felt that there could be no greater or more profitable blessing than a period of peace, which would enable him to carry out various reforms and also to consolidate his own interests. The negotiations finally took definite shape in the short-lived Treaty of Amiens. The British Government under the leadership of Addington lacked the genius and foresight of Pitt, consequently the balance of profit from the Treaty was on the side of France. The Egyptian question was to be settled by that country being restored to the Sultan; Malta was to be handed back to the Knights of St John, its former possessors; Great Britain was to retain Ceylon and Trinidad alone of her colonial conquests during the war. These were the principal items of the Treaty, the preliminaries of which were signed in London on the 1st October 1801. France was at peace with all the world.

Napoleon, whose term of office as First Consul had been extended for ten years (at a later period he was made Consul for life), now directed the whole of his powers on the internal government of France. Neither afraid of God nor man personally, he early discerned that religion had a deep political significance. France had tried to blot out Christianity, but as a result of her efforts the old forms of worship had merely given place to vague speculations and makeshifts. The Christian faith was re-established by the Concordat, a "treaty of peace with the Roman Catholic Church," as an eminent modern scholar terms it, the First Consul setting a good example by attending Mass at Notre Dame. This was followed by the inauguration of the Civil Code, a readjustment of laws involving the most arduous research on the part of those learned in the intricacies of jurisprudence.

Commerce received a fresh impetus, public works were undertaken, and social life revived. So great was the confidence of Englishmen that they again began to make the "grand tour" of the Continent, then deemed a necessary part of the education of members of the upper classes. The Diary of Robert Sym, clerk to his Majesty's Signet, affords us an interesting glimpse of Napoleon at this time. He writes in his quaint way as follows:—

"On the 'Quinze Thermidor' (Tuesday, August 3rd, 1802) we saw Bonaparte review in the 'Cour des Tuileries' what was certainly the flower of his army, for they were very different men from those we had seen on the road and at Calais. We never saw a finer body of men than these, nor finer horses and accoutrements, and all clothed and equipped in the most complete manner. The corps of Chasseurs and of the Gens d'Armerie, in particular, were very fine men. The corps of Guides, too, seemed to be all picked. These latter were commanded by young Beauharnais, the son of the wife of Bonaparte....

"About twelve o'clock Bonaparte came down the great stair of the Tuileries and one of our party, who happened to be right opposite the porch, told us that he mounted his horse from wooden steps. He then rode forward, accompanied by about fifteen or twenty generals and a Mameluke from Egypt. All his suite were dressed and powdered in the most showy manner, but Bonaparte himself wore a plain green coat with a narrow white cloth edging at the seams, such as servants in this country sometimes wear, and a cocked hat without any lace. His hair is very black and is cropped very close to his head and neck, so that his ears are all bare. It falls down over his brow. His complexion is swarthy, his face long, a fine nose, his eyes are very dark and his eyebrows fall, or are drawn down, much over his eyes. His cheek bones are high, and his cheeks sink between the bones of the face and those of the chin, which gives him a wasted, consumptive look. His upper lip projects in the middle of his mouth, considerably over the under one, and his chin is sharp and prominent. He does not seem to be above five feet six, and is very thin. He is thirty-three years of age. To me he appeared to have the look of anxiety, or rather of terror. He was mounted on a beautiful Arabian grey horse, one of the most perfect animals I ever saw. His saddle, or rather housing, on which he sat, was purple velvet, richly embroidered with gold and a great many nets and trappings.... Bonaparte was nearly an hour and a half on horseback on this occasion. During all that period he never once opened his lips, nor did he turn his head to the right or to the left. He looked straight over his horse's ears. No person spoke to him, nor was he cheered or huzzaed, either when he came into the Cour or when he departed."

The conquests of the Republic in Italy, Holland, Belgium, the left bank of the Rhine, and Switzerland imposed considerable responsibility upon the French, and it was necessary to reorganise the several governments. They were encumbered by tradition, with which Napoleon had little or no sympathy. As regards the independence which the inhabitants had every reason to expect by the terms of the Peace of Lunéville, the First Consul was rich in promise and poor in performance. Moderation was a quality distinctly lacking in Napoleonic statesmanship. The very thought of a national spirit was a nightmare to the man who was now bent on building a vast Empire of the West. Northern Italy was completely dominated by him; Piedmont, for long the football of Austria and France, was incorporated with the Republic, Parma and Placentia were occupied. The Cisalpine Republic speedily became the Italian Republic, a high-sounding name calculated to please, with Napoleon as President and a French army of occupation. Within certain limits the First

Consul's jurisdiction was beneficial, even though he ruled on despotic principles.

To Holland, now the Batavian Republic, he granted a constitution, but many of his measures were too arbitrary for the stolid Dutch; there was no end to their grievances, both fancied and real. Probably the provinces on the left bank of the Rhine, which were incorporated with France, gained more lasting advantages if only because they were less meddled with. Affairs on the opposite side of the river attracted more attention; in Germany there was something worth playing for. With the Czar's consent, Napoleon set about rearranging the various German States. This he did to his present satisfaction, Francis II. of the unwieldy Holy Roman Empire, of which these territories formed a part, meekly acquiescing, as befits a monarch who has no alternative but to grin and bear unpreventable misfortunes. Over two hundred independent States formerly belonging to bishops, abbots, and petty sovereigns were eventually annexed to their larger neighbours, the idea being to gain the good-will and friendship of the more important rulers.

Switzerland, a neutral State according to the Treaty of Lunéville but not held to be so by the First Consul, was more difficult of settlement. After several systems of government had been tried and failed, Napoleon himself drew up the Constitution of Malmaison. This he forced the country to accept in May, 1801, but it was amended in the following year. On the withdrawal of the French army of occupation, civil war broke out among the patriotic Swiss, Ney speedily quelling it, however, with a formidable body of troops. The Helvetian Republic was too important from a military point of view to be allowed to snap the fetters which linked it to France.

European affairs, it might be thought, would have been sufficiently exhausting to preclude colonial projects. But, to use an apparent paradox, Napoleon never had more time to spare than when he was most busy. He derived his recreation from change of work, shutting up one drawer in his mind to open another, to use his own simile. Of leisure and ease he had little; a visit to the theatre, a hunt occasionally, an hour's chat with Josephine and the ladies of the Consular Court, during which he would tell them the most creepy ghost stories, and a game of cards at which he cheated, sufficed him for pastime. He took exercise while working, restlessly pacing the study while he dictated a torrent of words on civil, military, and naval matters, or walking in the garden discussing affairs with a Minister of State.

At this period Napoleon's intellect and powers of exhaustive concentration were at their best, and it is characteristic of his marvellous energy that he could find time to devote to the possessions of the Republic overseas. He resolved upon an attempt to recover San Domingo, in the West Indies, then ruled by the famous negro President Toussaint L'Ouverture, the subject of one of Wordsworth's greatest sonnets: "Toussaint, thou most unhappy man of men." France had practically lost her supremacy of this important West India island owing to a revolt of the negroes, and there seemed a likelihood of Toussaint declaring its independence.

The First Consul sent off 21,000 troops under General Leclerc, who had married Pauline, the prettiest of the Bonaparte sisters, and the blacks were eventually routed. Some months later, when the yellow fever had laid low many of the French soldiers and England and the Republic were again at war, the cause of the negroes was taken up by the British, with the result that the independence of San Domingo was definitely established. Only one-fifth of the expeditionary army returned to France.

In a diary kept by Rear-Admiral Sir George Cockburn's secretary during Napoleon's voyage in the *Northumberland* to St Helena, a conversation is recorded in which the ex-Emperor referred particularly to the West Indies. He said that "had he continued at the head of the French Government, he never would have attempted the re-occupation of St Domingo; that the most he would have established with regard to that island would have been to keep frigates and sloops stationed around it to force the blacks to receive everything they wanted from, and to export all their produce exclusively to, France; for, he added, he considered the independence of the blacks there to be more likely to prove detrimental to England than to France. This latter remark is a reiteration of his feelings with respect to England, as in all the calculations he makes, the proportion of evil which may accrue to our nation seems to bear in his mind the first consideration."

In the early days of 1803 the First Consul's attention was distracted by events nearer home, and he had no alternative but to abandon his dreams of a Colonial Empire. If, as he afterwards stated, "the Saint Domingo business" was "the greatest error in all my government I ever committed," he had been able to obtain Louisiana from Spain in exchange for an extension of territory in Italy, and also to secure Guiana.

CHAPTER XV
THE DAWN OF THE EMPIRE (1803–1804)

WHILE neither party kept strictly to the terms of the Peace of Amiens, Napoleon's aggressive policy was such as to disturb other Powers as well as Great Britain. There was no knowing who might be the object of his unwelcome attentions. Frontiers seemed suddenly to have lost their significance and usefulness, treaties became of less value than the parchment on which they were written. Great Britain complained that whereas the Treaty of Lunéville had guaranteed the independence of the Batavian Republic, French troops were stationed within her borders, as well as in those of Switzerland. Napoleon retorted by saying that Great Britain still kept Malta. Eventually England declared war on the 18th May 1803, and it was to be a duel to the death.

Napoleon, usually so wide awake, was taken by surprise. He did not anticipate so quick a decision on the part of Addington's administration. He retaliated in an utterly senseless and cruel way by ordering that every British subject on French territory should be arrested and imprisoned. Small wonder that English newspapers vilified the First Consul as the Corsican Ogre, that the pens of Gillray, Cruikshank, Woodward, and a host of lesser artists caricatured him almost out of recognition; that poets poured forth vituperation in minor verse, and that Scott and Wordsworth wrote battle cries. Few people in England entertained the sympathy and admiration for the ruler of France shown by Dr Parr. "Sir," he once remarked, "I should not think I had done my duty if I went to bed any night without praying for the success of Napoleon Bonaparte."

To strike a mortal blow at the very heart of the British Empire and to ruin her commerce on the Continent now became the consuming object of Napoleon's ambition. He would cross the Channel, march on London, subjugate the United Kingdom, and while preparations for this bold move were being made, close the ports of Europe against her. "They want to make us jump the ditch, and we'll jump it," to quote an expression he used at an audience of ambassadors on the 1st May 1803. Frenchmen joyfully anticipated the triumph of the man with so bold an ambition; Englishmen armed themselves as eagerly to defend hearth and home. A Territorial Army of which posterity may well be proud quickly came into being. In March 1805 no fewer than 810,000 troops—Militia, Volunteers, and Fencibles—were prepared to defy Napoleon. The politician and the publican, the ploughboy and the squire, joined hands in the mutual cause as though no difference of class existed. George III. announced his intention of leading the troops in person if necessary. Pitt was acting-colonel of a regiment, and Charles James Fox became a humble private.

On the Sands at Boulogne

By A. C. Gow, R.A.

By permission of the Berlin Photographic Co., London, W.

Fortunately Great Britain had a navy, while Napoleon had practically to create one. Many of his finest ships were far away in the West Indies, and the Dutch fleet was small and of little consequence. England lost no time in maritime preparations: she was ready; Napoleon wished to gain every minute he could. While the sound of the shipwright's hammer rang through the coasts of France, the white sails of Old England kept watch to prevent all entry or exit from her harbours. The most important command, that of the Mediterranean, was given to Nelson. Cornwallis was stationed off Brest, the great western arsenal of France, while Keith patrolled the North Sea and the Straits of Dover. In addition, there were various smaller squadrons cruising about ready for instant action.

Three-deckers were laid down in many of the most important French seaports, cities and towns vying with each other in offering money to the Government for men-of-war. Smaller centres contributed in proportion to their means; naval stores, artillery, and ammunition were also supplied at the public expense. At Boulogne a flotilla of small vessels of various kinds was collected, some fitted with artillery, others for the conveyance of horses. Rowing boats were built on the river banks for the transportation of the troops. Fishing smacks were purchased and converted into miniature warships; the doings of smugglers were winked at, provided they brought information about the English coast likely to be of use. If ever a man was in earnest, Napoleon certainly was during the time of the Great Terror. He formed a vast camp at Boulogne, detailed battalions of soldiers to construct a mammoth basin to hold part of the flotilla, and others to build forts and learn to row. He showed himself frequently, inspiring the men by his terse phrases of encouragement, and consulting Admiral Bruix and others who had charge of the preparations on the most insignificant detail. He tested cannon, made short voyages in the different types of vessel, and lived for days at a stretch in a little château at the top of a cliff.

In the early stages of the war Napoleon had thought it would be possible to convey his troops in the small craft without making use of the navy proper. He hoped that on a dark or foggy night it might be possible to elude the vigilance of the British cruisers and land on the south coast of England before the enemy was aware of his intention. Later, he recognised that a successful crossing was impossible without the protection of the men-of-war, and the necessity for this added immensely to his many difficulties.

Napoleon did not content himself solely with preparations for the campaign in England. He sent Mortier to overrun Hanover, the hereditary territory of George III., seized the important commercial cities of Bremen and Hamburg, and closed the rivers Elbe and Weser against British commerce. In Italy the ports of Tarentum and Leghorn, with which British merchants did a considerable amount of trade, were also occupied. Not content with these drastic measures, Napoleon decreed that any ship which had so much as called at a British port was liable to be captured. With great good fortune the majority of the vessels from San Domingo eventually reached home ports, but several put in at the harbours of Coruña and Cadiz. Spain, unluckily for herself as it afterwards appeared, allowed supplies to be sent to the blockaded ships. Spain, indeed, helped France in other ways, including the payment of an annual subsidy. Portugal also agreed to disburse £640,000 a year.

Beloved though he was by the majority of the nation, Napoleon had enemies. Several attempts were made to take his life. In one of these, he narrowly escaped being blown to pieces by an infernal machine in the Rue St Nicaise, the plot being promoted by the Royalists of La Vendée. Napoleon showed his vindictive nature by seizing the opportunity to teach a lesson to the Jacobins, who had no hand whatever in the affair, and a hundred and thirty innocent persons were sentenced to transportation for life. Another Royalist conspiracy was that of Georges Cadoudal and Pichegru. These men tried to implicate Moreau, but without success. The famous Republican general, however, was arrested, with the ringleaders; Pichegru was found strangled in prison, Georges Cadoudal was guillotined, and Moreau was banished to America. The last was entirely innocent, but he had the misfortune to be Napoleon's rival, and that was sufficient condemnation. He had won his spurs in the early days of the Revolution by placing himself at the head of a battalion of Breton volunteers, and he was popular with the army. An instance of his sterling integrity, one of many which redound to his credit, may be given. When the landed property of the aristocracy was sold as belonging to the nation, an estate owned by M. d'Orsay, adjoining that of Moreau, was sold to the Republican general at an absurdly low figure. Not only did the new owner inform his former neighbour of the transaction, but he insisted on paying him what he considered was a legitimate price.

The Duc d'Enghien, son of the Duc de Bourbon, was even more unfortunate than Moreau. He also was charged with complicity in the Royalist plot, and although no evidence was produced against him, he was shot and buried in a grave dug before his trial, by a so-called special military commission, in the fortress of Vincennes. The story of the way in which the young duke's father heard the news is pathetic. He was an exile in London, living at the time in a small suite of rooms with one valet. As breakfast did not appear at the prescribed hour one morning, and no notice being taken of his repeated ringing of the bell, he entered the kitchen and found his servant bowed down with sorrow. On the table was a newspaper containing particulars of the grim tragedy. For two hours the sorely stricken parent was overcome by agonising grief in the humble little room. The Comtesse de Boigne, one of the many French emigrants who sought a refuge in England, relates the above, in her entertaining "Memoirs," adding that this excessive grief was "accompanied by fits of rage and cries for vengeance."

"This was the only means I had of leaving no doubt as to my intentions, and of annihilating the hopes of the partisans of the Bourbons," Napoleon wrote callously to his brother Joseph. "If what I have done were still to be done," he continues, "I would do it again, and if I had a favourable opportunity I would get rid of the rest." Fouché's caustic comment, "it was worse than a crime, it was a blunder," has passed into a proverb.

The conspiracy of Cadoudal and Pichegru was made a pretext on the part of the Senate for sending a deputation to the First Consul, who was told that, as he was founding a new era, he ought to perpetuate it. "We do not doubt but this great idea has had a share of your attention," said the President during the course of his short and flattering address, "for your creative genius embraces all and forgets nothing. But do not delay: you are urged on by the times, by events, by conspirators, and by ambitious men; and in another direction, by the anxiety which agitates the

French people. It is in your power to enchain time, master events, disdain the ambitious, and tranquillise the whole of France by giving it institutions which will cement your edifice, and prolong for our children what you have done for their fathers. Citizen First Consul, be assured that the Senate here speaks to you in the name of all citizens."

The question was duly debated in the Tribunate, Carnot alone voting against the proposal, and by a decree of the Senate Napoleon was declared Emperor of the French on the 18th May 1804. That a conspiracy and a "judicial murder" should herald so important an event was looked upon by some as of evil omen. A few of the more sober members of the nation began to whisper among themselves that France was being more and more absorbed in Napoleon. Perhaps the remark made by the Duc de Raguse to the Comtesse de Boigne in 1814 would not have been inapplicable if uttered ten years before. The duke was explaining his connection with the Emperor. "When he said: '*All for France*,' I served with enthusiasm; when he said: '*France and I*,' I served with zeal; when he said: '*I and France*,' I served with obedience; but when he said: '*I without France*,' I felt the necessity of separating from him."

CHAPTER XVI
THE THREATENED INVASION OF ENGLAND AND ITS SEQUEL (1804–1805)

NAPOLEON'S first thought after he became Emperor was of the army, in very truth the main support of his throne. He had seen too much of life to believe that his great commanders lived solely to carry out his will without reference to personal ambition. Experience had taught him that "men are fond of toys, and are led by them." He had remarked on the fact when opposition had been raised to the institution of the Legion of Honour in 1802, and he saw no reason to change his opinion. Now was the moment for him to show that those who had contributed to the success of his designs upon the Imperial throne were not to be forgotten. He therefore elevated eighteen generals to the rank of Marshals of the Empire, namely, Augereau, Bernadotte, Berthier, Bessières, Brune, Davout, Jourdan, Kellermann, Lannes, Lefebvre, Masséna, Moncey, Mortier, Murat, Ney, Pérignon, Soult, and Serrurier. By honouring the heads of the army, Napoleon not only flattered them and pleased the troops they commanded, but wove a silken cord which he hoped would bind them to himself. Some failed him in the evil days of 1814–1815, but the majority were worthy of the distinction and of his confidence.

A host of other dignitaries were created apart from the Bonaparte family, whose members assumed the title of Imperial Highness, their mother being called Madame Mère, which was as simple and dignified as the good soul herself. There was a Grand Elector, Arch-Chancellor of the Empire, Arch-Chancellor of State, and High Constable, to mention only a few of the many titles conferred at this time.

Napoleon paid frequent visits to Boulogne, and in August 1804 the vast camp was the scene of a grand review at which the crosses of the Legion of Honour were distributed to those who had been awarded this coveted distinction. The most intense enthusiasm was aroused: the ancient throne of Dagobert, King of France eleven centuries before, was used by the Emperor, and the platform on which it stood was gaily decorated with two hundred flags. Unfortunately a catastrophe marred the occasion. A flotilla of new boats for the projected invasion was to arrive from Holland and elsewhere at the height of the proceedings. Several of them struck a portion of the new harbour-works and were swamped, causing Napoleon to lose his temper. The enjoyment of the open-air dinner was also marred by heavy rain.

Arrangements for an even more imposing ceremony were soon proceeding. This was the coronation of the Emperor, which took place in the cathedral of Notre Dame on Sunday, the 2nd December 1804, and the Pope, thinking it prudent to respond to Napoleon's wish, graced the service with his presence. As the Emperor crowned both Josephine and himself, the Sovereign Pontiff had to be content with anointing Napoleon and blessing the sword and sceptre. "Vive l'Empereur!" thundered through the magnificently decorated cathedral, cannon were fired, and in the evening illuminations blazed forth all over Paris. It is said that when Napoleon retired to his apartment at the end of the day's proceedings he exclaimed in tones of scorn worthy of Cromwell on a celebrated occasion, "Off! Off with these confounded trappings!" His language always seemed more in keeping with the camp than with the court.

Napoleon giving the Eagles to his Army, December 5, 1804

By L. David

One of Napoleon's first acts after his coronation was to write to George III. on the subject of peace, just as he had done when taking the reins of office as First Consul; it was his way of throwing dust in the eyes of the enemy. War had broken out between Great Britain and Spain at a most inopportune moment, for Pitt, who had again come into power, had energetically entered into negotiations with some of the more important European Powers for a third Coalition against France. In April 1805, Russia signified her assent, and was followed in August by Austria. Great Britain agreed to replenish the war-chests of her allies, and, in addition, to furnish men, arms, and ships. The political chess-board was in active use again, and with his usual astuteness Napoleon made several moves before his opponents were aware that the game had begun. On the 26th May he became King of Italy, placing the crown on his own head in Milan Cathedral, and appointing Josephine's son, Eugène Beauharnais, to the important and scarcely enviable post of Viceroy. Early in June the Ligurian Republic was united with France, followed later by Parma and Piacenza; and Lucca and Piombino were created a principality, the Emperor's sister

Élise being recognised as Hereditary Princess. Napoleon was "consolidating his interests," just as Pitt was following the same principle under somewhat different conditions. These aggressive measures had an extremely irritating influence on Austria. But although her pride was severely shaken, she was slow to move. The army was encumbered by tradition, and the people, having been bitten, were twice shy. The old proverb, "Better half a loaf than no bread," fairly summed up the situation from their point of view. But what if the half loaf were taken? That side of the question had also to be considered.

Shipbuilding still continued to proceed with unabated vigour along the coasts of Holland and of Northern France. Three-deckers, gay with new paint, left the slips and took their first plunge into sea-water. In the Texel, and at Brest, Rochefort, and Toulon, squadrons came into being, but, like unfledged birds in a cage, they had little opportunity to try their wings. The men on England's floating bulwarks saw to that, watching every movement. When the various blockading squadrons had to vacate their station, as occasionally happened, the frigates, "the eyes of the fleet," as Nelson happily termed them, were usually present, although he complained that he had far too few of these useful vessels at his disposal.

Napoleon never thoroughly understood the difficulties of naval warfare. He was disposed to think that a naval squadron could carry out a manœuvre with the almost mathematical exactness of a regiment. Tides and wind meant little or nothing to him; Sir Neil Campbell, the Commissioner at Elba for Great Britain during Napoleon's short-lived rule of that island, perceived and noted this in his diary. And yet it must be conceded that the strategy which the Emperor had been secretly conceiving for the concentration of his scattered fleets was as clever as it was bold. "The wet ditch that lay around England" was not to be crossed by the flotilla alone; he had long since abandoned that plan as impracticable. The navy proper was to have a share in the downfall of the United Kingdom. By feints in directions calculated to deceive the enemy as to his real designs he hoped to assemble sufficient ships to command the Channel, if only for a few days. This would enable him to slip across with his army, although how he proposed to get out of England is not quite clear. A sufficient military force was to be left in France to provide for the possibility that other enemies might take advantage of so favourable an opportunity to cross the French frontiers.

Napoleon's general design was changed again and again as circumstances dictated, and twice an attempt was made to rally the naval forces. Suffice it to say that Missiessy with the Rochefort squadron eluded the English fleets and reached the West Indies, where he was to be joined by Villeneuve, his colleague at Toulon, the idea being that while the British were chasing them the ships at Brest under Ganteaume should land a force in Ireland and afterwards return to convoy the flotilla. Villeneuve, owing to stress of weather, was forced to return to port, Ganteaume being hemmed in by Cornwallis, a hero who has not had full justice done to him, largely because the naval annals of the time are dominated so completely by Nelson. Even the latter was deceived when he found Toulon empty, and he chased an entirely spectral fleet in the direction of Egypt, sufficient proof of the cleverness of Napoleon's elusive plan.

In the early days of 1805 the Emperor determined to delay no further. He who said that "God is on the side of the biggest battalions" probably thought that the same maxim applied to fleets. The Spanish naval resources were now allied to those of France, making them numerically stronger than those of the enemy, although decidedly deficient in fighting qualities and seamanship. In brief, Napoleon's last desperate attempt at the invasion of England was as follows: Villeneuve with the Toulon squadron, after joining that at Cadiz, was to make for the West Indies, there to be met by Missiessy. Ganteaume, escaping from Brest, was to call at Ferrol for the vessels lying there and join the others, making fifty-nine first-class ships in all, excluding frigates. The combined fleets were then to make a dash across the Atlantic and appear before Boulogne, where the flotilla would be in readiness to sail.

Villeneuve carried out his part, but Missiessy and Ganteaume failed, the latter because he was unable to pierce the British cordon. Napoleon, not to be discouraged, sent word to Villeneuve to come back, drive the British from their station off Ferrol, secure the fourteen ships in that harbour, repeat the operation at Brest, where there were twenty-one ships, and then make for Boulogne. Nelson had given chase and been outwitted, but by sending a swift-sailing brig to Plymouth to inform the authorities of his misfortune and the approach of the French fleet on its homeward voyage, they were enabled to order the British ships off Rochefort and Ferrol to leave their position and intercept Villeneuve. This, under Admiral Calder, they were successful in doing, two Spanish ships being lost in the action that was fought. Owing to fog and want of confidence on Calder's part, however, the contest was indecisive, and the Frenchman reached the Spanish fort of Vigo, afterwards creeping into Ferrol, where fourteen sail-of-the-line awaited him, the total force now being twenty-nine. Meanwhile five French ships which had been hemmed in at Rochefort, taking advantage of the absence of the British, were likely to join them, thus placing thirty-four vessels at Villeneuve's disposal for a dash to Brest. He made the attempt and failed, neglected to inform the commander of the Rochefort squadron, who was vainly searching for him, and retreated to Cadiz, where six Spanish ships were added to his squadron.

Calder and Collingwood "sat tight" outside the harbour with one eye on the enemy and the other searching for signs of the British ships which they knew would be with them before long. Nelson, after spending a short time in England, hove in sight off Cadiz on the day before his forty-seventh birthday and assumed supreme command. The officers trooped into his cabin to congratulate him. "The reception I met with on joining the fleet," he declared, "caused the sweetest sensation of my life."

On the 19th October the signal, "The enemy are coming out of port," flew from the mast-heads of the frigates stationed to watch the goings-on in the harbour. Thirty-three sail-of-the-line, five frigates, and two brigs had passed out by the following day. Nelson's force consisted of twenty-seven men-of-war, four frigates, a schooner, and a cutter. The enemy therefore had the advantage as regards numbers of six first-class ships. In armament the combatants were nearly equal, as in bravery and daring, but the French were very inferior in seamanship and general *morale*. The 21st October 1805, on which the Battle of Trafalgar was fought, is a red-letter day in the history of the British Empire, perhaps of the world. The story belongs rather to the life of Nelson than of Napoleon, and as such cannot be dealt with here. Eleven ships only escaped of the thirty-three which had ventured to contest England's command of the sea. The conflict in Trafalgar Bay was Napoleon's maritime Waterloo. It cost the life of the greatest naval commander of modern times, but it sealed the supremacy of his country on the element which she has made particularly her own. On land, success still remained with the man whose gigantic schemes for invasion were so completely shattered; at sea, it was never to attend his efforts.

CHAPTER XVII
THE WAR OF THE THIRD COALITION (1805–6)

SWIFT decision was as essentially a characteristic of Napoleon as was his policy of having an alternative scheme to fall back upon should the first and more important plan miscarry. A typical example in which both are to be seen is afforded by a study of the War of the Third Coalition, against the allied Powers, Austria, Russia, and Great Britain. Disappointed at the failure of his preparations for the invasion of England, but clinging to his pet project, the humiliation of that country, the Emperor suddenly, and with apparently little forethought, led his legions in the opposite direction. England remained unviolated, but he saw a chance of stealing a march on Austria, her faithful friend.

Napoleon decorating his Soldiers at Boulogne

By F. G. Roussel

Photo Neurdein

On the 26th August, 1805, two days after the Elector of Bavaria had signified his intention of casting in his lot with France, the Army of England, never destined to get nearer to the land whose name it bore than its headquarters at Boulogne, and now known as the Grand

Army, began its long march from the coasts of the English Channel to the banks of the Danube. Napoleon's forces soon reached the enormous total of 200,000 men, the majority of whom, braced up by their long sojourn by the sea, were more fit physically for an arduous campaign than any other army in Europe. Despite defects in organisation and the free-and-easy methods of some of its officers, the Grand Army was the army of achievement. It carried the eagles of France, not to one victory only, but to many. No armament since the dawn of history has failed to be criticised for its imperfections. It is easy to be drill-perfect, and yet to fail in the field.

That the invasion of England was a mere feint has often been asserted, whereas the weight of evidence is on the other side. The multitude of orders issued by Napoleon, the reckless expenditure of money on the flotilla and the enlargement of Boulogne harbour, the medal struck to commemorate the achievement destined never to be used, the determination with which he waited until the last moment for the appearance of his fleets, are surely sufficient proofs of his sincerity in the matter. Moreover, on its first campaign the Grand Army had to plunder or to starve because the commissariat arrangements were hopelessly inadequate, the greater part of the provisions being left on the coast. This in itself shows with what haste the camp was broken up and the march begun.

The army was divided into seven corps commanded by tried warriors of France, namely, Ney, Lannes, Soult, Davout, Bernadotte, Marmont, and Augereau. Murat was placed at the head of the cavalry. With the Emperor was the magnificent Imperial Guard, at once the pride of Napoleon and of the whole army. The Bavarians numbered some 27,000.

The Imperialists had two principal forces. That in Italy numbered nearly 100,000 troops, who were under Archduke Charles; the other in Germany totalled 76,000, and was commanded in theory by Archduke Ferdinand. As the latter was a youth of nineteen summers the real work devolved on General Mack, chief of the staff, although the Archduke was responsible to the Emperor. Unfortunately Mack was not particularly popular, and consequently received but weak support from his immediate subordinates.

The Austrian service was steeped in tradition and crowded with aristocratic nobodies. To be sure some of the cleverest officers had studied the men and methods of the all-conquering French armies since the last campaign, but the quick movements of the enemy at once dismayed and deceived the slow-moving Imperialist columns. Augsburg was speedily occupied by the French; at Wertingen, Lannes cut up a division; and Ulm, Mack's headquarters, was so completely at the mercy of the enemy's army owing to the rapid concentration of troops under Lannes, Soult, and Marmont that the unfortunate general speedily capitulated. He was made a scapegoat, court-martialled, deprived of his rank, and placed in a fortress for two years.

All these events happened within one month, and were the work of men who had been forced to provide themselves with most of their necessities. Bad weather had added to their troubles, marches had been made in torrents of rain, and the wind had sometimes been so boisterous as to prevent their lighting a fire by which to dry their soaking uniforms. Says a contemporary officer whose information is beyond dispute:—

"To surround Ulm it was necessary to concentrate. Numerous columns defiled upon the same road, appeared at the same point. 100,000 men, fatigued by long marches, destitute of provisions, come to take up a position which grows more and more confined. They are now no more allowed to straggle from their post, for then the whole enterprise would fail. What a critical moment! The resources of the country occupied by this mass are consumed in an hour."To enhance the difficulty, the heavens seem to dissolve. A heavy rain, continuing for many days, floods the country. The streams burst their banks. The roads are frightful, and in more than one place altogether disappear. The army marches in mud, and bivouacs in water; it is ready to perish with misery and hunger; discouragement and murmuring spread through it. What is to be done? A proclamation is read at the head of each column, which praises, flatters, and caresses the army, pours eulogy on its constancy, tells it the enemy is enclosed, and that only a few moments more of perseverance are needed. Thus the soldiers are kept quiet; but as they must have bread, active and intelligent officers are sent through all the neighbouring districts, to obtain it by threats, if requests fail. All yields to the power of requisition, and in twenty-four hours bread is procured, and the horses and vehicles of the inhabitants are used to bring it in.... Ulm is invested, blockaded, capitulates, and the French army reap the fruit of its endurance and of its incredible activity."

Napoleon next turned his attentions to the Russians under Kutusoff, who had now entered the field on behalf of their allies, trusting to disappoint their hopes as speedily as he had dispersed those of the Austrians. Time was all-important, as extensive reinforcements were shortly expected by the enemy. Without scruple or qualms of conscience some of the French forces under Bernadotte were therefore marched through the neutral territory of Prussia. It was unjustifiable, of course, but Napoleon made no apologies for treading on national corns. By the middle of November the Emperor was in Vienna, no opposition being offered. In Italy all was not quite so well. Masséna was unable to overcome the Austrian forces under Archduke Charles at Caldiero, which retreated in good order to Laybach. There they concentrated with Archduke John, who had been driven from Tyrol with severe losses by Ney and the Bavarians. After failing to bring hostilities to a conclusion by diplomatic measures, and foreseeing a winter campaign which would in all probability prove a protracted one, Napoleon determined, as on many other occasions, to put all to the hazard in an attempt to bring the contest to an end by a crushing victory. His forces were necessarily widely scattered, but 65,000 troops were available, whereas the allies had some 90,000. On the morning of the 2nd December, 1805, the rays of the sun quickly dispelled the mist which hung about the plateau of Pratzen—"the sun of Austerlitz," as the Emperor frequently termed it in later campaigns. Rapp, with the authority of an eye-witness, thus describes "The Day of the Anniversary," as many of the soldiers called the battle, because Napoleon had been crowned just twelve months before:—"When we arrived at Austerlitz, the Russians, ignorant of the Emperor's skilful dispositions to draw them to the ground which he had marked out, and seeing our advanced guards give way before their columns, they conceived the victory won. According to their notions, the advanced guard would suffice to secure an easy triumph. But the battle began—they found what it was to fight, and on every point were repulsed. At one o'clock the victory was still uncertain; for they fought admirably. They resolved on a last effort, and directed close masses against our centre. The Imperial Guard deployed: artillery, cavalry, infantry were marched against a bridge which the Russians attacked, and this movement, concealed from Napoleon by the inequality of the ground, was not observed by us. At this moment I was standing near him, waiting orders. We heard a well-maintained fire of musketry; the Russians were repulsing one of our brigades. Hearing this sound, the Emperor ordered me to take the Mamelukes, two squadrons of Chasseurs, one of Grenadiers of the Guard, and to observe the state of things."I set off at full gallop, and, before advancing a cannon-shot, perceived the disaster. The Russian cavalry had penetrated our squares, and were sabring our men. In the distance could be perceived masses of Russian cavalry and infantry in reserve. At this juncture, the enemy advanced; four pieces of artillery arrived at a gallop, and were planted in position against us. On my left I had the brave Morland, on my right General d'Allemagne. 'Courage, my brave fellows!' cried I to my party; 'behold your brothers, your friends butchered; let us avenge them, avenge our standards! Forward!' These few words inspired my soldiers; we dashed at full speed upon the artillery, and took them. The enemy's horse, which awaited our attack, were overthrown by the same charge, and fled in confusion, galloping, like us, over the wrecks of our own squares. In the meantime the Russians rallied; but, a squadron of Horse Grenadiers coming to our assistance, I could then halt, and wait the reserves of the Russian Guard.

"Again we charged, and this charge was terrible. The brave Morland fell by my side. It was absolute butchery. We fought man to man, and so mingled together, that the infantry on neither side dared to fire, lest they should kill their own men. The intrepidity of our troops finally bore us in triumph over all opposition: the enemy fled in disorder in sight of the two Emperors of Austria and Russia, who had taken their station on a rising ground in order to be spectators of the contest. They ought to have been satisfied, for I can assure you they witnessed no child's play. For my own part ... I never passed so delightful a day. The Emperor received me most graciously when I arrived to tell him that the victory was ours; I still grasped my broken sabre, and as this scratch upon my head bled very copiously, I was all covered with blood. He named me General of Division. The Russians returned not again to the charge—they had had enough; we captured everything, their cannon, their baggage, their all in short; and Prince Ressina was among the prisoners."

The total loss of the allies reached the amazing figure of 26,000, or not quite four times as many as that sustained by the victors. The story told of Napoleon that when the fugitives of the defeated armies were endeavouring to cross the frozen surface of Lake Satschan he ordered the artillery of his Guard to fire on the ice, thereby drowning the poor wretches, has now been proved apocryphal.

The Night before Austerlitz

By A. Dawant

By permission of Messrs. Goupil & Co.

Those who have read Macaulay's "Essays" will perhaps remember an anecdote introduced to show that exact fulfilment of certain rules does not necessarily constitute success. "We have heard of an old German officer," he relates, "who was a great admirer of correctness in military operations. He used to revile Bonaparte for spoiling the science of war, which had been carried to such exquisite perfection by Marshal Daun. 'In my youth he used to march and countermarch all the summer without gaining or losing a square league, and then we went into winter quarters. And now comes an ignorant, hot-headed young man, who flies about from Boulogne to Ulm, and from Ulm to the middle of Moravia, and fights battles in December. The whole system of his tactics is monstrously incorrect.' The world is of opinion in spite of critics like these, that the end of war is to conquer, and that those means are the most correct which best accomplish the ends." Napoleon was great enough to break rules which a man of mediocre ability would not dare to defy. This is the secret of the Emperor's skill in warfare, of his short but decisive campaigns which astonished officers of less intuition and daring.

After Austerlitz an armistice was arranged, followed on the 26th December 1805, by the signature of the Peace of Pressburg. Venetia, Istria, and Dalmatia were ceded by Austria to Italy; Bavaria gained Tyrol and Vorarlberg; Baden and Würtemberg also came in for a share of the spoil, and their rulers, hitherto styled Electors, became Kings. Prussia, deeming it wiser to appear as a strong ally than as a weak neutral, attached herself to the Nation of Conquests, although Frederick William had been within an ace of declaring war before Austerlitz. An offensive and defensive alliance was first drawn up, then the former clause was struck out, it being arranged that the respective territories of the countries should be held sacred. Hanover was handed over to Prussia in exchange for the territories of Clèves and Neuchâtel, Anspach was ceded to Bavaria, and the principal rivers were closed to British commerce.

This high-handed action was partly nullified by a strict blockade on the part of Great Britain and Sweden, and many Prussian ships were secured as prizes. King Frederick William III. speedily began to regret his bargain with Napoleon, and with the genius for double-dealing so often characteristic of weak men, he came to a secret understanding with the Czar, promising among other things that he would refuse to attack Russia should he be called upon to do so by Napoleon. On his part, Alexander was to come to the help of the House of Hohenzollern should it need assistance. Time was to teach them, as it does most individuals, that "no man can serve two masters."

Napoleon now parcelled out territory for the special benefit of his family and friends. Joseph Bonaparte became King of the Two Sicilies in April 1806, Naples having been occupied by French troops under Saint-Cyr. In the following June Louis ascended the throne of Holland. Caroline Bonaparte, now married to Murat, was granted the Grand Duchy of Berg and Clèves the same year. Pauline was given the miniature Duchy of Guastalla, near Parma. To Berthier Napoleon presented the principality of Neuchâtel, to Talleyrand that of Benevento. Their power was somewhat limited, it is true, but it pleased the recipients of the honours for a time, and put gold in their purses, which was perhaps even more desirable from their point of view.

Napoleon was putting into practice the theory he had propounded in 1804 when he said "there will be no rest in Europe until it is under a single chief—an Emperor who shall have Kings for officers, who shall distribute kingdoms to his lieutenants, and shall make this one King of Italy, that one of Bavaria, this one ruler of Switzerland, that one Governor of Holland, each having an office of honour in the Imperial household."

CHAPTER XVIII
THE PRUSSIAN CAMPAIGN (1806)

PITT breathed his last soon after the defeat of the allies at Austerlitz, and three months after the death of Nelson. Lord Chatham's son, no less a martyr to his country than the hero of Trafalgar, had been bent "on putting Europe to rights." Scarcely had 1806 been ushered in before the Emperor of the French gave fresh evidence to the world that he, too, had a similar ambition. Austria, still smarting from the wounds inflicted by the lash Napoleon had so unsparingly used, an invalid not yet convalescent, and unable to offer any resistance, was again the victim.

For many centuries the ruling King of Austria had been Emperor of the Holy Roman Empire, although many of the German States had become practically independent in all but name. It was here that the ruler of France did not hesitate to wound. To strengthen his position he formed the Confederation of the Rhine, whereby sixteen states of various sizes, including Bavaria, Würtemberg, Baden, and Hesse-Darmstadt severed themselves from the Germanic Empire and entered into an offensive and defensive alliance with him as Protector. The new arrangement added 63,000 soldiers to Napoleon's reserves, and provided additional barriers against his enemies. On his part he agreed in case of war to put 200,000 men in the field on behalf of the Confederation. Well might the Prussian minister at Paris assert that his master "saw around his territories none but French soldiers or vassals of France, ready to march at her beck." Prussia was almost hemmed in by the new Confederation; moreover the Grand Army continued to remain in Germany.

For a month or two there was a faint glimmer of hope that the continued war between France and England might cease. Charles James Fox, Foreign Secretary and leading figure in the Grenville administration, was not without admiration for Napoleon, and more or less informal negotiations for peace were opened. There was an exchange of courtesies, Fox sending particulars of a plot to assassinate the Emperor to Talleyrand, Napoleon releasing a few British prisoners from French fortresses. When Napoleon really showed his hand he disclosed a suspicious eagerness to obtain Sicily, the possession of which would be of great importance in his cherished scheme of establishing the supremacy of France in the Mediterranean. The Emperor hungered and thirsted after sea-power; it was the one world left for him to conquer.

Hanover was held out as bait to Great Britain, quite regardless of anything Prussia might have to say in the matter. It was this unscrupulous juggling with other folk's possessions on the part of Napoleon that kept the Continent in so unsettled a state. None knew who next might be bartered or overrun by French troops, irrespective of previous agreements. When Napoleon played cards he cheated; in political matters his morality was no more conspicuous. His sense of right and wrong had long since given way to an egotism which recognised no law, and placed himself above all codes of ordinary conduct. De Tocqueville said of him: "He was as great as a man can be without virtue."

The peace overtures came to nought. The King of Prussia entered into an alliance with Russia, and began to mobilise his army. His soldiers were for up and doing regardless of the consequences, and effected a foolish disdain of their antagonists which is well shown by Varnhagen von Ense, then a student at Halle, in his "Memoirs."

"During the whole summer," he relates, "we had heard of warlike movements interrupted by hopes of peace; but after Napoleon had obtained a firm footing in Germany by means of the Rhenish Confederation, all idea of peace was at an end, and every one in Prussia called loudly for war. Prussian troops were to be seen in and near Halle on their way to the south and west, and the desire for war grew stronger every day. Some hot-headed fellows were furious if peace was hinted at, or if the superiority of the Prussians over the French was not at once acknowledged. I distinctly remember meeting an officer who asserted that the war was as good as ended—that nothing could now save Bonaparte from certain destruction. When I attempted to talk of French generals, he interrupted me by saying, 'Generals! whence should they spring? We Prussians, if you like it, have generals who understand the art of war; who have served from their youth up: such men will drive the tinkers and tailors, who date only from the Revolution, before them like sheep....' This put me out of temper, and I answered bluntly, that a man became a general not by accident of birth, but by actual service; that a man's former condition was nothing; a tinker or a tailor might make as good a general as a drill sergeant."

The reference to "accident of birth" is to the fact that before the battle of Jena (1806) practically every Prussian officer was an aristocrat, a rule which it will be remembered from a previous reference in this work obtained in the French army before the Revolution.

During a journey to Berlin, undertaken in his holidays, Varnhagen tells us that he was "reminded all along the road, that we were on the eve of some great event; in every direction we met soldiers in larger or smaller detachments, with artillery and baggage waggons. In Treuenbriezen I saw old Field Marshal von Müllendorf on his way to join the army; war was no longer doubtful, and it was thought that the presence of one of Frederick the Great's heroes would fill the troops with the enthusiasm of that period, and incite them to fresh victories. I saw him with a smiling countenance making the most confident promises of victory out of his carriage window to the surrounding crowd; he then drove off amid the loud huzzas of the assembled multitude. The soldiers were singing jovial songs, and rejoicing that at last they were to be led against the enemy; everywhere were to be seen the stragglers and others rushing to join the army. The noise died away after leaving Potsdam—an unusual stillness prevailed, and the fine summer weather soon banished from my thoughts all save the objects and expectations which more immediately concerned myself."

Music and merriment were not to last for long. All too soon sunshine turned to rain, pride of race to national disaster. But it taught the Prussians a lesson they never forgot, even if they were slow to learn, and the full fruits of it were reaped on the field of Waterloo nine years later.

At first Napoleon felt confident that the military preparations in Prussia were nothing but bluff, and although war was decided upon at Berlin on the 7th

August 1806, and an ultimatum sent to Paris on the 25th September, it was not until the 7th October that Napoleon heard of it, for he was then with his army. By the following day many of his troops had crossed the frontier. His fighting force numbered, in all, some 190,000 men, that of his opponents some 40,000 less, under the chief command of the Duke of Brunswick, a veteran over seventy years of age who had seen service in the wars of the Warrior King. With the French eagles marched many soldiers of the Confederation, evidence of the value of the policy of Napoleon to surround himself with vassal states. It was a somewhat one-sided bargain, for it was considerably more likely that he, in pursuing his aggressive projects, would call upon his allies more frequently than they upon him. Prussia was aided by Russia in the later stages of the campaign, for it was not until after the battle of Jena that the Czar's slow-moving forces were available. Saxony completed what might have been a most formidable triple alliance.

The Prussian general's great hope was that he might be able to cut off Napoleon's communications with France, but he was far too cumbersome in his movements to catch so nimble an adversary. The Emperor divined the plan, gave orders for an immediate concentration of his troops, and turned the tables by threatening the Prussian communications with Berlin. To Bernadotte was given the task of clearing the way for the main army. On the 9th October an affray took place between Saalburg and Schleiz, where there was an extensive wood, and the Prussians were forced to give way after a lengthy resistance. The French afterwards marched to Schleiz and carried the place. Murat, who had put himself in possession of Saalburg on the previous day, also accomplished much difficult work. More important was the action fought near Saalfeld between Lannes and Suchet and Prince Louis Ferdinand of Prussia, in which the young prince—he was but thirty-three years of age— lost his life while fighting against desperate odds. The infantry he commanded fell into disorder, and soon got altogether out of hand. The Prince had now but five squadrons of cavalry on which he could rely, and he determined to die rather than surrender. He gave the order to charge, was wounded in several places, and at last fell from his horse, the victim of a fatal sword-thrust from a hussar. He certainly exhibited the contempt for death which Napoleon recommended to his chasseurs about this time. "My lads," said he, "you must not fear death; when soldiers brave death, they drive him into the enemy's ranks."

The campaign was speedily decided. While the Emperor was closing upon the allied forces concentrated near Weimar and Jena under the King and Prince Hohenlohe respectively, a very foolish movement was decided upon. A large portion of the Prussian forces were detached for the relief of Naumburg, leaving but 47,000 men to face the French should they appear. The unexpected happened; for on the same day the Landgrafenberg, a steep hill whose summit, well-nigh inaccessible but commanding a magnificent bird's-eye view of the army Napoleon had marked for destruction, was unexpectedly occupied by the French. Almost superhuman exertion was required to haul up the heavy artillery so that it might be placed in the most advantageous positions for the coming conflict. Napoleon invariably discarded his trappings of state during a campaign and assumed the duties of a common soldier when necessity demanded, as on this occasion. He showed himself ready and willing to take his share in what the troops called "the dirty work." He laid mines for the blasting of rocks which blocked progress up the rugged heights, tugged at the ropes by which the cannon were hauled to the wind-swept ridge, and did not retire to his tent until he was perfectly satisfied in his own mind that nothing had been left undone which might contribute to the discomfiture of the enemy.

The story is told by Marbot, who, if he tells the truth, performed prodigies of valour worthy of D'Artagnan himself. A village priest pointed out the path which enabled the French troops to ascend the Landgrafenberg. "Up this path," the genial Marshal relates, "he led some officers of the staff and a company of voltigeurs. The Prussians, believing it to be impracticable, had neglected to guard it. Napoleon judged otherwise, and, on the report of the officers, went himself to see it, accompanied by Marshal Lannes and guided by the *curé*. He found that between the top of the path and the plain occupied by the enemy, there was a small rocky platform; and on this he determined to assemble a part of his troops, who should sally forth from it, as from a citadel, to attack the Prussians. For any one except Napoleon, commanding Frenchmen, the task would have been impossible; but he, sending to the engineers and artillery for four thousand pioneer's tools, set the infantry to work to widen and level the path, the battalions taking it in turn, each one for an hour, and as it finished its task, advancing in silence and forming on the top of the hill.... The nights were very long at this season of the year, and there was plenty of time to make the path practicable not only for columns of infantry, but for artillery and ammunition waggons; so that before daybreak the troops were massed on the Landgrafenberg. The term *massed* was never more correct, for the breasts of the men in each regiment were almost touching the backs of those in front of them. But the troops were so well disciplined that, in spite of the darkness and the packing of more than 40,000 men on the narrow platform, there was not the least disorder, and although the enemy who were occupying Cospoda and Closevitz were only half a cannon-shot off, they perceived nothing."

In the plain below the flaming bivouac fires winked and blinked like watch-dogs at the Prussian soldiers. Some had already taken an unconscious farewell of the stars as their weary eyelids closed upon a scene of natural beauty marred by the stacks of arms, parks of artillery and baggage waggons, which told of imminent strife and bloodshed.

At four o'clock in the morning, ere the faintest streak of dawn had pierced the sky, the French camp was astir, and Napoleon with it. Had a dragon breathing fire and brimstone presented itself on the field of Jena Prince Hohenlohe could not have been more surprised than when the French advance guard suddenly appeared out of a heavy, rolling, autumn mist. The death-dealing guns began their work, the cavalry and infantry on either side fought with desperation, and the battle inclined first to the one side, then to the other. The Prussian troops showed that notwithstanding long years of inaction there was still some of the blood and iron of *Unser Fritz* left in them; but before the reserve of 20,000 under Rüchel, for whom Hohenlohe had sent, came up, he had been obliged to write a second despatch urging haste, and confiding the news that the French cavalry "has driven into one confused mass the infantry, cavalry, and artillery." When the reserve appeared on the field the addition of so large a number of men tended to steady the Prussians, and it was on seeing them that an impetuous young French officer, noting the effect, shouted: "Forward! Forward!" to the Imperial Guard, which had not yet been used. "How now?" asked Napoleon. "What beardless boy is this who ventures to counsel his Emperor? Let him wait till he has commanded in thirty pitched battles before he proffers his advice!"

The day was definitely decided by a magnificent cavalry charge led by Murat, which caused a rout that only ended at Weimar, the home of the immortal Goethe, six leagues away.

"The Emperor," says Savary, "at the point where he stood, saw the flight of the Prussians, and our cavalry taking them by thousands. Night was approaching; and here, as at Austerlitz, he rode round the field of battle. He often alighted from his horse to give a little brandy to the wounded; and several times I observed him putting his hand into the breast of a soldier to ascertain whether his heart beat, because, in consequence of having seen some slight colour in his cheeks, he supposed he might not be dead. In this manner I saw him two or three times discover men who were still alive. On these occasions, he gave way to a joy it is impossible to describe."

At the same time another battle had been fought and lost by the Prussians not more than twelve miles distant from the scene of this terrible carnage. Davout had received instructions to march to Jena by a route which would enable him to fall on the enemy's rear while Napoleon was engaging them. In endeavouring to carry out this manœuvre the Marshal came directly upon Frederick's army before Auerstädt. As regards material strength, the condition of things at Jena was completely reversed. Here, as we have seen, the Prussians were in the minority; at Auerstädt the French were very much weaker. Both sides fought well, and proved themselves worthy of their countrymen who were engaged in a similar struggle only a few leagues away, but when the survivors of the two Prussian armies met it was as fugitives with the common desire to put as great a distance between them and their pursuers as possible. The King, Prince Henry, Prince William, and Marshal Möllendorf were wounded, the Duke of Brunswick and General Schmettau died as a result of injuries they received, and despite the inability of Davout to continue the pursuit of the stricken enemy, the corpses of 20,000 Prussians covered the fields of Jena and Auerstädt, lay in ditches, or almost blocked the roads. Many guns and colours fell to the spoil of the victors. What would have happened had Bernadotte and his cavalry come up is too horrible to contemplate.

It is almost impossible to overstate the dreadful position in which the people of Prussia now found themselves. Mr (afterwards Sir) George Jackson, who had been sent by Fox to obtain accurate information as to what was passing in Germany, confides to his Diary under date Hamburg, October 23rd: "Everybody is in despair, everything is upset by the late disaster that has fallen on the country.... The letters from Berlin speak of a state of ferment that is indescribable."

On the 25th October the French entered the capital. In their despairing condition the good folk of Berlin appear rather to have welcomed the invaders than otherwise. We will let our friend the Halle student tell us what happened. "I saw the first French who entered the town," he writes. "At about midday an officer, in a blue uniform, accompanied by three or four chasseurs, rode into the town; they stopped their horses, hurriedly asked the way towards the municipality, or the mansion-house, told the idlers to stand off, and galloped away again. There they were then! Many people still maintained that these were not French, but Russians. This was evident, said they, from their green uniforms. But in a quarter of an hour there was no longer room for doubt; large bodies of cavalry and infantry entered the town, and on the following day Berlin was filled with Marshal Davout's troops. And now began a totally new life among the half-stupefied inhabitants of Berlin. We breathed again; for, instead of wild unprincipled plunderers, we found a well-disciplined gay soldiery, who were disarmed by being addressed in French, and whose officers were, for the most part, remarkable for courteous manners. This first favourable impression was not effaced by subsequent rough conduct, although it was difficult to satisfy the pressing want of so many people. We still found that we had to thank God, if we were to have enemies quartered upon us, that they were not worse than these. Nevertheless, the slovenly, dirty, ragged appearance of these little, mean-looking, impudent, witty fellows, was a strange sight for eyes which, like ours, had been used to the neatness and admirable carriage of the Prussians, and we were the more astonished how such rabble—for they almost deserved the name—could have beaten such soldiers out of the field....

"On the 27th October," he continues, "I was taking my usual evening walk by the so-called Lustgarten, or park, when I was struck by a new sight. The whole space in the middle, which had been always kept carefully mown, and even the side-walks towards the palace, were covered with innumerable watch-fires, round which the soldiers of the Imperial Guard were grouped in all kinds of attitudes. The huge fires shone upon these handsome men and their glittering arms and accoutrements, and the eyes were attracted by the incessantly recurring national colours of red, blue and white. About 10,000 men were moving about in this glowing bivouac, near the gloomy-looking palace in which Napoleon had taken up his abode. The whole scene made a strong impression upon me, and when I examined the small details—for every one was allowed to go among the troops—my wonder was increased; each soldier, in appearance, manner, and authority, was like an officer—each man seemed a commander, a hero. The men sang, danced, and feasted till late in the night, while every now and then small detachments, in an admirable state of discipline, marched to and fro with drums and music. It was such a sight as I had never beheld. I stayed there for hours, and could scarcely leave the spot. The Imperial Guard remained there for some days, and all eyes were riveted by the beautiful but hated spectacle. But no subsequent impression equalled that of the first night: the fires burned more dimly; part of the troops had been detached elsewhere; and at length, small bodies of cavalry, with their horses ready saddled and bridled for instant service, were the only troops left in this encampment. The numerous body-guard in the court of the palace was quite sufficient for Napoleon's personal safety."

But we must return to war and to misery. Strongholds which had hitherto been thought well-nigh impregnable fell with sickening regularity. Magdeburg, for instance, surrendered ingloriously to Marshal Ney, and the garrison of 24,000 able-bodied men marched out and laid down their weapons, as did 10,000 troops at Erfurt. Custrin, reputed to be one of the strongest fortresses on the Oder, was handed over to some forty chasseurs, Stettin surrendered in the same despicable manner. Soult at Nordhausen, Bernadotte at Halle, and Murat and Lannes at Prenzlow won important victories which still further weighed down the scales against Prussia. It seemed as though the army which had started out with so much noise and bragging would disappear almost to a man. One fragment still remained, that under Blücher, the rugged old soldier who was to be in the chase when the fox was at last run to earth at Waterloo. His total force amounted to about 24,000 men, against whom 60,000 troops under Soult, Murat, and Bernadotte were pitted. On the 6th November 1806, the latter slaughtered many of the harassed Prussians in the narrow streets of Lübeck, but Blücher did not capitulate until the following day, when he was absolutely compelled to do so by the limits of Prussian territory.

CHAPTER XIX
THE POLISH CAMPAIGN (1806–7)

HAVING deprived the Elector of Hesse-Cassel, the Duke of Brunswick, and the Prince of Orange of their possessions; concluded an alliance with Saxony, whose Elector was raised to the dignity of King and joined the Rhenish Confederacy; and compelled the Prussian provincial authorities to swear allegiance preparatory to leaving General Clarke as Governor-General, Napoleon turned his unwearied attention to Poland. There he anticipated meeting the slow-moving Russian army before it reached Germany. The Commander-in-chief of the Czar's forces was Marshal Kamenskoi, a man of eighty years of age, who shortly afterwards became insane, and was succeeded by Bennigsen, on whom the soldiers placed considerably more reliance.

The partition of Poland by Russia, Austria and Prussia in 1795—a wound by no means healed—afforded an opportunity, had Napoleon decided to take advantage of it, for an appeal to the national spirit of the Poles to assert itself to regain their country's independence, an aspiration which is alive to-day. The Emperor sought to temporise, and when an influential deputation waited upon him to ask his assistance for the Poles, he evaded the point by a skilful answer which neither said yea nor nay to their request, but was nicely calculated to secure their enthusiasm on his behalf. The truth is, that while Napoleon did not disdain Polish recruits for the French army, he perceived that it would have been dangerous to further exasperate Russia, Prussia, and Austria. Indeed, Austria was arming already, Prussia was endeavouring to recuperate, and Russia was preparing a surprise.

The numerical strength of the various armies was, as far as can be ascertained, as follows: France, 145,000; Russia, 100,000; Prussia, 15,000. The Emperor's first headquarters were at Posen, but on Murat entering Warsaw at the end of November 1806, after some desultory fighting, he decided to move to that city, where he arrived with his staff on the 18th December. At

Pultusk, Lannes experienced a severe check at the hands of Bennigsen, whose troops outnumbered the French by 5000. A violent snow-storm made the work doubly heavy for both contestants, but the Russians had fewer difficulties to contend with than the attacking party, which was obliged to wade through slush that numbed the soldiers to the bone. They quitted themselves well, however, and forced the enemy to retreat until the cavalry and reserve were brought into action, when the French were forced to give up the unequal contest with the loss of 6000 men, one thousand more than that of the Russians. At Golymin, a somewhat similar disaster occurred to Davout, Augereau, and Murat, and these two misfortunes largely determined Napoleon to suspend hostilities for a time. Both armies therefore took up winter quarters, Napoleon on the forest-clad banks of the Vistula, the Russians near the Narew.

Bennigsen, now in chief command, knowing the almost desperate situation of the King of Prussia, who was shut up in Königsberg, upon which the divisions of Ney and Bernadotte were slowly closing, saw what he thought was an excellent opportunity to surprise Napoleon. He would assume the offensive, relieve the important fortress of Graudentz, then feebly held by a Prussian garrison, and protect Königsberg. But the Emperor, whilst enjoying the social life of Warsaw, was not to be caught quite so easily, and was speedily on the march. Through a despatch from Bernadotte, which was intercepted by a band of Cossacks, the Russian general got to know of the enemy's movements, and perforce had to give up his former plan or run the risk of a disastrous defeat. Many a game of military hide-and-seek followed, often accompanied by severe losses. Matters were brought to a crisis on the 7th February 1807, when both armies bivouaced within sight of each other at Eylau, the French to the number of 50,000 entering the town after an affray with the Russians, who probably totalled about 75,000. The corps under Ney, Bernadotte, and Davout, having been ordered to join the main force, were expected to afford valuable help.

Never was there a more keenly-contested field. It was snowing heavily when the first shells began to plough the opposing ranks. In a single charge nearly half the men in

Augereau's corps were annihilated, and their commander wounded. Davout returned the compliment, and was on the point of succeeding when the Russians received reinforcements and compelled him to fall back. Ney, who had duly arrived, and Murat, were more successful, but at the end of eighteen hours' fighting it was difficult to tell who had secured the advantage. Napoleon frankly confessed that it was quite possible he might have retreated, but when the next morning dawned, leaden and sullen, it was found that the Russians had disappeared, leaving him in possession of the field. On the 14th, Napoleon wrote to the Empress: "The country is covered with the dead and the wounded. This is not the pleasant part of war," while to his brother Joseph, he related some of the hardships of the campaign. "The officers of the staff," he says, "have not undressed for two months, many not for four months. I myself have not taken off my boots for a fortnight. We are in the midst of snow and mud, without wine, brandy, or bread. We have nothing but potatoes to eat; we make long marches and countermarches—no pleasant experience. We have to fight with the bayonet under a tremendous fire of grape, the wounded have then to be carried back 150 miles in open sleighs."

An incident which occurred at this period exemplifies very clearly how Napoleon could rebuke an officer and show at the same time that he had not forfeited his trust in him. It should be added that the Emperor did not always deal so leniently with a subordinate as he did with this particular individual.

One evening a bundle of despatches was delivered to Napoleon. "Surely these despatches have been a long time on their way!" he remarked to his attendant. "How is this? Tell the orderly officer who brought them that I wish to speak to him."

The officer entered, mud-bespattered and obviously ill at ease.

"Sir," said the Emperor, "at what hour were these despatches placed in your hands?"

"At eight o'clock in the evening, sire."

"And how many leagues had you to ride?"

"I do not know precisely, sire."

"But you ought to know, sir. An orderly officer ought to know *that*. I know it. You had twenty-seven miles to ride, and you set off at eight o'clock. Look at your watch, sir. What o'clock is it, now?"

"Half-past twelve, sire. The roads were in a terrible state. In some places the snow obstructed my passage——"

"Poor excuses, sir—poor excuses. Retire, and await my orders."

As the door closed behind the unfortunate messenger, whose unhappy frame of mind it is not difficult to realise, Napoleon remarked, "This cool, leisurely gentleman wants stimulating. The reprimand I have given him will make him spur his horse another time. Let me see—my answer must be delivered in two hours. I have not a moment to lose."

He replied to the communications and recalled the officer who had brought the despatches.

"Set off immediately, sir," said the Emperor; "these despatches must be delivered with the utmost speed. General Lasalle must receive my orders by three o'clock. You understand?"

"Sire, by half-past two the general shall have the orders of which I have the honour to be the bearer."

"Very well, sir, mount your horse—but stop!" he added, as the officer was about to make his exit. "Tell General Lasalle," and a magnetic smile lit up the Emperor's face for an instant, "that it will be agreeable to me that you should be the person selected to announce to me the success of these movements."

After the terrible fight at Eylau, which proved that the French arms were not invincible and added considerably to the prestige of the Russian army, Napoleon felt compelled to concentrate his forces still further. Although he was within an easy march of Königsberg, upon which Bennigsen had retreated, and had promised his soldiers before the action that "their fatigue will be compensated by a luxurious and honourable repose" at that city, he determined to try Fortune no further. He put down the sword of war and took up the pen of peace, writing a letter to the King of Prussia calculated to woo him from his allies. After the triumph of Jena Napoleon had asked half of Prussia as the price of peace, now he was willing to give back all the conquered territory east of the river Elbe, and at the same time to release Prussia from any future strife he might have with Russia.

We have already noted that Frederick William III. possessed little strength of will, of which fact the Czar as well as Napoleon was fully aware. Alexander determined to make the alliance between Russia and Prussia still more binding, feeling confident that Eylau was the beginning of the end so far as the Corsican upstart was concerned. The diplomacy of Napoleon received a check, and a treaty between Russia and Prussia was arranged at Bartenstein in April 1807, which, while it provided for eventualities which might follow the defeat of Napoleon, had the more immediate effect of strengthening the wavering purpose of the Prussian monarch.

CHAPTER XX
FRIEDLAND AND TILSIT (1807)

NAPOLEON saw every reason for a speedy and more vigorous prosecution of the war, which threatened to be prolonged indefinitely. The ranks of his army had been seriously thinned, and although he had obtained 80,000 conscripts but five months before, he found it necessary to call for a second levy of the same number, a very serious drain on the resources of France, for in the natural order of things the young men would not have been called upon until September 1808, eighteen months later. The urgency of the demand is shown in the Emperor's despatch to Cambacérès: "It is very important that this measure should be adopted with alacrity. A single objection raised in the Council of State or in the Senate would weaken me in Europe, and will bring Austria upon us. Then, it will not be two conscriptions, but three, or four, which we shall be obliged to decree, perhaps to no purpose, and to be vanquished at last." To talk of defeat was not usual with Napoleon, and although he added that he was not going "to wage war with boys," he most certainly did so. In June 1807 the total force at his disposal amounted to 310,000 troops, that of the allies 130,000 men.

The capture of Königsberg not being practicable at the moment, the fall of Danzig, an important strategic point, was eagerly anticipated by Napoleon. The place had already endured several notable sieges, and notwithstanding Lefebvre's energetic measures he was not able to send the good news that he had accomplished his purpose until the end of May 1807. The slow progress was partly due to the number of young, inexperienced soldiers with whom Lefebvre had to work, and also to a certain jealousy he manifested towards the engineers, the grenadiers being his favourites. "Your glory is in taking Danzig," Napoleon wrote to the old spit-fire. As 900 pieces of artillery were captured on the fall of the great fortress at the mouth of the Vistula, it must be conceded that the work was done well, if all too slowly for the patience of the Chief.

On the 5th June Ney was surprised by a Russian force, the Marshal losing 2000 men. Five days later the troops under St Cyr and Legrand met with disaster, and 12,000 of the rank and file were killed, wounded, or taken prisoners. These reverses were followed by the frightful field of Friedland, fought on the 14th June, the situation for France being alone saved by the intrepidity of Victor. The Russians under Bennigsen, seconded by Prince Bagration, behaved with exceptional bravery, retreating through water which reached nearly as high as their arms. Fifteen thousand of the enemy, including many who were drowned in their last desperate attempt to reach the opposite shore, were slain on this the anniversary of Marengo, and nearly 8000 Frenchmen fell.

Jackson, who had remained in the ill-fated city of Königsberg until the last moment, tells the story of Friedland in his Diary, and as he had every opportunity of obtaining facts at first hand, we will let him relate further particulars of the tragedy:—

"However great the loss sustained by the allies at Friedland, and it cannot be put at less than twenty-four thousand in killed, wounded, prisoners and missing, yet everything that valour and bravery could effect was achieved by them; and had the activity and ability of their leader borne any proportion to the courage of his troops, this battle, as disastrous as that of Austerlitz or Auerstädt, would have been as glorious for us, and as important in its consequences, as those were for the French; but these reflections are now as useless as they are sad. On the night of the 11th, Bennigsen, crossing the Alle, began his retreat from Heilsberg, which, with little intermission, he continued until he arrived on the evening of the 13th opposite Friedland. There he found a few squadrons of the enemy, who were driven across the river without much difficulty. He himself followed, and took up his quarters that night in the town, in front of which is a plain flanked by a wood; detaching a few regiments just before Friedland, to secure the safety of his quarters.

The Battle of Friedland

By Horace Vernet

"At between three and four in the morning, the enemy, masked and covered by the wood, began his attack on the right wing, supported by troops that came by degrees from the other side of the river; over which there was but one bridge and two pontoons. Notwithstanding these disadvantages, the Russians each time successfully repulsed the attacks of the French, both on their right and centre, with great loss to the enemy—with the one exception of a battery, carried in the first instance but immediately retaken—until seven in the evening, when Bonaparte came up with ten thousand fresh troops against their left. This decided the fate of the day. The Russians, worn out, as well by their late hard marchings and want of food, as by the fourteen hours of incessant fighting they had sustained, could not make a stand against this new shock, and in less than an hour began a very disorderly retreat. The general confusion was increased by the difficulty of recrossing the Alle, and the necessity of again passing through the town, which was on fire in several parts from the enemy's shells. Numbers were drowned in fording the river; being hardly pressed by the French.

"The extent of our losses both in men and cannon should be attributed to these circumstances rather than to any decided superiority of the French in the field. Their effect, too, on the troops, who had fought and had borne up so bravely through the day, was discouragement and dismay, and converted what might still have been, under abler leadership, a well-conducted retreat into a disorderly rout and precipitated flight.

"The Russian officers were unanimous in their reprobation of Bennigsen, who has betrayed the army, they say, if not by downright treachery, at least by the grossest ignorance and utter want of energy. 'If he is not removed,' says every military man, even the warmest of the war party, 'we had better make peace to-morrow; for to attempt to fight a battle with him as their leader is only to sacrifice the lives of brave men without any possible chance of success.'... The French entered Tilsit yesterday afternoon, and commenced firing at the Russians across the river. The fate of Europe is probably decided."

The immediate effects of the battle of Friedland was the capitulation on the 15th June of Königsberg, which had been admirably defended by the Prussian general L'Estocq, and an armistice between the French and Russians, in which Prussia was graciously allowed to share several days later when Napoleon and Alexander had talked over the matter together. Their meeting-place was a raft in the river Niemen, where they remained for nearly an hour alone, the conference being extended two hours longer on the admittance of the Grand Duke Constantine, Bennigsen, and Kalkreuth. King Frederick William, who had left Königsberg for Memel a short time before the fall of the former town, had to content himself with riding up and down the shore in the rain. A more humiliating position for a successor to the throne of the hero of the Seven Years' War, who never received an insult tamely, is difficult to conceive. Napoleon despised the weak monarch, and by his subsequent conduct showed that he had no better liking for the beautiful Queen Louisa. On the following day the King was admitted to the Council, but when the fate of Europe was under discussion the two Emperors repaired to their raft alone.

Napoleon paid delicate attentions to the Autocrat of all the Russias. He walked about with him arm in arm, and reviewed his troops before him, a compliment which Alexander duly returned.

Méneval, one of Napoleon's secretaries, who was present at Tilsit, affords us an interesting little glimpse of the two monarchs as they fraternised. "So intimate did the two Emperors become," he says, "that, when on returning from their excursions the Czar was to dine with Napoleon, the latter would not allow him to go home to change his dress. He used to send somebody to the house where Alexander lived to fetch the things he needed. He used to send him his own cravats and handkerchief through his valet. He placed his big gold travelling bag at his disposal, and as Alexander had praised the carvings of the various fittings, and the way in which the bag was arranged, Napoleon made him a present of it before they separated. When they returned before the dinner hour it was for the sake of a free *tête-a-tête*. On such occasions they used to leave the King of Prussia, and go into a little gallery which adjoined the Emperor's work-room. Sometimes Napoleon would bring the Czar into his study and ask for his maps, which included one of Turkey in Europe. I have seen them bending over this map and then continuing their conversation as they walked up and down. Schemes of partition were occupying them. Constantinople was the only point on which they were not visibly agreed."

It seemed like a case of love at first sight, but the wooer sought more than peace and good-will; he aimed at a definite alliance with Russia. This he achieved, and although the Czar is to be blamed for having broken faith with Great Britain and Austria so speedily, much must be forgiven him if only because both Powers had done little more than applaud the performer in the great war drama which had just ended. Prussia, as might be expected, came off very badly in the final settlement. Silesia and the provinces on the right bank of the Elbe were given back to her; those on the left bank, with the Duchy of Brunswick and the Electorate of Hesse-Cassel were formed into the Kingdom of Westphalia and handed over to Jerome Bonaparte; nearly the whole of Prussian Poland was added to the possessions of the King of Saxony, and became the Grand Duchy of Warsaw. The remaining province, that of Bialystok, was added to the Czar's territory. The war which had been proceeding between Russia and Turkey was to end, Russia withdrawing from the Sultan's Danubian Provinces. French troops were no longer to be quartered in Prussia.

These are the chief clauses of the famous Peace of Tilsit, signed between France and Russia on the 7th July 1807, and between France and Prussia two days later. A secret treaty was also assented to by Alexander and Napoleon, who not only agreed to join their armies in mutual support should either of them decide to make war on any European Power, but mapped out the Eastern Hemisphere as future spoil, Napoleon's particular plunder being Egypt and the coasts of the Adriatic Sea, which would be extremely useful in French designs against England. The reigning Kings of Spain and Portugal were to be deposed for the special benefit of the Bonaparte family. The Czar also promised that if peace were not made with Great Britain, whereby she recognised the equality of all nations on the ocean highway and handed back the conquests made by her since the year of Trafalgar, Russia and France would together renew the war against England. In that event Denmark, Sweden, Austria and Portugal would also be compelled to join the allies and close their ports against British ships. If the great Sea Power consented to the arrangements so thoughtfully made on her behalf, Hanover was to be given back to George III. England successfully disposed of, the complete domination of the Eastern Hemisphere might come within the range of practical politics.

CHAPTER XXI
NAPOLEON'S COMMERCIAL WAR
WITH GREAT BRITAIN (1807)

FROM the terms of the secret understanding between Napoleon and Alexander at Tilsit, it is obvious that the former had made up his mind to stand or fall in a last desperate encounter with Great Britain. Secure in her island home, that Power alone had been successful in thwarting Napoleon. Her ships and her money were constant menaces to the accomplishment of his over-lordship of the Continent. England's wooden walls barricaded the principal harbours; by her gold she largely helped to provide the sinews of war which enabled her allies to resist the oppressor. To make war on the sea, to drive it home to the coasts of the enemy, was not possible in the shattered condition of the French marine.

How then was her downfall to be brought about? Before his war with Prussia, Napoleon had taken a preliminary step by compelling Frederick William III. to forbid British vessels the use of the ports of his Kingdom and of Hanover. On the 21st November 1806 he augmented his plan by the stringent regulations of the Berlin Decree, so called because it was issued from that city. His powerful rival was to be cut off from all further intercourse with Europe. No letters were to pass, all commerce was to cease, every British subject in France or any country allied to her, or occupied by French troops, was liable to be declared a prisoner of war.

In theory the United Kingdom was in a state of blockade. By excluding her goods, the sale of which amounted to an enormous sum every year, from the countries of his allies and those directly under his control, Napoleon hoped that she would be forced to give up the unequal contest. Great Britain had retaliated speedily and effectually upon Prussia by seizing several hundred of her ships then lying in British harbours, by blockading her coasts, and by declaring war. She met the Berlin Decree by turning the tables on France, proclaiming France and her allies to be in a state of blockade, and providing that any ship which had not set out from, or touched at, a British harbour should be considered a lawful prize. Napoleon retorted by his Milan Decree of the 7th December 1807, whereby ships that had issued from or touched at British ports were put at the mercy of the French privateers which scoured the seas; "all ships going to or coming from any harbour in Great Britain or her colonies, or any country occupied by British troops, should be made a prize."

The banning of British goods and the fostering of home manufactures were the main planks of the great Continental System. Started with the ostensible purpose of ruining Great Britain, it contributed largely to Napoleon's downfall. In order to make Europe self-contained it was necessary to add conquest to conquest, and an interminable war does not contribute to happiness or make for prosperity. Eventually the French themselves lost their zest for strife, and the real meaning of nationality began to make itself felt in countries whose inhabitants groaned under the intolerable burden of a foreign task-master. The System, which Bourrienne calls "an act of tyranny and madness" which was "worthy only of the dark and barbarous ages," was applied to France, Italy, Switzerland, Holland, Austria, Russia, Prussia, the Rhenish Confederation, Denmark, Spain and Portugal. If you glance at the map of Europe you will see that there were few States to which the Napoleonic rule in some way or other did not apply. The people who benefited chiefly by this cutting off of England were the smugglers, who plied a magnificent trade both on sea and land. Thousands of persons were engaged in the business of contraband, conveying goods into French territories and assisting the sending of Continental productions to Great Britain. The cost of many articles went up to an extravagant figure. For instance, in France cotton stockings ranged from six shillings to seven shillings per pair; sugar varied from five shillings to six shillings per pound, while the same quantity of coffee sold at from ten shillings to eleven shillings. When we compare the last commodity with the price which obtained in England the difference is astounding. In 1812 coffee could be purchased in Liverpool for one-fifteenth of the price paid in Paris.

"Take especial care," the Emperor wrote to Junot, "that the ladies of your establishment use Swiss tea. It is as good as that of China. Coffee made from chicory is not at all inferior to that of Arabia. Let them make use of these substitutes in their drawing-rooms, instead of amusing themselves with talking politics like Madame de Staël. Let them take care, also, that no part of their dress is made of English merchandise. If the wives of my chief officers do not set the example, whom can I expect to follow it? It is a contest of life or death between France and England. I must look for the most cordial support in all those by whom I am surrounded."

Napoleon's tariff reform, instead of materially benefiting the manufacturers, tended to decrease the consumption of raw materials, because they could not be obtained. When uniforms were required for the French troops in the Eylau campaign they had to be purchased in England! Gradually the barriers began to break down, and by the sale of licenses for the bringing in of hitherto forbidden goods with the proviso that French manufactured goods must be taken in exchange, Napoleon replenished his war chests preparatory to the next campaign. It was the Czar's abandonment of the Continental System which led to the Emperor's disastrous Russian campaign. After that mammoth catastrophe, the whole scheme gradually fell to pieces, but not before all concerned, including Great Britain, had suffered very considerably.

On the Emperor's return to Paris from Tilsit in July 1807, he gave his attention for a short time to home affairs. He had been away for ten months, and the keenest enthusiasm for him was shown on all sides. The Great Nation was indeed worthy of the name which had been given to the French long before Napoleon and his armies had proved their right to it, and his subjects shared in the glamour of victory if not in the spoil. They furnished him with troops, were the props which supported his throne, and if they gave their sons to be victims of war they did not show on festive occasions that they regarded this as aught but a cruel necessity. The French love glory above everything, and to have a son serving with the eagles was a matter of pride to every true Frenchman.

Chancellor Pasquier attended the *Te Deum* to celebrate Napoleon's triumphs which was sung at the cathedral of Notre Dame, and he tells us in his "Memoirs" that he sat almost opposite the throne; from which point of vantage he studied the Emperor's face with quiet persistency. "He was obviously pleased with the religious sanction," the judge relates, "which, in the eyes of the people, consecrated his glory and omnipotence; he set a price on it, all the greater from the fact that up to the time of his coming it had been absolutely denied to all the works of the Revolution, and that it distinguished him from all that had preceded him.

"I am of opinion," adds the same authority, "that at no moment of his career did he enjoy more completely, or at least with more apparent security, the favours of fortune. Generally, in the midst of his greatest successes, he affected an anxious air, as if he wished it to be understood that his great designs were not yet accomplished, and that people ought not to think that there remained nothing more to do. The observation which I here record has been repeatedly made by those who have come into close contact with him, and who never found him less approachable than at times when it was reasonable to suppose that some most fortunate happening would open his soul to the sentiments of a more expansive good nature.

"Generally speaking, it was better for one having a favour to ask of him to approach him in his moments of worry, rather than on the days of his most brilliant successes. His character did not err on the generous side. I think I see him still, as he was on that day, dressed in his State costume, which, though a little theatrical, was noble and fine. His features, always calm and serious, recalled the cameos which represent the Roman Emperors. He was small; still his whole person, in this imposing ceremony, was in harmony with the part he was playing. A sword glittering with precious stones was at his side, and the famous diamond called the *Régent* formed its pommel. Its brilliancy did not let us forget that this sword was the sharpest and most victorious that the world had seen since those of Alexander and Cæsar. I remember that M. Beugnot, who sat by me, gave utterance to this thought.

Both of us were then far from dreaming that less than seven years would suffice to break it."

The following is an instance in support of Pasquier's statement regarding favours. When the Emperor was deeply engrossed in the Austrian campaign of 1809, one of his servants, named Fischer, went out of his mind. His master refused to fill his post, and paid the poor fellow, who had to be put in an asylum, his full salary of 12,000 francs a year until the end of 1812, when Napoleon gave him an annual pension of 6000 francs. Such kindness on the part of the man who might well be pardoned for forgetting or overlooking some claim, real or fancied, on his good-will was not rare but common.

Napoleon soon settled down to work, forsaking the hubbub of war for the quietness of the study. He established the University of France, which included every school both large and small, the primary object being to train the children in patriotism. In a word, he sought to dominate the mind. "There will never be fixity in politics," the Emperor averred, "if there is not a teaching body with fixed principles. As long as people do not from their infancy learn whether they ought to be republicans or monarchists, Catholics or sceptics, the State will never form a nation: it will rest on unsafe and shifting foundations, always exposed to changes and disorders." The first effort of the Council of the University was to compile the "Imperial Catechism," one of the articles of the Napoleonic faith being that "Christians owe to the princes who govern them, and we in particular owe to Napoleon I., our Emperor, love, respect, obedience, fidelity, military service, and the taxes levied for the preservation and defence of the Empire and of his throne. We also owe him fervent prayers for his safety and for the spiritual and temporal prosperity of the State."

The founder took the greatest possible interest in the work of the University, delighting to pay surprise visits to the schools. On one occasion he was somewhat nonplussed by a girl of whom he had asked the question: "How many needlesful of thread does it take to make a shirt?" "Sire," she replied, "I should need but one, if I could have that sufficiently long." The Emperor gave the witty scholar a gold chain as a reward.

It was not fated, however, that the arts of peace should for long occupy first place in the attention either of Napoleon or his people, and soon the country was again engrossed in rumours of war. British agents had not been asleep on the Continent, indeed, on the 15th July 1807, less than a week after the signature of peace between France and Prussia, Jackson confided to his "Diary" that he had "been positively assured that Bonaparte has sent eventual orders to Denmark to shut the Sound against us." A secret article of the Tilsit treaty was to the effect that should Sweden refuse to close her ports to England and to declare war against her, Denmark should be compelled to fight the former. This was to take effect if the negotiations for peace between Great Britain and Russia failed, but recent research shows that Canning, our Foreign Minister, was not correctly informed on this matter, and believed that the arrangement was to take effect immediately. England determined not to be forestalled, and proposed that Denmark should hand over her fleet until a general peace was proclaimed. The Prince Royal positively refused to entertain the proposition. As a land expedition was contemplated by Great Britain thousands of peasants were enlisted to defend Copenhagen, the garrison there consisting of some 4000 troops ill-provided with artillery. An army of 27,000 strong under Lord Cathcart sailed from Yarmouth in a fleet commanded by Admiral Gambier and disembarked on the morning of the 16th August some ten miles north of the Danish Capital. Batteries were erected, but little actual progress was made until Arthur Wellesley, who had recently returned from India, attacked a corps of 4000 of the militia at Kioge, 900 of whom were killed or wounded, and 1500 taken prisoners. Jackson's description of them is anything but picturesque. "The men are on board prison ships," he writes, "and miserable wretches they are, fit for nothing but following the plough. They wear red and green striped woollen jackets, and wooden *sabots*. Their long lank hair hangs over their shoulders, and gives to their rugged features a wild expression. The knowing ones say that after the first fire they threw away their arms, hoping, without them, to escape the pursuit of our troops. In fact, the *battle* was not a very glorious one, but this you will keep for yourself.... The Danes have not yet been put to any severe trial; but they show symptoms of a resolute spirit, and seem determined to fight it out with us. They have already burnt their suburbs and destroyed every house that was likely to afford shelter to our people."

The bombardment of the capital began on the 2nd September, 1807, and ended on the 5th, when the British took possession of the citadel and arsenals. The Danish fleet was surrounded and convoyed to England the following month. Jackson thus describes the contest, beginning with the preliminary passage from Landscrona to the fleet off Copenhagen, which occupied two hours and a half.

"It was nearly dark when we sailed out of the harbour; and in about half an hour afterwards we saw a great many rockets in the air, succeeded by shells on either side. The wind was so violent that we heard nothing until we were actually in the midst of the fleet, though we saw everything distinctly. Several shells fell in our direction, and so frightened our boatmen, that they repeatedly urged us to turn back. This, of course, we would not hear of; and at last we succeeded in getting alongside the flag-ship, where we found the Admiral and my brother in the stern gallery looking at the conflagration—for the city was on fire in three places. I never saw, nor can well conceive, a more awful, yet magnificent spectacle. It was the beginning of the bombardment *in forma*. We saw and heard it going on until daylight, as we lay in our cots; and as the work of destruction proceeded, I cannot describe to you the appalling effect it had on me. Our cabin was illuminated with an intensely red glow, then suddenly wrapped in deep gloom, as the flames rose and fell, while the vessel quivered and every plank in her was shaken by the loud reverberation of the cannon. Alas! poor Danes! I could not but feel for them.

"Lord Cathcart told me the next morning that he had thrown two thousand shells into the town, besides the fire from our gun-boats and the famous catamaran rockets. And this sort of work was to begin again at night....

"In the afternoon the firing began again with greater fury than ever, and for two or three hours there was a tremendous blaze. The wind was high; the flames spread rapidly, and towards night vividly illumined the horizon, so that at the distance of five miles from the city we could see each other on the quarter-deck as if it had been broad daylight, and into the city in the same manner; the intervening ships forming very picturesque objects.

"... Ere I left, the fire had increased to a prodigious height, the principal church was in flames, looking like a pyramid of fire, and the last I saw and heard of the ill-fated city was the falling-in of the steeple with a tremendous crash, and the distant loud hurrahs it occasioned along our line.

"I own that my heart ached as I thought of the many scenes of horror that must inevitably take place in the midst of all this—and soon there would be but a heap of ruins instead of a city to take."

Few people were surprised when Denmark definitely allied herself to France and declared war against Great Britain, as did Russia, after some show of negotiations, in November. In the following spring war was declared upon Sweden by the Czar without any just cause. Finland was overrun by his troops, but the resistance of the brave inhabitants led to an Act of Guarantee whereby the Czar promised to uphold the old laws. Still eager to share in the dismemberment of the Turkish Empire, Alexander clung to the Danubian provinces of Moldavia and Wallachia which were to have been restored to the Sultan by the terms of the Treaty of Tilsit, and Napoleon, on his part, continued to keep Prussia full of French soldiers. Thus both parties were unfaithful to their most solemn promises, but this did not preclude a joint expedition to India to be undertaken by France, Russia, and Austria from being mooted.

Napoleon now took occasion to visit Italy, with the usual results. Etruria, whose king was a grandson of Charles IV. of Spain, became a department of France, the young monarch being promised a province in Portugal with the title of King of Northern Lusitania, and the Papal States were filled with French troops and shortly afterwards absorbed in the kingdom of Italy.

CHAPTER XXII
THE GENESIS OF THE
PENINSULAR WAR (1808)

ALTHOUGH the crown of Spain was not yet worn by a nominee of Napoleon its present holder, or rather Manuel Godoy, an adventurer who in five years had risen from private in the Guards to chief Minister, was careful not to offend the Emperor. Portugal, on the other hand, was a friend of England, with whom she did a very large trade. Unfortunately her means of resistance were so weak and unorganised that when the Emperor of the French called upon the Prince Regent to close the harbours to British ships and declare war against England he had no alternative but to obey. A constant menace in the form of 28,000 troops had been stationed at Bayonne, and did not admit of argument. This Army of the Gironde was composed for the most part of young and inexperienced conscripts, but they were French, and therefore held to be invincible. The confiscation of British property was also demanded by Napoleon, but on this point the Prince Regent temporised, thus giving the majority of the British residents time to leave the country, to the wrath of the Emperor. Sufficient of the story of Napoleon has been told to show that he was no believer in half measures; when a State hesitated to do his will, swift retribution usually followed. Orders were immediately issued for Junot to proceed to Spain, where he would be joined by troops of that nationality, and enter Portugal. On the other side of the French frontiers the march was only accomplished with much difficulty, the trackless mountains, swollen rivers, and almost incessant rain making progress extremely slow and hazardous.

Stricken with panic, the Queen, the Regent, the Royal Family, the Court and many members of the nobility sailed for Brazil under the protection of a British fleet commanded by Sir Sidney Smith, the brilliant young officer who had already crossed Napoleon's path in Syria. So great was the fear of the French that no fewer than fourteen cartloads of plate were left on the quay at Belem.

But for the impassable state of the river Zezere, which prevented Junot from making rapid progress, the royal fugitives would have been prevented from escaping to Rio Janeiro.

Lisbon was occupied by Junot's ragged regiments without much trouble. A strong resistance could scarcely have been expected, seeing what a poor example had been given to the people by those who ruled them. For a time it appeared as if everything connected with the French occupation would be settled satisfactorily. The proclamation issued by Junot, now Duke of Abrantès and Governor of Portugal, on the 1st February 1808, made no secret of Napoleon's intentions.

"The House of Braganza," it runs, "has ceased to reign in Portugal; and the Emperor Napoleon, having taken under his protection the beautiful kingdom of Portugal, wishes that it should be administered and governed over its whole extent in the name of his Majesty, and by the General-in-Chief of his army."

This must have been bitter reading to Godoy. In a secret treaty signed at Fontainebleau on the 27th October 1807, he had been promised the southern Portuguese provinces of Alemtejo and Algarve as a Principality for his connivance and assistance in the downfall of Portugal. Napoleon was paying him back in his own coin. During the Prussian campaign Godoy had cherished hostile designs against France, hoping for the co-operation of either England or Russia. In a proclamation dated the 5th October 1806, he had summoned the Portuguese nation to arms and but thinly disguised the name of the prospective enemy. The brilliant field of Jena, however, so radically changed the political aspect that it was necessary to make other plans, and Godoy put forth every effort possible to placate Napoleon. The Emperor had not forgotten, however; he never did, and he returned evil for evil. Having had the assistance of Spanish troops and the use of Spanish territory for the passage of his own soldiers, the Emperor found it inconvenient to complete his part of the bargain, and so the Prince of the Peace, to give Godoy his official title, went empty away.

Things were far from well with the Royal house of Spain. Charles IV. and his son Ferdinand, Prince of the Asturias, had quarrelled, the King going so far as to have his heir arrested on the charge of plotting against the throne. The main cause of disagreement was the Prince's detestation of Godoy, who at every turn came between him and his father, and might conceivably rob him of his succession to the throne. Napoleon, ever eager and willing to make an advantage out of another's disadvantage, surmised that the quarrel would enable him to settle the affairs of the eastern portion of the Peninsula to his liking. Hence another army of 25,000 men was concentrated at Bayonne which, without warning, crossed into Spanish territory towards the end of November 1807. Further corps followed until more than 100,000 French soldiers had traversed the Pyrenees. Citadels and fortresses were seized, often by bribery or cunning, that of Pampeluna by over-eagerness on the part of the garrison to secure the French soldiers as contestants in a snowball-fight. The opportunity was not allowed to slip, and while the Spaniards were off their guard the new arrivals took possession of the fort, and remained there till 1813.

The nation correctly associated Godoy with the indignities it was suffering. His palace at Aranjuez was sacked, and the Favourite was fortunate in not being lynched by the mob. Finally the King abdicated in favour of his son, an act which caused more rejoicing than had been accorded any other event during his reign.

Murat and his troops entered Madrid the day previous to the state entry of the young monarch. Little interest was shown in the arrival of the French soldiers, but Ferdinand received an astounding ovation, women in their enthusiasm scattering flowers before him as he rode. Forty-eight hours after the event Napoleon offered the Crown of Spain to his brother Louis, King of Holland.

On one pretext and another Ferdinand, whom Napoleon called "the enemy of France," was persuaded to meet the Emperor at Bayonne. During the interview he was informed that he could have the choice of two evils. If he would resign his throne the Emperor would give him Etruria as some kind of compensation, if not he would be deposed. To complicate the difficulty, Charles IV., at

Napoleon's instigation, withdrew his abdication, which he declared had been wrung from him by fear, and did everything in his power to induce his son to accept Napoleon's offer. At last the Emperor lost patience, and Ferdinand was given a few hours to make up his mind whether he would submit or be tried for high treason. Accordingly, on the 6th May 1808, the King, who had reigned less than two months, surrendered his throne, as he believed, to its former occupant, totally unaware that Napoleon had exacted the resignation of Charles IV. on the previous day. Few more despicable acts are recorded in history, certainly no better example could be found of Napoleon's lack of a sense of honour in political matters.

Spain was now at the Emperor's disposal. Louis had refused the kingdom, and so it was handed over to Joseph, Naples being given to Murat, his brother-in-law. The Emperor lived to repent the day, as did Joseph, who had endeared himself to the Neapolitans but could never persuade his Spanish subjects that he was anything but a vulgar upstart trading on the reputation of his brilliant brother.

Baptiste Capefigue, the eminent French historian, has tersely summed up the cause of Napoleon's ultimate failure, and the passages quoted here have special reference to the events we are now studying. "Napoleon," he says, "did not fail through the governments opposed to him, but through the people; it was when he attacked national feelings that he met with a stubborn resistance; he had strangely abused his dictatorial power over Europe; he crushed down nations by his treaties, and he gave up the populations to kings of his own creation; he broke territories into fractions, separating that which was before united, and joining together those parts which were separated; he transformed a republic into a kingdom; of a free town he made a district of one of his prefectships; he united the high lands to the plain; simple, primitive populations to old and corrupt ones, without regard to diversities of language, or manners, or to religious antipathies. In Germany, above all, his policy appears most tyrannical; he takes away a province from one monarchy and gives it to another; he plays with the masses as if they were chessmen; he creates a kingdom of

Westphalia out of more than twenty States or fragments of States; he detaches Tyrol from Austria, heedless of traditional customs, institutions, and manners; Holland, a mercantile republic, he changes into a kingdom; to Naples, at the extremity of Italy, he sends one of his brothers. His is an unparalleled despotism, without reason or excuse. The people are for him like a mute herd of cattle; he pens them up, or drives them before him with his terrible sword. Add to this the French spirit, the French character, which, in his pride of a founder of a great empire, he wished to force upon all Europe, together with his own code of laws. God has imparted to each of the various nations a character which is its own; for good or for evil, it is unwise to run counter to it. Germany has its own morals and manners; Spain has its inveterate habits—perhaps they dispose to indolence—but what is that to strangers? Uniformity may be a plausible idea in mathematics; but in the moral organization of the human kind, harmony is the result of diversities."

What is probably a typical summing up of the case from the distinctly British point of view is afforded us in a letter written by Francis Horner on the 13th June 1808, in which he says: "I cannot but rejoice that a people who bear such a name as the Spaniards should make a struggle at least for their independence; the example cannot be otherwise than beneficial, even if they should entirely fail, to their posterity at some future day, and to all the rest of mankind. It is the most detestable of all the enormities into which Bonaparte's love of dominion has plunged him, and more completely devoid than any other of all the pretence of provocation or security. If I were a Spaniard, I should consider resistance, however desperate in its chances of success, and however bloody in its immediate operation, as an indispensable duty of discretion and expediency; to put the proposition in its most frigid form of expression.... What a moment for a Spaniard of political and military genius!"

Pending the arrival of the new monarch, Murat was assigned the important post of Lieutenant-General of the kingdom. He was a good cavalry leader beyond question, but as a statesman he did not shine during the period in which he was dictator of Spain. He let it be seen that he regarded the nation as already conquered, and it is not surprising that his tactless rule should have roused bitter resentment. On the 2nd May there was a riot in Madrid, short and furious, but indicating the passionate nature of the citizens. Eight hundred insurgents fell in the streets, perhaps half that number of soldiers were laid low, and two hundred Spaniards were afterwards shot by Murat's orders for having taken part in the rebellion. Many of the populace had been armed with sticks and stones only, others with muskets which they used to good effect, both in the squares and from the housetops. It was only when additional soldiers, including the Mamelukes, the chasseurs, and dragoons, were brought up that the crowd realised the hopelessness of the task they had undertaken. If "the blood of the martyrs is the seed of the church," the blood of those who fell in Madrid on that May day in 1808 was the seed from which the harvest of disaster for Napoleonic statesmanship was reaped. The despot did not realise the possibility at first, but at St Helena, when frankness was not always a despised virtue, he told Las Cases that the Spanish war "was the first cause of the calamities of France." The self-confidence of Murat, who said, "My victory over the insurgents in the capital assures us the peaceable possession of Spain," a sentiment in which the Emperor agreed, was speedily dispelled. "Bah!" exclaimed Napoleon when he was told by an eye-witness of the revolution at Madrid and the sullen courage of the people, "they will calm down and will bless me as soon as they see their country freed from the discredit and disorder into which it has been thrown by the weakest and most corrupt administration that ever existed."

While the officials in Madrid were bowing to Joseph, the people in the provinces were showing by open rebellion that they neither desired him as king nor wished for Napoleon's assistance in the ruling of their country. The priests told the people of the Emperor's ungenerous treatment of the Pope, how a French force had entered Rome in the previous February, and that his Holiness had lost almost every vestige of his civil power. Every little township began to take measures of offence and defence. Innumerable miniature armies roamed among the mountains like bandits, awaiting an opportunity to annihilate a French outpost, to interrupt communications, or to fall on a division as it marched along to join one of the army corps now being poured into Spain. General actions were not encouraged, and usually ended in disaster. Assassinations and massacres became the order of the day on both sides, forcing the French commanders to realise that they had to face a novel kind of warfare—a nation in arms. At the end of May 1808, when the people were actively organising, there were nearly 120,000 French troops in Spain and Portugal. In the first few engagements the Spaniards, who possibly numbered 100,000, including the regulars, were routed. When towns were besieged the French met with less success, and the defence of Saragossa under young Joseph Palafox, whose daring soon raised him to the dignity of a national hero, is a most thrilling episode. A name which must be coupled with his is that of Augustina (or Manuela) Sanchez. A battery had been abandoned by the Spaniards, and this brave girl, one of the many inhabitants who helped to defend their city, found that the hand of a dead gunner still grasped a lighted match, whereupon she seized it and fired the gun, thereby attracting the attention of the fugitives, who returned to the fight. The first siege of Saragossa lasted for nearly eight weeks, but the place eventually surrendered to Lannes.

Duhesme and his French soldiers met with even worse fortune, being forced to take refuge in Barcelona, where the Spaniards kept them secure for nearly four months. At Medina de Rio Seco the insurgents under La Cuesta and Blake, an Irishman, were completely routed by Bessières. This event might have weakened the national cause very considerably had not Dupont's army been entrapped among the Sierra Morena mountains by Castaños. In the fighting that took place 3,000 French were either killed or wounded, and 18,000 troops were forced to lay down their arms at the subsequent capitulation of Baylen. When Napoleon heard of the victory at Medina de Rio Seco, he wrote: "Bessières has put the crown on Joseph's head. The Spaniards have now perhaps 15,000 men left, with some old blockhead at their head; the resistance of the Peninsula is ended!" His reception of the news of Dupont's surrender was very different. "That an army should be beaten is nothing," he burst forth after reading the fatal despatch, "it is the daily fate of war, and is easily repaired, but that an army should submit to a dishonourable capitulation is a stain on the glory of our arms which can never be effaced. Wounds inflicted on honour are incurable. The moral effect of this catastrophe will be terrible." The luckless Dupont was promptly imprisoned on his return to France, and remained so until 1814.

This trouble did not come singly. It was followed shortly afterwards by the news that Joseph, feeling that Madrid was no longer secure, had deemed it advisable to retire in haste to Burgos, behind the Ebro, and within comparatively easy distance of the frontier. Some three weeks later Castaños at the head of his troops marched into the capital. The position of Ferdinand's successor was speedily becoming untenable. "I have not a single Spaniard left who is attached to my cause," he tells his brother. "As a General, my part would be endurable—nay, easy; for, with a detachment of your veteran troops, I could conquer the Spaniards, but as a King my position is insupportable, for I must kill one portion of my subjects to make the other submit. I decline, therefore, to reign over a people who will not have me." He adds that he does not wish to retire conquered, but pleads for an experienced army that he may return to Madrid and come to terms with his rebellious subjects ere seeking the quiet of Naples.

In Portugal Junot, by dint of extreme severity, had succeeded in disarming the populace and securing the principal fortresses, his troops being dispersed about the country. His success made him feel so self-satisfied that he entertained the hope that Napoleon would confer the crown of Portugal upon him. As a preliminary step he endeavoured to win over the nobles and clergy. The Emperor had different views, and while recognising Junot's unquestionable ability he was not blind to his shortcomings.

At the same time as King Joseph was retreating from Madrid, 9000 British soldiers under Sir Arthur Wellesley had reached the mouth of the Mondego River, and, in spite of many difficulties, had effected a landing. The future Duke of Wellington was not to retain supreme command, although he had started out with that expectation. After leaving England he learned that three other officers, namely, Sir Hew Dalrymple, then Governor of Gibraltar; Sir Harry Burrard, a Guardsman of some experience; and Sir John Moore, who had previously taken part in Paoli's descent on Corsica and seen much honourable service in the West Indies and Ireland, were to join the expedition. Wellesley was not pleased at being superseded, but he was too good a soldier to show resentment. "Whether I am to command the army or not," he told the home authorities, "or am to quit it, I shall do my best to secure its success, and you may depend upon it that I shall not hurry the operations or commence them one moment sooner than they ought to be commenced, in order that I may reap the credit of success." Nothing that he ever wrote or said reveals more truly the unswerving honour and loyalty of the Iron Duke.

Junot was not particularly perturbed by the news of Wellesley's arrival. Small British expeditionary forces had landed again and again in various parts of the continent since 1793, and usually had been only too glad to return to England. The French commander noted with pleasure that the Portuguese showed little sympathy with their allies, so much so that Sir Arthur had the utmost difficulty to persuade them to lend assistance. Lisbon was still too disturbed to warrant Junot leaving it, and he accordingly directed Loison and Laborde to concentrate near Leiria. Wellesley, however, outmarched them, and prevented them from combining their forces immediately. On the 15th August he had a smart skirmish with Laborde, and two days later was victorious at Roleia, where a stiff battle was fought with the same commander. Unfortunately Wellesley's forces were not sufficiently strong to make the victory decisive or to stop the two forces of the enemy from uniting later.

Junot now found it necessary to assume personal command. Leaving Madrid with a garrison of 7000 soldiers, he gathered his available forces, including those of Loison and Laborde, and came up with the British at Vimiero on the 21st August. Wellesley's strength was some 18,000 troops in all, and although Sir Harry Burrard was the senior officer, he did not exercise his authority until the battle was almost concluded. In infantry Sir Arthur had the advantage, but Junot, while having but 13,000 men for the task he had undertaken, was considerably better off in cavalry. One incident in particular relieves the sordid story of the fight. In a charge made by the 71st and 92nd British regiments a piper, who was wounded in the thigh, fell to the ground. He continued to blow his pibroch, declaring that "the lads should nae want music to their wark." The day remained with the British, and had Wellesley been allowed to pursue the French, probably Lisbon would have fallen. It is said that when Wellesley heard Burrard's order to abstain from following the enemy, he remarked to his staff: "There is nothing left for us, gentlemen, but to hunt red-legged partridges!"

On the suggestion of Junot an armistice was agreed upon. This ended in the ill-considered Convention of Cintra, signed on the 30th August 1808, whereby Portugal was relieved of 25,000 French invaders. The troops were conveyed back to France by British ships. Junot was disgraced in the eyes of the Emperor and received no further command until the Russian campaign of 1812. His wife, when reviewing this campaign, says with justice, "Everything which was not a triumph he (Napoleon) regarded as a defeat." As no clause was inserted in the Convention to the effect that the troops should not serve again, it is not difficult to understand why a popular outcry was raised in Great Britain against the three generals. It soon became evident that Wellesley did not merit the attacks made upon Dalrymple, Burrard, and himself in the Press and elsewhere. An inquiry into the affair was instituted by command of George III., and its finding was favourable to the decision of the signatories of the Convention, but only Wellesley saw active service again. The command in Portugal was given to Sir John Moore, and meantime Sir Arthur took his seat in the House of Commons and resumed his work as Irish Secretary, little thinking that in a few months he would return to the South as Commander-in-Chief.

A caricature by Woodward, published in February 1809, very ably sums up British opinion of the affair. It can be understood by the following humorous lines, in imitation of "The House that Jack Built":—

These are the French who took the Gold
that lay in the City of Lisbon.
This is Sir Arthur (whose Valour and skill
began so well but ended so ill) who
beat the French who took the Gold that
lay in the City of Lisbon.
This is the *Convention* that Nobody owns,
that saved old Junot's Baggage and Bones,
altho' Sir Arthur (whose Valour and skill
began so well but ended so ill,) had beaten
the French who took the Gold that lay in the
City of Lisbon.
This is John Bull, in great dismay, at the
sight of the Ships which carried away the
gold and silver and all the spoil the French
had plundered with so much toil after the
Convention which nobody owns, which saved
old Junot's Baggage and Bones, altho' Sir Arthur
(whose Valour and skill began so well but ended so ill)
had beaten the French who took the Gold
that lay in the City of Lisbon.

CHAPTER XXIII
GLORY AT ERFURT AND
HUMILIATION IN SPAIN (1808–1809)

THE cloud of misfortune which overshadowed the French armies in Spain and Portugal gradually grew in size and density until it covered practically the whole of Europe. Encouraged by the success of the insurgents in the Iberian Peninsula and the triumph of British arms in Portugal, both Austria and Germany took courage and prepared to throw off the yoke. In Austria a *landwehr*, or local militia, designed to number 180,000 of the young men of the country, came into being; in Prussia patriotic clubs sprang up on all hands, while such able statesmen as Stein, who had been Minister of State for Trade, and Scharnhorst, a skilful officer and organiser, worked nobly in the interests of military reforms which were destined to bear much good fruit in due course.

Napoleon was more immediately concerned with the intentions of the former Power. To a certain extent he had clipped the wings of the Prussian eagle by forcing the King into an undertaking that for the next ten years his army should not exceed 40,000 troops. This did not prevent many civilians being quietly drafted into a reserve for future service, or the formation of a school of thought with the highest patriotic ideals. The Emperor's policy was thoroughly sound. By still holding the fortresses of Glogau, Stettin, and Küstrin, and reducing the number of national troops to a minimum, the French troops which had been kept in Prussia since the campaign of her humiliation were set free for service in the South. Napoleon already knew of Austria's warlike disposition, and was even a little uncertain as to Russia. Suspicion was mutual, and as he was about to set out for Spain to take command of his troops, he thought it advisable to "sound" the temper of his ally personally.

It was arranged that the Emperor and the Czar should meet at the little town of Erfurt towards the end of September 1808. No fewer than seventy sovereigns and princes came to the meeting, including the Kings of Saxony, Bavaria, Würtemberg, and Westphalia, the Grand Duke Constantine of Russia, Prince William of Prussia, the Dukes of Saxe-Weimar, Saxe-Gotha, and Holstein-Oldenburg, together with distinguished marshals and courtiers. There were reviews, plays in the theatre acted by the most talented artists in France—Talma having been promised "a parterre full of kings"—and a stag-hunt on the battle-field of Jena. Costly presents were exchanged, one of the Czar's gifts being a magnificent Persian horse, silvery grey in colour, which Napoleon afterwards used by a strange coincidence in the battles of Vitebsk, Smolensk, and Borodino during the Russian campaign. The animal also accompanied him to Elba.

This great diplomatic performance was magnificently staged. If less dramatic than Tilsit, it was no less important. The festivities and conferences between the Emperor and Alexander lasted seventeen days. They parted on the 14th October, the anniversary of the great fight which did so much to make Napoleon master of Prussia. The terms of the Peace of Tilsit had not been kept too scrupulously by either monarch, and when one is uncertain as to one's own morality, a strong suspicion is usually entertained as to that of others. Alexander had not withdrawn his troops from the Danubian Provinces, which suggested that he still had in view the partition of the Ottoman Empire, while Napoleon, until his misfortunes in the Peninsula, had seen fit to keep a large number of troops in Silesia. Spain and Portugal were stepping-stones to the East as well as necessary acquisitions for the enforcement of his Continental System, facts quite well comprehended by the Czar of all the Russias. Napoleon, who was as well informed concerning his ally's weak spot, threw out suggestions for an expedition to India, and consented to Finland, Moldavia, and Wallachia being added to the Russian Empire. Alexander returned these courtesies by approving of Napoleon's recent moves regarding Naples, Tuscany, and the Peninsula, and promised to lend his aid should Austria come to blows with France. "We talked of the affairs of Turkey at Erfurt," the Emperor told Las Cases at St Helena. "Alexander was very desirous that I should consent to his obtaining possession of Constantinople, but I could never bring my mind to consent to it. It is the finest harbour in the world, is placed in the finest situation, and is itself worth a kingdom." As a concession to Prussia, probably because of the Czar's wish, Silesia was to be returned to her former possessor.

Chancellor Pasquier says of Napoleon at Erfurt that "On no other occasion, perhaps, did the suppleness and craftiness of his Italian spirit shine to more brilliant advantage." Boutourlin avers that notwithstanding these qualities Alexander felt that when the interests of Napoleon were adversely affected the friendship would not last, "that the grand crisis was approaching which was destined either to consolidate the universal empire which the French Emperor was endeavouring to establish on the Continent, or to break the chains which retained so many Continental States under his rule."

Mention must be made of the interviews which took place at this time between Napoleon and Wieland and Goethe, two of the greatest literary geniuses which Germany has given to the republic of letters. Both poets were fascinated by the magic personality of Napoleon, and both have left us some record of their conversation with the man who at this period was in very truth a ruler of kings.

"I had been but a few minutes in the room," Wieland says, "when Napoleon crossed it to come to us. I was presented by the Duchess of Weimar. He paid me some compliments in an affable tone, fixing his eye piercingly upon me. Few men have appeared to me to possess, in the same degree, the power of penetrating at a glance the thoughts of others. I have never beheld anyone more calm, more simple, more mild, or less ostentatious in appearance. Nothing about him indicated the feeling of power in a great monarch. He spoke to me as an old acquaintance would speak to an equal. What was more extraordinary on his part, he conversed with me exclusively for an hour and a half, to the great surprise of the assembly. He appeared to have no relish for anything gay. In spite of the prepossessing amenity of his manners, he seemed to me to be of bronze. Towards midnight I began to feel that it was improper to detain him so long, and I took the liberty to request permission to retire: 'Go, then,' said he in a friendly tone. 'Good-night.'"

The Emperor conferred the Cross of the Legion of Honour on Wieland, a mark of Imperial favour which he likewise showed to Goethe. The interview between Napoleon and the latter took place on the 2nd October 1808, in the presence of Talleyrand, Daru, Berthier, and Savary. "You are a man!" he exclaimed, either in a burst of admiration or of flattery, and then he asked the poet his age and particulars of his work, adding that he had read "Werther" seven times and had taken the volume to Egypt. "After various remarks, all very just," says Goethe, "he pointed out a passage, and asked me why I had written so, it was contrary to nature. This opinion he developed in great clearness. I listened calmly, and smilingly replied that I did not know whether the objection had been made before; but that I found it perfectly just.... The Emperor seemed satisfied and returned to the drama, criticising it like a man who had studied the tragic stage with the attention of a criminal judge, and who was keenly alive to the fault of the French in departing from nature. He disapproved of all pieces in which Fate played a part. 'Those pieces belong to a dark epoch. Besides, what do they mean by Fate? Politics are Fate!'"

Even more interesting perhaps, because it so essentially reveals Napoleon's outlook on life, was a remark he made at a later meeting at which both Wieland and Goethe were present. He wished the latter to treat of the "Death of Cæsar." "That," he said, "should be the great task of your life. In that tragedy you should show the world how much Cæsar would have done for humanity, if only he had been allowed time to carry out his great plans." When we reflect on the events which had immediately preceded this notable utterance, on the grandiose schemes which were then being actively promulgated by the speaker for the conquest of Europe and the advancement of his Empire of the West, we can understand why Napoleon wished to woo this literary giant to his cause. "Come to Paris," Napoleon said in his abrupt, commanding way, "I desire it of you. There you will find a wider circle for your spirit of observation; there you will find enormous material for poetic creations." But it was not to be; Goethe had other wishes and ideals. Had he acceded to the despot's request the result would have been no more felicitous than that which had attended Voltaire's removal to the Court of Frederick the Great. Goethe loved Prussia too well to desert her, and while he admired Napoleon in some ways he did not admire him in all.

Peace with Great Britain was suggested by the two Emperors at Erfurt, but England had far too much to lose to seriously entertain such an overture. In his reply Canning made it perfectly clear that George III. was not prepared to break faith with his Portuguese, Sicilian, and Spanish allies. Both the King and his Minister fully realised the nature of the undertaking upon which they had embarked, and having put their hands to the plough there was to be no turning back. Their course gave rise to many blunders abroad and many heartburnings at home, yet they loyally followed the precept of the great man whose ashes were now lying in Westminster Abbey. "England," said Pitt in his last public speech, "has saved herself by her exertions, and will, as I trust, save Europe by her example."

We must now glance across the Pyrenees at the strife still going on in the Peninsula. Had Sir John Moore secured the active and loyal assistance of the people, as he clearly had a right to expect, all might have been well with the cause of the allies. The preliminary successes of the Spaniards, however, had made them over-confident, and over-confidence is a sure prelude to disaster. Of all their many mistakes most fatal was their preference for fighting with independent corps, each under a Captain-General. Instead of joining together in the common cause there was considerable rivalry and many misunderstandings between the various forces. As a consequence when Napoleon, feeling comparatively secure from Austrian menaces because of the Russian alliance, determined to lead his armies in person, the Spaniards were but ill organised. Their antagonist, on the contrary, soon had at his disposal 300,000 trained soldiers divided into eight corps under his most skilled generals. "In a few days," the Emperor said before leaving Paris, "I shall set out to place myself at the head of my army, and, with the aid of God, crown at Madrid the King of Spain, and plant my eagles on the towers of Lisbon." The Spaniards could not muster at the moment more than 76,000 men, and whereas their cavalry totalled 2000, that of Napoleon was at least twenty times the number. A reserve of nearly 60,000 Spaniards was gathering in the rear, but would not be available for the first desperate onslaught, on the result of which so much would depend. The British army of some 30,000 was, by a series of misfortunes, in three divisions and unable to come up with any of the Spanish armies, which were also separated.

Napoleon began his movements and got into action while his opponents were thinking of what was likely to happen. Blake's ragged patriots were scattered by Lefebvre early in November after having been defeated at Tornosa and Reynosa. Soult defeated the army under the Count de Belvidere at Burgos on the 10th November, the Spaniards suffering a loss of 2000 men and 800 prisoners, as well as their ammunition and stores. The town, after having been pillaged, became the Emperor's headquarters. On the 22nd of the same month Castaños' forces, augmented by the men under Palafox, and amounting in all to 43,000, were routed by the 35,000 troops opposed to them by Lannes. After such a series of defeats it was not difficult for the Emperor to push towards Madrid, the outskirts of which he reached, after forcing the Somosierra Pass, on the 2nd December. The inhabitants made some show of resistance, but they were so badly organised as to preclude any possibility of serious defensive measures. Wishing to spare the city from bombardment, Napoleon sent a flag of truce, and a capitulation was speedily signed.

A soldier who was present thus relates the entry of the French into Madrid: "A heavy silence," he says, "had succeeded that confusion and uproar which had reigned within and without the walls of the capital only the day before. The streets through which we entered were deserted; and even in the market-place, the numerous shops of the vendors of necessaries still remained shut. The water-carriers were the only people of the town who had not interrupted their usual avocations. They moved about uttering their cries with the nasal, drawling tone, peculiar to their native mountains of Galicia, *'Quien quiere agua?'*—Who wants water? No purchasers made their appearance; the waterman muttered to himself sorrowfully, *'Dios que la da,'*—It is God's gift,—and cried again.

"As we advanced into the heart of the city, we perceived groups of Spaniards standing at the corner of a square, where they had formerly been in the habit of assembling in great numbers. They stood muffled in their capacious cloaks, regarding us with a sullen, dejected aspect. Their national pride could scarcely let them credit that any other than Spanish soldiers could have beaten Spaniards. If they happened to perceive among our ranks a horse which had once belonged to their cavalry, they soon distinguished him by his pace, and awakening from their apathy, would whisper together: *'Este caballo es Español'*—That's a Spanish horse; as if they had discovered the sole cause of our success."

On the 7th December 1808, Napoleon issued a proclamation which was largely a fierce tirade against England and the English, whose armies were to be chased from the Peninsula. In the constitution which he framed for the nation he abolished the iniquitous Inquisition, and the old feudal system which had held Spain in its shackles for so long, reduced the number of monasteries and convents by two-thirds, improved the customs, and endeavoured to institute reforms which would have been beneficial. "It depends upon you," the Emperor told the people, "whether this moderate constitution which I offer you shall henceforth be your law. Should all my efforts prove vain, and should you refuse to justify my confidence, then nothing will remain for me but to treat you as a conquered province and find a new throne for my brother. In that case I shall myself assume the crown of Spain and teach the ill-disposed to respect that crown, for God has given me the power and the will to overcome all obstacles."

The concluding words are noteworthy. Napoleon now regarded himself as little less than omnipotent. Impelled by the force of his own volition, into a dangerous situation, he was to find it impossible to draw back when the nations which he had treated with contempt felt that self-confidence which alone made Leipzig and Waterloo possible. The Peninsular War was indeed what Talleyrand prophesied, "the beginning of the end."

After considerable hesitation, due to the varying and oftentimes contradictory accounts which he received as to what was actually happening in the field, Sir John Moore, having concentrated his troops, cautiously began to close upon Soult's army on the banks of the river Carrion. When Napoleon heard of this he speedily decided to crush the friends of Spain and Portugal by sheer force of numbers, God, according to him, being "on the side of the biggest battalions," a parallel remark to Nelson's "Only numbers can annihilate." Winter had set in with severity, but disregarding the inclemency of the weather, the Emperor marched with his 40,000 men along the Guadarrama Pass through the blinding sleet, traversing no fewer than twenty miles a day for ten days. Meanwhile Moore had given up hope of attacking and had decided to retreat as rapidly as possible. Unfortunately his troops did not follow the example of their noble commander; they broke away from every restraint, drinking and pillaging whenever they had opportunity. It is only just to add, however, that at Lugo, when there seemed an opportunity to contest Soult, who was following in their track, they stood to arms with a confidence and precision worthy of the best disciplined regiment in the British service. Lord Paget's corps, which covered the retreat, behaved with conspicuous bravery, and succeeded in worsting some of the chasseurs, the "Invincibles" of the French army.

"Before our reserve left Lugo," writes a soldier of the 75th Regiment who endured the hardships of this terrible retreat, "general orders were issued, warning and exhorting us to keep order, and to march together; but, alas! how could men observe order amidst such sufferings, or men whose feet were naked and sore, keep up with men who, being more fortunate, had better shoes and stronger constitutions? The officers in many points, suffered almost as much as the men. I have seen officers of the Guards, and others, worth thousands, with pieces of old blanket wrapped round their feet and legs; the men pointing at them, with a malicious satisfaction, saying 'There goes three thousand a year'; or 'There goes the prodigal son, on his return to his father, cured of his wanderings.'"

On the 11th January 1809, Coruña was reached, and several days afterwards the welcome sails of the British troop-ships made their appearance, ready to convey the survivors of the battle to be fought on the 16th to England and to home. Soult had the advantage of 4000 more troops and of a better position, but lacked ammunition, while the British general had been able to obtain a supply of new muskets from the vessels which rode at anchor in the Bay.

It was round the little village of Elvina that the fight raged most fiercely, for a French battery of eleven guns was placed on a ridge not more than 600 yards off, and from this commanding position shells were hurled at the British defenders with ruthless fury. Elvina was taken by the French and re-captured by the gallantry of Charles Napier, who led the fearless Irishmen of the 50th regiment. He then endeavoured to secure the French battery, but without success, and during the charge he was wounded and made prisoner.

"My brave 42nd," cried Moore, when the enemy was again advancing on the village, "if you have fired away all your ammunition, you have still your bayonets. Recollect Egypt! Remember Scotland! Come on, my brave countrymen!"

"Sir John," according to an eye-witness, "was at the head of every charge." Indeed, he had several narrow escapes before he received his death-wound. He was talking to Napier when, records the latter, "a round shot struck the ground between his horse's feet and mine. The horse leaped round, and I also turned mechanically, but Moore forced the animal back, and asked me if I was hurt. 'No, sir.' Meanwhile a second shot had torn off the leg of a 42nd man, who screamed horribly and rolled about so as to excite agitation and alarm in others. The General said, 'This is nothing, my lads; keep your ranks. My good fellow, don't make such a noise; we must bear these things better.' He spoke sharply, but it had a good effect, for this man's cries had made an opening in the ranks, and the men shrank from the spot, although they had not done so when others had been hit who did not cry out. But again Moore went off, and I saw him no more."

Sir John was struck by a cannon-ball which tore his flesh in several places and precluded all possibility of recovery. "I hope the people of England will be satisfied: I hope my country will do me justice," were the noble words which passed his parched lips as he lay dying on the field of victory.

"We buried him darkly at dead of night,
The sods with our bayonets turning;
By the struggling moonbeam's misty light,
And the lantern dimly burning."

CHAPTER XXIV
THE AUSTRIAN CAMPAIGN (1809)

ON a certain memorable occasion, Walpole is said to have made the remark, "They are ringing the bells now; they will be wringing their hands soon!" with reference to a universal outcry for war on the part of Great Britain. Had it been uttered by an Austrian statesman at the beginning of 1809, it would have been equally apposite. Thinking men recognised that the army was not yet prepared to meet Napoleon, despite the fact that since the Austerlitz campaign of 1805 the improvement of her military forces had engrossed the attention of Archduke Charles, the Commander-in-chief. He was convinced that his troops were not ready to take the field, and he led the peace party solely on this account. The war party, however, headed by Count Stadion, the able and energetic Minister of Foreign Affairs, and aided by the Empress, who had considerable influence over her august husband, proved more powerful. Its supporters felt confident that as the war in Spain necessarily occupied so much of Napoleon's attention, and had drawn off such a large proportion of his troops, the time to strike was come. Austrian diplomatists had vainly endeavoured to woo both Russia and Prussia without success; the Czar had no wish at that moment to break with his ally; Frederick William trembled for his throne.

In January 1809, war was imminent. Napoleon, deceived as to the real state of affairs in Spain, set out on his return journey to France on the 16th. He at once began to organise his forces, Berthier being placed in command until the Emperor's arrival at the seat of war. Napoleon's explicit instructions were as follows:—

"By the 1st April the corps of Marshal Davout, which broke up from the Oder and Lower Elbe on the 17th March, will be established between Nuremberg, Bamberg, and Baireuth: Masséna will be around Ulm: Oudinot between Augsburg and Donauwörth. From the 1st to the 15th, three French corps, 130,000 strong, besides 10,000 allies, the Bavarians in advance on the Iser, and the

Würtembergers in reserve, may be concentrated on the Danube at Ratisbon or Ingolstadt. Strong *têtes-de-pont* should be thrown up at Augsburg, to secure the passage of the Lech at Ingolstadt, in order to be able to debouch to the left bank of the Danube; and above all at Passau, which should be able to hold out two or three months. The Emperor's object is to concentrate his army as soon as possible at Ratisbon: the position on the Lech is to be assumed only if it is attacked before the concentration at the former town is possible. The second corps will be at Ratisbon by the 10th, and on that day Bessières will also arrive with the reserve cavalry of the Guard: Davout will be at Nuremberg: Masséna at Augsburg: Lefebvre at one or two marches from Ratisbon. Headquarters then may be safely established in that town, in the midst of 200,000 men, guarding the right bank of the Danube from Ratisbon to Passau, by means of which stream provisions and supplies of every sort will be procured in abundance. Should the Austrians debouch from Bohemia or Ratisbon, Davout and Lefebvre should fall back on Ingolstadt or Donauwörth."

On the 9th April, when hostilities began, the strength of Napoleon's forces was as follows:—His newly-named Army of Germany, on the Danube, numbered 174,000 troops, including some 54,000 of the Rhenish Confederacy; the Army of Italy consisted of 68,000; in Saxony there were about 20,000; in Poland 19,000; in Dalmatia 10,500. Consequently the Emperor had 291,500 troops at his disposal, some 275,000 of whom were ready to confront Austria by the middle of the month. This is an enormous number when it is remembered that he was still at war with Spain, where 300,000 men were engaged, but he had had recourse to his old plan of forestalling the conscription, whereby he had obtained 80,000 recruits.

The Austrian forces were divided into three armies: that of Germany, under Archduke Charles, consisting of 189,684 troops; of Italy, under Archduke John, totalling 64,768, including those for action in Tyrol under Chasteler; and of Galicia, under Archduke Ferdinand, with 35,400; in all 289,852. The Reserves, made up of the *landwehr* and *levées en masse* reached 244,247, but as Mr F. Loraine Petre points out in his masterly study of this campaign, only some 15,000 of the *landwehr* were used with the active army at the beginning of hostilities. "There was little of the spirit of war in the *landwehr*," he adds, "and discipline was very bad. One battalion attacked and wounded its chief with the bayonet. Two others refused to march. Eleven Bohemian battalions could only be got to march when regular troops were added to them. Even then they only averaged about 500 men each, and those badly equipped and armed." But while this organisation was of little practical service at the moment, it was creating a healthy public opinion which could not fail to be beneficial in the years to come.

Already Napoleon's military glory was beginning to decline. In some of his principles he "became false to himself," he omitted to make his orders to his subordinates sufficiently clear, and on one occasion, in the early stage of the campaign, threw away "chances of a decisive battle which would then probably have made an end of the war." He also exhibited the utmost contempt for a country which "had profited by the lessons he had taught her," with the result that "her armies, and her commander-in-chief, were very different from the troops and leaders of 1796 and 1805," when he had crossed swords with Austria.

Yet another failing is pointed out by Mr Petre. "Napoleon's wonderful successes in every previous campaign," he notes, "and the height to which his power had risen, by the practical subjugation of all Europe to his dominion, tended to fan the flame of his pride, to make him deem himself invincible and infallible, to cause him to assume that what he desired was certain to happen. The wish now began to be father to the thought. Of this we shall find numerous instances in this campaign, the most notable, perhaps, being when, notwithstanding Davout's positive assertions that the greater part of the Austrian army was in front of himself, the Emperor persisted in believing that Charles was in full retreat on Vienna by the right bank of the Danube. His constant over-estimates of his own forces, not in bulletins but in letters to his generals and ministers, are other examples of this failing."

The campaign opened in Bavaria, where 176,000 Austrians assembled early in April 1809. Berthier, doubtless acting for the best as he conceived it, instead of concentrating at Ratisbon, Ingolstadt or Donauwörth according to orders, had seen fit to scatter his forces, "in the dangerous view," as Alison puts it, "of stopping the advance of the Austrians at all points." As a result of Berthier's blunder Davout at Ratisbon and Masséna at Augsburg were thirty-five leagues from each other, and Archduke Charles with 100,000 troops were interposed between them. About Ingolstadt were the Bavarians under Wrede, Lefebvre, and the reserve under Oudinot, the only forces available to oppose the Austrians, whose march, fortunately for the French, was extremely slow.

The Emperor arrived at Donauwörth on the 17th April, and at once saw the danger. "What you have done appears so strange," he wrote to Berthier, "that if I was not aware of your friendship I should think you were betraying me; Davout is at this moment more completely at the disposal of the Archduke than of myself."

It was Napoleon's task to bring the two armies in touch with each other so that a combined movement might become possible. "One word will explain to you the urgency of affairs," the Emperor wrote to Masséna on the 18th. "Archduke Charles, with 80,000 men, debouched yesterday from Landshut on Ratisbon; the Bavarians contended the whole day with the advanced guard. Orders have been dispatched to Davout to move with 60,000 troops in the direction of Neustadt, where he will form a junction with the Bavarians. To-morrow (19th) all your troops who can be mustered at Pfaffenhofen, with the Würtembergers, a division of cuirassiers, and every man you can collect, should be in a condition to fall on the rear of Archduke Charles. A single glance must show you that never was more pressing occasion for diligence and activity than at present. With 60,000 good troops, Davout may indeed make head against the Archduke; but I consider him ruined without resource, if Oudinot and your three divisions are on his rear before daybreak on the 19th, and you inspire the soldiers with all they should feel on so momentous an occasion. Everything leads us to the belief that between the 18th, 19th, and 20th, all the affairs of Germany will be decided."

On the 19th Davout withdrew from Ratisbon, leaving only the 65th French infantry to guard the bridge over the Danube, and after a severe but indecisive action at Haussen, reached Abensberg in the evening, thereby effecting his junction with Lefebvre. At Pfaffenhofen Masséna defeated a body of the enemy and remained there. Archduke Charles had foolishly divided his army, and while he was marching on Ratisbon, Archduke Louis and Hiller, with 42,000 troops forming the Austrian left wing, were brought to action at Abensberg by Napoleon on the 20th. The day remained with the French, who numbered 55,000, their enemies losing over 2700 killed and wounded, and some 4000 prisoners. According to Mr Petre, about 25,000 soldiers only on either side came into action. The defeated Austrians retreated in the direction of Landshut, several of the energetic Bavarian battalions following them. After a spirited fight, during which ammunition ran out and many men were killed and wounded, the solitary regiment which held Ratisbon was forced to surrender on the same day, half the troops of the 65th being taken prisoners.

On the morning of the 21st Napoleon renewed the battle against the Austrian left. About 9000 men were added to the enemy's already extensive losses, and it had the desired effect of preventing them from joining the main army. Davout and Lefebvre also engaged the Austrian centre, which retreated, leaving many wounded and dead on the field.

The Emperor was now ready to give attention to Archduke Charles who, with 74,000 troops, was bent on destroying Davout. The French Marshal was in a tight corner, the Austrian main army being opposed to him, and not to Napoleon, as the Emperor had supposed on the morning of Abensberg. As we have seen, it was only the left wing which he had defeated on the 20th.

When the Archduke heard that Napoleon was on his track he abandoned the idea of attacking Davout and made his dispositions to meet the Emperor. Immediately they came up, the bridge, village, and château of Eckmühl were captured by the French. The heights were stormed in truly magnificent style, and a brave attempt was made by the Bavarian cavalry to capture the enemy's battery on the

Bettelberg, which was doing considerable execution. They were driven back, but an hour later a French cuirassier regiment captured the greater part of the guns, with the result that Rosenberg, the commander of the fourth Austrian army corps, was forced to retreat. The Emperor then ordered the cavalry and infantry to pursue the unfortunate Imperialists, who broke away almost in a panic.

It now became evident that a general retreat was necessary, the Austrian left wing making in the direction of the river Isar, the main army, after a further sharp conflict with the enemy, reaching the Danube, the idea being to retire into the forests of Bohemia. It is calculated that nearly 10,000 Austrians were killed, wounded, or taken prisoners on this terrible day.

At St Helena, where, like the old soldiers in Chelsea Hospital, Napoleon so often "fought his battles o'er again," he frequently referred to the battle of Eckmühl. On one occasion he called it "that superb manœuvre, the finest that I ever executed," attributing its indecisiveness to his lack of sleep on the previous night.

Under cover of night, and during the early hours of the morning of the 23rd, the cumbersome baggage of the Imperialists was hurried across the bridge which spans the Danube at Ratisbon. This was followed by the retreat of part of the army over a pontoon bridge hastily put together, the Austrian rear-guard protecting the necessarily slow and somewhat difficult passage. Nine battalions only remained on the right bank of the river when Napoleon was making his final preparations to take the walled town of Ratisbon by assault. Fighting had already begun near the town. Ladders were secured, and the intrepid Lannes was soon within the old-time fortress, which speedily capitulated.

In his "Incident of the French Camp" Browning has sung of a lad who took part in the storming. He depicts Napoleon standing on a little mound

"With neck out-thrust, you fancy how,
Legs wide, arms locked behind,
As if to balance the prone brow
Oppressive with its mind."

The Emperor soliloquises that if Lannes "waver at yonder wall" his plans may miscarry, when—

"Out 'twixt the battery-smokes there flew
A rider, bound on bound
Full-galloping; nor bridle drew
Until he reached the mound.

"Then off there flung in smiling joy,
And held himself erect
By just his horse's mane, a boy:
You hardly could suspect—
(So tight he kept his lips compressed,
Scarce any blood came through)
You looked twice ere you saw his breast
Was all but shot in two.

"'Well,' cried he, 'Emperor, by God's grace
We've got you Ratisbon!
The Marshal's in the market-place,
And you'll be there anon
To see your flag-bird flap his vans
Where I, to heart's desire,
Perched him!'"

Napoleon's eye flashed with the pride of victory, but presently:

"Softened itself, as sheathes
A film the mother-eagle's eye
When her bruised eaglet breathes;
'You're wounded!' 'Nay,' the soldier's pride
Touched to the quick, he said:
'I'm killed, Sire!' And his chief beside
Smiling the boy fell dead."

The Emperor himself was slightly wounded while directing operations. A spent musket-ball struck his right foot and caused him considerable pain. "Ah! I am hit," he remarked quietly, adding with grim humour, "It must have been a Tyrolese marksman to have struck me at such a distance. Those fellows fire with wonderful precision." The matter soon got noised abroad; the news was passed from rank to rank that the "little Corporal" was wounded. Anxiety was evident in almost every face. Men who had seen many a comrade struck down and had not so much as moved a muscle of their features took on a look of care and of pain until reassured that the Emperor's injury was a mere contusion. A louder cheer was never raised during the whole of his career, than when Napoleon rode along the lines a little later. Not till then were "his children" convinced of his safety.

Thus ended what has been called the Campaign of Ratisbon, during the five days of which, according to Major-General August Keim, the Imperialists lost nearly 40,000 troops in killed, wounded, and prisoners. Truly a prodigious number and eloquent proof of the valour and energy of their opponents.

There was now nothing to prevent Napoleon from presenting himself before Vienna, but while his troops, flushed with success, were marching towards that picturesque city, their leader heard grave and disquieting news. The Bavarians under Wrede had been defeated on the 24th April by the retreating Austrians+ under Hiller, who was endeavouring to come up with Archduke Charles. Bessières had also been forced to retire. In addition Prince Eugène and the army of Italy had met with disaster at the hands of Archduke John at Sacile eight days before, and had not an immediate concentration of the various Austrian armies become essential for the defence of Vienna the consequences must have been serious.

Marshal Macdonald points out in his "Recollections" that a defeat in Italy was of secondary importance; the decisive point was Germany. There is, however, a moral point of view to be taken into consideration in warfare, to which he also draws attention. "It might have a bad effect," he says, "upon the Italian mind, already prejudiced against us, kept under as they were, but not conquered; and upon that of the Germans and their armies, although they had been so often beaten, and their territory so often invaded by us. But they were like the teeth of Cadmus; no sooner was one army destroyed than another came to take its place. They seemed to rise out of the ground." Napoleon was aware that the Tyrolese had broken out in revolt, and that similar movements were expected in other places.

It is unnecessary to follow all the Emperor's movements on his march to the Imperial city. Bessières, with comparatively few troops at his disposal, came in conflict with a much larger force under Hiller, and was repulsed. The Marshal somewhat retrieved this mishap by crossing the Inn at Passau, where he took several hundred prisoners. These "affairs" were but skirmishes to the battle of Ebelsberg (sometimes spelt Ebersberg) on the 3rd May 1809 between General Hiller and the French vanguard under the impetuous Masséna, at which Napoleon was not present. Hiller had taken up his position at Ebelsberg, crossing the long wooden bridge over the turbulent Traun, a tributary of the Danube, to which admittance was only gained by an extremely narrow gateway beneath a tower, while the whole structure was at the mercy of the guns in and near the castle on the heights above. For purposes of defence the situation approached the ideal, the only thing needed being a skilful commander. The day proved that the Austrian general was lacking in nearly all the qualities possessed by the French officers who opposed him, and was unworthy the men who fought in the ranks. A desperate struggle led by the fearless Coehorn took place on the bridge; men were flung into the surging waters below, while the Austrian artillerymen, perhaps not knowing that many Austrians were on the frail structure, fired at the combatants on the bridge with disastrous results to their own side. To make matters worse several ammunition waggons blew up. It was a repetition of the scene on the Bridge of Lodi, only the carnage was more terrible. Once across, the castle became the next objective of the French, but it was not captured until many a gallant soldier had lost his life in a hand-to-hand struggle in the town below. Hitherto only a comparatively small number of Masséna's troops had maintained the fight, but the Marshal now hurried fresh men across the bridge to support those engaged with the enemy. Gradually the men fought their way to the castle, and Mr Petre tells us that of one regiment which appeared before it, Colonel Pouget, who commanded, alone escaped without a wound.

"The entrance to the castle," Mr Petre writes, "was by a vaulted archway open at the outer end, but closed by a strong wooden gate at the inner end. Above was a window, closely barred with iron and with loopholes on either side. From all of these there poured a heavy fire, especially from the grated window. The losses of the besiegers, as they stood and returned the fire from the exposed space between the archway and the mouth of the hollow road, were fearful. Men crowded up to take part in the fight, which was directed by Pouget from the angle of the archway, whence he could both see his own men and the grated window. The French infantry fired as quickly as they could; some even used the dead bodies of their comrades to raise them more on to a level with the window. Then Pouget sent for a well-known sportsman, Lieutenant Guyot, who, taking post within five yards of the window, poured in shots as fast as loaded muskets could be handed to him by the soldiers. Other picked marksmen joined him, and, at last, the Austrian fire began to fail. Sappers had now arrived and were at work breaking in the thick gate.

"In the enthusiasm of the fight Colonel Baudinot and Sub-Lieutenant Gérard of the 2nd battalion had managed to get forward, though most of their battalion was blocked in the narrow road behind. These two intrepid men, followed by a few others as brave as themselves, managed to find a way by the cellar ventilators, whence they got into the castle. Between Gérard and a grenadier of the garrison, who entered a room on the first floor simultaneously, there was a desperate encounter, which was not interfered with by the entrance of a third visitor in the shape of an Austrian round shot. Just at this moment the gate was broken in, and the garrison, including, presumably, Gérard's grenadier, very soon surrendered as prisoners of war."

Surely no more thrilling adventure than this is to be found in any story book? And yet it is but one of many that might be related of this campaign alone, could this volume be extended beyond the present limits.

But the storming of the castle of Ebelsberg was not yet over. The burning town had been cleared of the Imperialists, who were now pouring a veritable hail of shot on the besiegers from the surrounding heights, and their situation was perilous in the extreme, cut off as they were from their friends and surrounded only by their foes.

Why the Austrians should have begun to retreat when such an opportunity was offered them to annihilate the enemy is beyond comprehension. Such was the case, and they hastened towards Enns, leaving two thousand killed and wounded, and over that number of prisoners. The French also lost very heavily. Late in the afternoon Napoleon came up, and in company with Savary, entered the town. He was by no means pleased with the terrible sights which met him on all sides, and bitterly lamented the heavy losses which his troops had suffered. Savary states that the Emperor remarked: "It were well if all promoters of wars could behold such an appalling picture. They would then discover how much evil humanity has to suffer from their projects." If he did thus speak, it shows how blinded he had become by his own egotism; for Napoleon had certainly forced the war on unhappy Austria, now sorely discomfited by the turn events had taken.

CHAPTER XXV
THE AUSTRIAN CAMPAIGN—CONTINUED (1809)

ON the 10th May 1809, the French were before Vienna, and preparations were made for a vigorous attack. Late in the evening of the 11th the Emperor's artillerymen began to hurl shells into the city, which was but ill-defended by Archduke Maximilian, who thought too much of his own skin to be of any considerable service, and speedily retired with his troops from the capital. Within forty-eight hours of the first shot being fired many of the French troops were in Vienna, the Emperor taking up his quarters in the palace of Schönbrünn near by.

Here he issued a decree annexing Rome, to which Pius VII. retorted with a Bull of excommunication. Napoleon, always an admirer of Charlemagne, referred to that monarch as "our august predecessor." He had already hinted that the Pope should be no more than Bishop of Rome, as was the case under the rule of the founder of the Empire of the West. Several weeks later the Holy Father was escorted from the Quirinal to Avignon, and thence to Savona, in which quiet retreat the Emperor hoped he would come to his senses, in other words, to Napoleon's way of thinking. This is exactly what the aged and determined Pontiff did not do, however. He preferred to remain virtually a prisoner and to pray for the recovery of his temporal kingdom rather than to submit to the dictatorship of the Emperor. The latter did not see fit to relent until 1814, the Pope then being at Fontainebleau. He offered to restore a portion of his states, but Pius VII. refused to discuss any terms except from Rome, to which city he returned on the Emperor's abdication.

Decisive victory over his Austrian foes had yet to be gained by Napoleon, and while Hillier was slowly endeavouring to unite with Archduke Charles on the left bank of the Danube, the Emperor was laying his well-conceived plans before his generals.

The following interesting anecdote is related of this campaign. It shows how a raw recruit may become imbued with a keen sense of responsibility after spending a few months in the ranks.

A sentinel, Jean Baptiste Coluche, was stationed by two paths near the Emperor's temporary headquarters on a certain night. He had been told to allow no one to pass, so when his quick ears detected a scrunch on the gravel some distance away, he carried out his instructions without question. Jean shouted to the intruder to stop. No notice was taken; the heavy, measured steps drew nearer. Again he repeated his summons, and bringing his carbine to his shoulder, prepared to fire. At that moment the outline of a dark and unmistakable figure approached. It was the Emperor himself. When the guard, alarmed by the cries, came up to render assistance, they set to chaffing Coluche, but the only reply of the peasant conscript was: "I've carried out my orders."

This was by no means the only occasion on which the Emperor appeared when least expected, and he was wont to reward the soldier whom he found on the *qui vive* under such circumstances. It was not so with the faithful Coluche. But in 1814 the much-coveted Cross of the Legion of Honour was pinned on his breast for his heroism at the battle of Arcis-sur-Aube, when the man whom he had ordered to halt before the walls of Vienna was forced to beat a retreat.

Bourrienne relates another interesting anecdote told to him by Rapp, the Emperor's aide-de-camp during the Austrian campaign. It concerns "one of those striking remarks of Napoleon," to quote Bourrienne, "which, when his words are compared with the events that follow them, would almost appear to indicate a foresight of his future destiny. The Emperor, when within a few day's march of Vienna, procured a guide to explain to him the names of every village, or ruin, however insignificant, that presented itself on his road. The guide pointed to an eminence, on which were still visible a few remaining vestiges of an old fortified castle. 'Those,' said the guide, 'are the ruins of the castle of Diernstein.' Napoleon suddenly stopped, and remained for some time silently contemplating the ruins, then turning to Marshal Lannes, who was with him, he said: 'See! yonder is the prison of Richard Cœur de Lion. He, too, like us, went to Syria and Palestine. But Cœur de Lion, my brave Lannes, was not more brave than you. He was more fortunate than I at St Jean d'Acre. A duke of Austria sold him to an emperor of Germany, who shut him up in yonder castle. Those were the days of barbarism. How different the civilisation of our times! The world has seen how I treated the Emperor of Austria, whom I might have imprisoned—and I would treat him so again. I take no credit to myself for this. In the present age crowned heads must be respected. A conqueror imprisoned!'" and yet that is exactly what happened to the speaker but a few years later.

At last Archduke Charles and Hillier joined forces on the Marchfeld, intent on regaining the lost capital. Napoleon had made up his mind to fight in the very camp of the enemy by crossing the Danube. For this purpose he built a succession of bridges consisting of boats and pontoons from Ebersdorf to the three islands in the river, and linked the last and largest of these, that of Lobau, to the opposite bank.

The first troops to cross occupied the stone-built villages of Aspern and Essling, which served somewhat as fortified places. The French found themselves confronted by quite double the number of Imperialists. Both villages were attacked with feverish energy, the assault on Aspern being the more severe. It was ably defended by Masséna, while Lannes at Essling fought as he had never done before. When night fell, the latter still successfully defied the Austrians, while the white coats, after making repeated unsuccessful attempts to capture Aspern, had effected a lodgment in the church and the graveyard. This was partly due to the energy of Archduke Charles, who led the last attack of the day in person.

Good use was made of the succeeding night by Napoleon. He hurried over as many troops as possible to the bank of the Danube occupied by the Imperialists, a necessarily slow process owing to the frequent breaches made in the temporary bridges by obstructions floated down the rapidly-rising river by the Austrians. These difficulties taxed the resources of the engineers, but they stuck manfully to their task, while the troops cared little if the pontoons were under water provided they could reach the opposite bank. Early on the 22nd May there were 63,000 troops ready to advance against the Imperialists who, not having been called upon to labour so arduously through the night as the French had done, were considerably fresher for the day's work. Fighting at Aspern and Essling had been resumed long since, if indeed it had left off, the first charge of the day being against the Austrian centre by Lannes. The French battalions sustained a raking fire from the enemy's artillery, some of whose infantry, however, soon showed such signs of weakness that Archduke Charles, as on the day before, caught up a standard and shouted to the grenadiers to follow him. They did so to such good purpose that further progress of the French infantry was impossible. Nor did their comrades of the cavalry, sent to their relief under Bessières, fare better. According to some accounts, when victory seemed almost in the grasp of Napoleon's men, the Austrians were reinforced in the nick of time and Bessières compelled to retire.

Other disasters of an even more serious nature were in store for the French. The bridge between the right bank and the island of Lobau was severed, thus cutting off all connection with the Emperor's troops and those fighting against the Austrians.

Meanwhile the Archduke took advantage of his enemy's discomfiture by attacking the two villages which had figured so prominently in the contest of the previous day with greater energy than ever. Still the French fought on. Many a brave man fell in the desperate struggle, which finally resulted in Aspern being held by the Austrians and the French retaining Essling. The gallant Lannes had both his knees almost carried away by a shot when the battle was beginning to slacken. He had defended Essling with all his native genius and the most consummate bravery, amply retrieving his somewhat inglorious doings in the Spanish Campaign. The Emperor frequently visited the stricken Marshal, who shortly before he passed away feebly murmured: "Another hour and your Majesty will have lost one of your most zealous and faithful friends." This was on the last day of May, 1809, and the master whom he had served so well wrote to Josephine in words which show how keenly he appreciated the fallen warrior: "The loss of the Duke of Montebello, who died this morning, deeply affects me. Thus all things end. Adieu, my love. If you can contribute to the consolation of the poor Marchioness, do it." At St Helena the fallen King-maker said, "I found Lannes a dwarf, but I made him a giant!"

On the following day (the 23rd), the bridge being now repaired, the French retired to well-wooded Lobau, soon to be re-named the Ile Napoléon. The honours of the fight remained with the Austrians; the great Napoleon had been defeated! True to his creed, the Emperor announced a victory, "since we remain masters of the field of battle," and admitted simply that the fight had been "severe," in which latter contention he was indisputably correct. Success or failure, it proved to his enemies that either Napoleon's genius for war was failing or that he had undertaken more than he could carry out. This disaster, added to those which had occurred in the Peninsula, was regarded as proof positive in certain quarters that Napoleon's star was setting. They took little account of the fact that the French forces had been greatly outnumbered both in men and munitions of war, remembering only that they had retreated. Beaten many times before, a defeat or two more did not affect the prestige of the Imperialists, but for the hitherto invincible warrior no excuse was found.

Encouraged by the French reverse, an alliance between Austria and Prussia was now mooted, but Frederick William showed his usual indecision, and consequently the negotiations collapsed, to the great disappointment of the Emperor Francis's hope of an almost unanimous rising in Germany.

Had the King of Prussia possessed some of the pluck displayed by several officers who had served in his army, and now attempted to raise the standard of revolt against Napoleon in Westphalia and Saxony, Frederick William III. would have been a less sorry figure in the history of his country. For instance, Baron von Dörnberg headed a campaign against the unpopular King Jerome, while Major Frederick von Schill, after attempting to capture Wittenberg and Magdeburg, laid down his life for the national cause in the assault on Stralsund. Neither of these soldiers of fortune accomplished anything of importance, mainly because the means at their disposal were abnormally small, but they displayed a spirit of true patriotism. Duke Frederick William of Brunswick-Oels succeeded in occupying Dresden and Leipzig and in forcing Jerome to retreat, but in the end the enthusiastic volunteer and his Black Band were compelled to seek refuge on British ships and sail for England.

For seven weeks after the battle of Aspern the two armies prepared for the next contest, but in expedition and thoroughness Napoleon far outstripped his opponents. If occasional fighting sometimes occurred it was usually no more than an affair of outposts. Both sides were far too busily engaged in repairing their misfortunes, securing reinforcements and additional supplies, to waste men and ammunition in conflicts which could not be other than indecisive. Napoleon took good care to see that the new bridges were more solidly constructed than those which had contributed so much to his defeat. Not only were his arrangements for their protection more complete, but gunboats were stationed in suitable positions for their defence. Lobau was entrenched and fortified; nothing was to be left to chance on the next occasion.

CHAPTER XXVI
THE WAR IN POLAND AND TYROL
(1809)

AT the beginning of July Napoleon's movements showed that a battle was imminent. By means of feints he succeeded in making the enemy believe that his plan was similar to that which had obtained at the battle of Aspern. Thus while the Austrians were occupying their attention with the bridge of Aspern, Napoleon's forces were crossing by movable bridges lower down the river, near Enzersdorf. This was accomplished during a tremendous thunderstorm, the rain soaking the poor fellows to the skin. On the 5th July the greater part of the troops now at his disposal was ready for action, including those of Prince Eugène. The Emperor's step-son, successful against Archduke John at the battle of Raab on the 14th June—the anniversary of Marengo—had joined forces with Napoleon; his opponent was hastening to the assistance of Archduke Charles. Marmont and Macdonald, after desultory fighting, also arrived at Lobau. The French army now outnumbered its opponents by 30,000 men.

The battle of Wagram began on the 5th July, but the issue was not determined until the following day. Macdonald, who played a prominent part in the fighting, as will be narrated, thus describes it in a private letter:—

"The crossing of the Danube [on the 4th and 5th July] was a masterpiece of prodigious genius, and it was reserved for the Emperor to conceive, create, and carry it out. It was performed in presence of an army of over 180,000 men.2 The enemy expected the attempt to be made at the same point as that of May 21st.3 They had prepared tremendous entrenchments, and had brought up a formidable body of artillery; but, to their great surprise, they suddenly saw us attack their left flank and turn all the lines of their redoubts. We drove them back three leagues, and when, next day, they tried conclusions with us, they lost the game.

2 In reality about 140,000.

3 First day of the battle of Aspern.

"Never, sir, had two armies a mightier force of artillery, never was battle fought more obstinately. Picture to yourself 1,000 or 1,200 pieces of artillery vomiting forth death upon nearly 350,000 combatants, and you will have an idea of what this hotly-disputed field of battle was like. The enemy, posted upon the heights, entrenched to the teeth in all the villages, formed a sort of crescent, or horse-shoe. The Emperor did not hesitate to enter into the midst of them, and to take up a parallel position.

"His Majesty did me the honour of giving me the command of a corps, with orders to break through the enemy's centre. I, fortunately, succeeded, notwithstanding the fire of a hundred guns, masses of infantry, and charges of cavalry, led by the Archduke Charles in person. His infantry would never cross bayonets with mine, nor would his cavalry wait till mine came up; the Uhlans alone made a stand, and they were scattered.

"I pursued the enemy closely with bayonet and cannon for about four leagues, and it was only at ten o'clock at night that, worn out and overwhelmed with fatigue, my men ceased their firing and their pursuit.

"The same success attended us at all other points. His Majesty, who directed everything, amazed me by his coolness and by the precision of his orders. It was the first time I had fought under his eyes, and this opportunity gave me an even higher opinion than I already had of his great talents, as I was able to form my own judgment upon them...."

Napoleon had almost used up his reserves when the Austrian retreat began. No fewer than 24,000 dead and wounded Imperialists were left on the field, a loss of probably 6000 more than that sustained by the French. Not until daybreak on the 7th did the victorious troops lay down their arms. "I soon fell asleep," says Macdonald, "but not for long, as I was awakened by cries of 'Long live the Emperor!' which redoubled when he entered my camp. I asked for my horse, but he had been taken away. I had no other, as the rest were far behind. As I could not walk (the General had been kicked by the animal), I remained on my straw, when I heard someone enquiring for me.... He came by the Emperor's order to look for me. On my remarking that I had no horse and could not walk, he offered me his, which I accepted. I saw the Emperor surrounded by my troops, whom he was congratulating. He approached me, and embracing me cordially, said:—

"'Let us be friends henceforward.'

"'Yes,' I answered, 'till death.' And I have kept my word, not only up to the time of his abdication, but even beyond it. He added: 'You have behaved valiantly, and have rendered me the greatest services, as, indeed, throughout the entire campaign. On the battle-field of your glory, where I owe you so large a part of yesterday's success, I make you a Marshal of France' (he used this expression instead of 'of the Empire'). You have long deserved it.'

"'Sire,' I answered, 'since you are satisfied with us, let the rewards and recompenses be apportioned and distributed among my army corps, beginning with Generals Lamarque, Broussier, and others, who so ably seconded me.'

"'Anything you please,' he replied; 'I have nothing to refuse you.'"

In this abrupt but characteristic way Macdonald was created a Marshal—a well-merited distinction also conferred on Oudinot and Marmont for their services in this campaign. Napoleon's opening remark as to friendship referred to the five years of disgrace which the general had suffered by being unjustly implicated in the affairs of Moreau, a disfavour now to fall on Bernadotte, whose corps had behaved ill at Wagram and was dissolved. Thus almost at the same time as he gained a friend the Emperor made an enemy. It is interesting to note that Macdonald's father was a Scotsman who fought for the Pretender and his mother a Frenchwoman, and that he was born at Sedan.

Napoleon, usually the most active in following up a victory, did not actively pursue the Austrians after the battle of Wagram for the all-sufficient reason that his troops were worn-out with fatigue. If you want to know and see and *feel* what a battle-field is like, glance through the sombre pages of Carlyle's "Sartor Resartus" until you come to his description of that of Wagram. Here is the passage, and it is one of the most vivid in literature: "The greensward," says the philosopher, "is torn-up and trampled-down; man's fond care of it, his fruit-trees, hedge-row, and pleasant dwellings, blown-away with gunpowder; and the kind seedfield lies a desolate, hideous place of Skulls." There were two days of hard fighting at Znaym on the 10th and 11th July, in which Masséna and Marmont took part, Napoleon not coming up until the morning of the second day. On the 12th an armistice was arranged.

Brief notice must be taken of the course of the war in other parts of Europe. The formidable Walcheren Expedition, so called because of its disembarkation on the island of that name, was undertaken by Great Britain as a diversion against the French. The idea had been mooted and shelved three years before, to be revived when Austria pressed the British Government to send troops to Northern Germany in the hope of fostering insurrection there. The Duke of Portland's government, prompted by Lord Castlereagh, thought that Antwerp would be a more desirable objective. Instead of the troops pushing on immediately to that city, Flushing must needs be first besieged and bombarded. This detour lost much precious time, which was used to good advantage by Bernadotte and King Louis in placing the city in a state of defence.

The commanders of the English naval and military forces—Sir Richard Strachan and Lord Chatham respectively—now engaged in unseemly wrangling as to further movements, while meantime many of the soldiers fell victims to malarial fever. Eventually the army sailed for home, after an immense expenditure of blood and treasure, thousands of men dying and the cost amounting to many millions of pounds sterling. The expedition was for long the talk of the British people, the affair being epitomised in a witty couplet which aptly summed up the situation:—

Lord Chatham, with his sword undrawn,
Stood waiting for Sir Richard Strachan;
Sir Richard, longing to be at 'em,
Stood waiting for the Earl of Chatham.

In Spain things were going from bad to worse for Great Britain, and an expedition against Naples, commanded by Sir John Stewart, was eventually obliged to withdraw after some early successes. England felt the heavy hand of Napoleon very severely in the dark days of 1809.

We have noted that Archduke Ferdinand had troops to the number of 35,400 in Poland called the Army of Galicia. He was faced by Prince Galitzin and Prince Poniatovski, who had nearly 60,000 men, including Russians, Poles, and Saxons, under their command. Warsaw was secured by the Austrians after the battle of Raszyn, but following an attack on Thorn the Archduke was compelled to retreat, hostilities in Poland being terminated by the armistice of Znaym.

In Tyrol the peasant war was marked by many exciting events. The inhabitants of this picturesque land of forests and mountains were intensely patriotic and hated the Bavarians, under whose domination they had passed after Austerlitz, with an exceedingly bitter hatred. They felt that now was the time for revenge, for showing that the country was at heart still loyal to the Emperor Francis, descendant of a long line of monarchs who had exercised their feudal rights for over four centuries. A section of Archduke John's army, amounting to some 10,000 men under General Chasteler, was accordingly sent to aid the ardent nationalists, who appointed their own leaders, the most celebrated of whom was Andreas Hofer, an innkeeper and cattle-dealer of considerable substance. A signal was agreed upon; when sawdust was seen floating on the waters of the Inn the people of the villages through which the river flowed were to understand that a general rising was expected of them. There was no fear that the news would not reach outlying districts. The people did not fail their leaders, and Innsbruck, the capital of the province, then in the hands of the Bavarians, was attacked, and did not long resist the gallantry of the Tyrolese. Other garrisons met a similar fate, and in less than a week but one fortress still held out in Northern

Tyrol, so well had the rugged fellows performed their self-appointed task. Unhappily for the intrepid patriots—Napoleon with his usual partiality for misrepresentation called their leaders "brigands"—disasters succeeded their early victories, and Innsbruck was held for but six weeks before Lefebvre put himself in possession. Again fortune smiled on the Tyrolese. Wrede, who commanded the Bavarians, unduly weakened his forces by sending various regiments to join Napoleon. Taking advantage of their knowledge of this fact, 20,000 peasants presented themselves before the capital and regained it. Two more battles were waged outside the walls of Innsbruck, and innumerable skirmishes took place with the large army which the Emperor now poured into Tyrol before the flames were finally extinguished in December 1809. It is safe to say that the ashes would have continued to smoulder much longer had not Hofer been the victim of treachery. He was betrayed to the enemy by an ungrateful priest, and, after trial, executed on the 21st February 1810. Many of his colleagues availed themselves of an amnesty granted by Prince Eugène, but both Hofer and Peter Mayer preferred to fight to the end. The Emperor of Austria, grateful for the services rendered to him by the former innkeeper, provided the hero's widow with a handsome pension and ennobled his son.

On the 15th October 1809 peace was restored between France and Austria by the Treaty of Schönbrünn, sometimes called the Peace of Vienna, by which the former chiefly benefited. More than once the negotiations trembled in the balance, but ultimately the Austrian war party was obliged to give way. Archduke Charles had grown tired of fighting, the wily Metternich could see nothing but disaster by its continuance. Just as business people sometimes ask a higher price than they expect to receive for an article of commerce and are content to be "beaten down," so Napoleon made extravagant demands at first and was satisfied with smaller concessions. The apparent readiness to give way, for which he did not forget to claim credit, enabled him to pose as a political philanthropist. Nevertheless, three and a half million people were lost to Austria by the districts which she ceded to France, Bavaria, Russia, Saxony, Italy, and the Grand Duchy of Warsaw. Pursuing the same policy of army retrenchment he had followed with Prussia, Napoleon insisted that Austria should support not more than 150,000 troops. A big war indemnity was also exacted.

The Emperor afterwards maintained that this "pound of flesh" was insufficient. "I committed a great fault after the battle of Wagram," he remarked, "in not reducing the power of Austria still more. She remained too strong for our safety, and to her we must attribute our ruin. The day after the battle, I should have made known, by proclamation, that I would treat with Austria only on condition of the preliminary separation of the three crowns of Austria, Hungary, and Bohemia." As a matter of fact the abdication of the Emperor Francis had been one of his extortionate demands in the early stages of the negotiations.

If proof were necessary of the truth of the proverb that "truth is stranger than fiction" the marriage of Napoleon to the Archduchess Marie Louise of Austria, but a few months after he had threatened to dispossess her father of his throne, would surely justify it. Poor childless, light-hearted Josephine was put away for this daughter of the Cæsars. The Emperor had first asked for a Russian Princess, then as suddenly turned in the direction of the House of Hapsburg because his former suit was not immediately accepted. From that time Napoleon's friendship with Alexander began to wane perceptibly. The Czar was under no delusion when he prophetically remarked, on hearing of the Emperor's change of front in wooing an Austrian princess, "Then the next thing will be to drive us back into our forests."

Small wonder that in after years Napoleon referred to his second marriage as "That abyss covered with flowers which was my ruin."

To compare Napoleon's two consorts is extremely difficult, because their temperaments were essentially different. Josephine was vivacious, witty, fond of dress and of admiration, and brought up in a very different school of thought to that of Marie Louise. The former had witnessed, and to some extent felt, the terrors of the Revolution at their worst; she had mixed with all sorts and conditions of men and women, some good, many bad; the latter had been nurtured with scrupulous care, so shielded and safeguarded that she scarcely knew of the follies and sins which mar the everyday world. She once wrote to a friend that she believed Napoleon "is none other than Anti-Christ." When she heard that the man she felt to be "our oppressor" was to become her husband, she lifted her pale blue eyes to the skies and remarked that the birds were happier because they could choose their own mates! And yet, although she was so horrified, she had a certain nobility of character which enabled her to understand that in making the surrender she would be performing a double duty to her father and to her country: "This marriage gives pleasure to my father, and though separation from my family always will make me miserable, I will have the consolation of having obeyed his wishes. And Providence, it is my firm belief, directs the lot of us princesses in a special manner; and in obeying my father I feel I am obeying Providence."

But what were the reasons for Napoleon's dissolution of his first marriage when his love for Josephine is beyond question? Pasquier thus sums up the matter for us:

"For some time past," he says, "the greater number of those about him, and especially the members of his family, had been urging him to repudiate a union which could not give him an heir, and which precluded the idea of his dreaming of certain most advantageous alliances. As early as the time of his consecration as Emperor, the greatest pressure had been put upon him to prevent him from strengthening the bonds uniting him to Josephine, by having her crowned by his side; but all these endeavours had been neutralized by the natural and potent ascendancy of a woman full of charm and grace, who had given herself to him at a time when nothing gave any indication of his high destinies, whose conciliatory spirit had often removed from his path difficulties of a somewhat serious nature, and brought back to him many embittered or hostile minds, who seemed to have been constantly a kind of good genius, entrusted with the care of watching over his destiny and of dispelling the clouds which came to darken its horizon....

"I can never forget the evening," adds Pasquier, "on which the discarded Empress did the honours of her Court for the last time. It was the day before the official dissolution. A great throng was present, and supper was served, according to custom, in the gallery of Diana, on a number of little tables. Josephine sat at the centre one, and the men went round her, waiting for that particularly graceful nod which she was in the habit of bestowing on those with whom she was acquainted. I stood at a short distance from her for a few minutes, and I could not help being struck with the perfection of her attitude in the presence of all these people who still did her homage, while knowing full well that it was for the last time; that, in an hour, she would descend from the throne, and leave the palace never to re-enter it. Only women can rise superior to the difficulties of such a situation, but I have my doubts as to whether a second one could have been found to do it with such perfect grace and composure. Napoleon did not show as bold a front as did his victim."

The Archduchess was in her eighteenth year, Napoleon in his forty-first. She was not without personal charms, although Pasquier, who keenly sympathised with Josephine, scarcely does her justice. "Her face," he says, "was her weakest point; but her figure was fine, although somewhat stiff. Her personality was attractive, and she had very pretty feet and hands." The marriage was celebrated by proxy at Vienna on the 11th March 1810.

That Marie Louise grew to love the man of whom she once wrote that "the very sight of this creature would be the worst of all my sufferings" is very improbable, and in the end she played him false. She certainly showed no wish to join him at Elba, and shortly after his death married the dissolute Adam Albert, Graf von Neipperg, her third husband being the Comte de Bombelles. The Emperor believed in her faithfulness to the last. "I desire," he said to his physician, Antommarchi, "that you preserve my heart in spirits of wine, and that you carry it to Parma to my dear Marie Louise. Please tell her that I loved her tenderly, and that I have not ceased to love her."

CHAPTER XXVII
A BROKEN FRIENDSHIP AND
WHAT IT BROUGHT (1810–1812)

NAPOLEON now entered with renewed zest upon the work of perfecting his Continental System, and in so doing he quarrelled with his brother Louis, King of Holland. The young monarch had followed a liberal policy, devoting his time and energy to the interests of his people, and earning their respect if not their love. Napoleon always regarded the land of dykes and windmills as scarcely more than a province of France; Louis was determined that his country should be independent. He was no believer in the Emperor's plan to keep out British goods, so profitable a source of revenue, and as a consequence an extensive business was carried on between Holland and England. Napoleon threatened, Louis temporised, until the former, holding the trump card, finally settled to annex the Kingdom which so openly defied his wishes and commands. Louis was aware that this would probably be the end of the quarrel, for on the 21st September 1809, Napoleon had written a letter to him setting forth his many grievances. He charged the King with favouring Dutchmen who were well disposed towards England, with making speeches containing "nothing but disagreeable allusions to France," with allowing "the relations between Holland and England to be renewed," with violating "the laws of the blockade which is the only means of efficaciously injuring this Power," and so on.

"To sum up," he concluded, "the annexation of Holland to France is what would be most useful to France, to Holland, and to the Continent, because it is what would be most harmful to England. This annexation could be carried out by consent or by force. I have sufficient grievance against Holland to declare war; at the same time I am quite ready to agree to an arrangement which would yield to me the Rhine as a frontier, and by which Holland would emerge to fulfil the conditions stipulated above."

The Emperor began by annexing the island of Walcheren. Gradually the encroachments were extended until the left bank of the Rhine was wholly French. Troops were drafted to Holland, the Dutch bitterly resenting the interference of Napoleon in affairs which they held were no concern of his. There was talk of an insurrection, of arming the country to resist the arbitrary claims of the despot. Finally the unhappy Louis abdicated in favour of his son, and retired to the confines of Bohemia. Little more than a week later Holland was definitely annexed to the Empire, thereby adding nine departments to France. In the following month Jerome Bonaparte, King of Westphalia, was offended by the appearance of French troops at the mouths of the Elbe and Weser. Indeed, it would appear as if Napoleon was intent upon alienating the affection of the members of his own Imperial family. Perhaps the most tried brother was Joseph, who deserved all pity in the far from enthusiastic reception his new Spanish subjects were according him. Lucien had long since quarrelled with the Emperor, and although the latter attempted a reconciliation he was unsuccessful. On obtaining Napoleon's permission to retire to America, the ship on which he sailed was captured by an English frigate, and for several years he lived the life of a country gentleman in the land he had been brought up to hate. The hapless Josephine was in retirement at Malmaison; Murat failed to see eye to eye with his brother-in-law, so much so that later the Emperor threatened to deprive him of his throne. In 1810 Napoleon also lost the services and support of Bernadotte by his election as Crown Prince of Sweden.

But while his brothers and friends were thus falling away from him Napoleon felt amply compensated in March 1811 by the birth of a son, who was given the high-sounding title of King of Rome. It will be remembered that Charlemagne, founder of the Holy Roman Empire, was styled "King of the Romans." "Glory had never caused him to shed a single tear," says Constant, the Emperor's valet, "but the happiness of being a father had softened that soul which the most brilliant victories and the most sincere tokens of public admiration scarcely seemed to touch."

Supreme in war, Napoleon was also one of the greatest administrators of whom we have record. As the story of his life has progressed we have noted how he set about the reformation of the governments of the various countries he had conquered or where his word was regarded as law. "The State—it is I," said Louis XIV., and Napoleon summed up his own mode of life on one occasion by quoting the remark, which was no mere figure of speech. He seldom took recreation; when he was tired of thinking of battalions he thought of fleets, or colonies, or commerce. As Emperor he sometimes hunted, but more from a matter of policy than because he loved sport, just as he went to Mass to set a good example, and to the first act of a new play to gratify public curiosity. M. Frédéric Masson, the eminent Napoleonic historian, is authority for the statement that the Emperor once promised to attend a magnificent ball, and the most elaborate preparations had been made in his honour. Unfortunately the Imperial guest remained closeted with the Minister of Finance from eight o'clock in the evening until he heard a clock strike and was surprised to find that it was 3 A.M. The so-called pleasures of the table were miseries to him, and he ate his food with no regard whatever for convention or the menu. He would begin with an ice and finish with a viand.

The "Memoirs" of Napoleon's three private secretaries, Bourrienne, Méneval, and Fain, afford us intimate views of the great man at work. Those of Bourrienne are the least authentic because they are not entirely his writing. The Emperor had an unfortunate habit from his secretary's point of view of dictating his correspondence in full, and he spoke at such a rate that it was almost impossible to note what he said in its entirety. To interrupt him was a breach of etiquette. Fain found it necessary to leave blanks, which he filled up when he was transcribing with the help of the context.

M. Masson thus describes the Emperor's work-room at the Tuileries:—

"The room which Napoleon made into his study was of moderate size. It was lighted by a single window made in a corner and looking into the garden. The principal piece of furniture, placed in the middle, was a magnificent bureau, loaded with gilt bronze, and supported by two griffins. The lid of the table slided into a groove, so that it could be shut without disarranging the papers. Under the bureau, and screwed to the floor, was a sliding cupboard, into which every time the Emperor went out was placed a portfolio of which he alone had the key. The armchair belonging to the bureau was of antique shape; the back was covered with tapestry of green kerseymere, the folds of which were fastened by silk cords, and the arms finished off with griffins' heads. The Emperor scarcely ever sat down in his chair except to give his signature. He kept habitually at the right of the fireplace, on a small sofa covered with green taffeta, near to which was a stand which received the correspondence of the day. A screen of several leaves kept off the heat of the fire. At the further end of the room, at right angles in the corners, were placed four bookcases, and between the two which occupied the wall at the end was a great regulator clock of the same kind as that furnished in 1808 by Bailly for the study at Compiègne, which cost 4000 francs.... There were books also in the back study, books in the cabinet of the keeper of the portfolio, along the side of the bedroom, and books also in the little apartment.

"Opposite the fireplace, a long closet with glass doors, breast high, with a marble top, contained boxes for papers, and carried the volumes to be consulted and the documents in use; no doubt also the equestrian statuette of Frederick II., which the Emperor constantly had under his eyes. This statuette was the only work of art which he ever personally desired to have.

"In the recess of the window was the table of the private secretary. The room was furnished with a few chairs. At night, to light his bureau, Napoleon used a candlestick with two branches, with a great shade of sheet iron of the ordinary kind."

There was also a back study, where the Emperor usually received his Ministers of State, a topographic study, and two small rooms. From this suite of apartments Napoleon may be said to have directed Western Europe.

Brief mention must be made of the Emperor's "campaign" library. The volumes were contained in two mahogany cases fitted with shelves; each book was noted in a miniature catalogue and had its special place, changes being made from time to time. Novels, historical memoirs, poetry, and the classics were invariably represented. No fewer than six chests of volumes were conveyed to Waterloo.

Meanwhile the rearrangement of Europe, always to the advantage of France, continued almost without cessation by the addition of a strip of territory here, some miles of another man's possessions there. Soon every inch of coast line from the Rhine to the Elbe was under Napoleon's domination. Oldenburg, a Duchy ruled by one of the Czar's relations, was swallowed up, the Hanseatic towns and Valais were incorporated in the ever-growing Empire. The restoration of Polish independence by the Emperor of the French seemed not improbable and annoyed the Czar intensely. The latter had good ground for thinking that Napoleon contemplated this course in the recent territorial acquisitions of the Duchy of Warsaw according to the terms of the Treaty of Schönbrünn. When he boldly asked for an assurance that the kingdom of Poland should never be re-established, Napoleon politely declined, contenting himself with the statement that he would not assist anyone else to do it, thereby leaving a loophole for his own interference should he deem it necessary or desirable.

Such a reckless, or rather insane, policy made it evident that Napoleon no longer intended to share the world with the Emperor of all the Russias as he had suggested at Tilsit and Erfurt. We have already noticed that the Czar had entertained suspicions of his friend's loyalty, a doubt reciprocated by Napoleon, who was intensely annoyed that Russia had not kept strictly to the terms of the Continental System, the relaxation of which was considerably to the benefit both of Great Britain and of Russia. Alexander, also, had been at war with Turkey, and Napoleon, instead of aiding his ally, as the Czar had a certain amount of right to expect, endeavoured to prolong the contest to serve his own personal ends. This the Porte, suspecting ulterior motives, refused to do, and on the 28th May 1812 peace was restored, to be followed in July by peace between Russia and Great Britain. Sweden, coveting Norway and knowing that no help could be expected from France in the fulfilment of her hope, while possibly it might be received from Russia, also came to terms with the two reconciled Powers after hostile measures had been undertaken against her by Davout in Pomerania. Preparations for war were now made by France and Russia in real earnest. Following his usual plan Napoleon made overtures to England for a cessation of hostilities. His terms were that the present occupants of the thrones of Spain and Naples should be acknowledged by Great Britain and her troops withdrawn from their territory. He on his part undertook to recall his armies.

On the eve of the Emperor's departure for Dresden to dazzle and flatter his allies by a final display of grandeur worthy the Conqueror of Western Europe, Pasquier, his newly-appointed Prefect of Police, had an interview with him. The question of a shortage in the food supply of Paris had come up, and Pasquier had ventured to remark that the situation would be rendered more dangerous by the monarch's absence. "Napoleon appeared struck by these few remarks," Pasquier tells us. "When I had ended speaking, he remained silent, and pacing to and fro between the window and the fireplace, his arms crossed behind his back, like a man who is pondering deeply. I followed in his steps, when, facing me suddenly, he uttered the words which follow: 'Yes, there is doubtless some truth in what you tell me; it is one more difficulty added to the many I have to face in *the greatest, the most difficult* undertaking I have ever attempted; but I must fain bring to a termination what I have begun. *Farewell, monsieur le préfet.*'"

On the 9th May 1812, the Emperor and his consort set out on their journey to the capital of Saxony. It was one long series of festivities culminating in a Court of Kings which included the Emperor and Empress of Austria, the Kings of Prussia, Saxony, Naples, Würtemberg, and Westphalia, and the rulers of Saxe Weimar, Saxe Coburg, and Dessau. "His levée," says de Ségur, "presented a remarkable sight. Sovereign princes waited for an audience from the Conqueror of Europe; they were mixed up to such an extent with his officers that the latter were frequently on their guard lest they should accidentally brush up against these new courtiers and be confounded with them." His description may be a little exaggerated, but it showed to what a supreme height Napoleon had risen, and how marked had been the change in his ideas since the days when he would have willingly laid down his life for Republicanism. At St Helena he stated that at Dresden he "appeared as the King of Kings." This was not meant in any blasphemous sense, but was merely the Emperor's summing-up of the unique and all-powerful position he then occupied. The inhabitants of Dresden waited in the streets for hours on the chance of getting a fleeting glimpse of the "little great man" who had done so much and who was expected to do considerably more in the forthcoming campaign. "It was not his crown," says Count Philip de Ségur, "his rank, the luxury of his Court, but him—himself—on whom they desired to feast their eyes; a memento of his features which they were anxious to obtain: they wished to be able to say to their less fortunate countrymen and posterity that they had seen Napoleon." Englishmen who had every reason to hate him have left behind records which testify to the fascination exercised over them by the Emperor on various occasions. The Germans had nothing to thank him for, and yet they flocked in crowds to see their oppressor.

Far from giving way to the fears which he had confessed to Pasquier, the Emperor made light of the many difficulties which he knew to be insuperable to the task he had undertaken. To the Abbé de Pradt, Archbishop of Malines, whom he sent as envoy to Warsaw, he remarked, "I will destroy Russian influence in Europe. Two battles will do the business; the Emperor Alexander will come on his knees, and Russia shall be disarmed. Spain costs me very dear: without that I should be master of the world; but when I become such, my son will have nothing to do but to retain my place."

"Never was the success of an expedition more certain;" he assured his vassals, "I see on all sides nothing but probabilities in my favour. Not only do I advance at the head of the immense forces of France, Italy, Germany, the Confederation of the Rhine, and Poland, but the two monarchies which have hitherto been the most powerful auxiliaries of Russia against me, have now ranged themselves on my side: they espouse my quarrel with the zeal of my oldest friends." This was not strictly true, and savoured rather too much of his army bulletins and similar proclamations. Like the doctor with a nervous patient, he withheld some of the disagreeable features of the case. "The two monarchies," namely Austria and Prussia, had they dared, would have preferred to remain neutral, or if that were impossible, to come to terms with Russia, their last resource on the Continent against the aggressor who had treated them with such scant consideration. Prussia had "espoused" Napoleon's quarrel so far as to entertain hopes but a few months before of an alliance with either Russia or Austria.

The campaign of 1812 was to dwarf all Napoleon's previous efforts in magnitude; a mere summing-up of statistics can at most give but an inadequate idea of the immense armament which he deemed necessary if a death-blow was to be struck at the heart of the great Russian Empire. The flames of the Peninsular war were still flickering, which necessitated the locking-up of a large number of troops under Soult, Marmont and Suchet which Napoleon could have used to better purpose had affairs been more settled in that quarter. France was in very truth "a nation in arms." For home defence the ablebodied men from twenty-five to sixty years of age were divided into three classes, 900,000 of whom were to garrison the fortresses on the frontiers and watch the coasts, the remaining 300,000 to drill and make themselves efficient for immediate service whenever necessary. A rich man considered himself fortunate if he could secure a substitute for less than 8000 francs. The price of the Emperor's friendship was also a costly one to those Princes whom he deigned to favour with his attentions. The Confederation of the Rhine was called upon to furnish 147,000 men, Italy some 80,000, Poland 60,000. France contributed 200,000 strong, other countries brought the total to the stupendous figure of 680,000 troops. Prussia found herself called upon to furnish 20,000 troops for the invasion of the Czar's territory, and enormous quantities of oats, rice, wheat, and other provisions, in addition to hospital accommodation, horses and carriages. Austria was to supply 30,000 soldiers, but she did so on the distinct understanding that her Polish provinces should be kept inviolate. Prussia asked nothing and expected nothing.

Napoleon's new army was one of the most cosmopolitan that ever came into being. There were French, Austrians, Prussians, Bavarians, Poles, Italians, Illyrians, Dutch, Swiss, even a sprinkling of Spaniards and Portuguese. These men did not all follow willingly. Indeed in 1811 no fewer than 80,000 French conscripts deserted or failed to answer the summons. A string of manacled recruits was not an uncommon sight in France. Napoleon was now "the common oppressor," the gold of glory had turned out to be tinsel.

While France was deploring, Napoleon was organising his forces. He brooked no delay, would listen to no arguments, was deaf to the entreaties of those who failed to see his reason for making war with Russia. "The Emperor is mad, quite mad," Admiral Decrès confided to a friend. "He will ruin us all, many as we are, and everything will end in a frightful catastrophe." Mad with ambition he certainly was, mad in intellect he certainly was not.

The army was divided into ten great corps. The first under Davout, the second under Oudinot, the third under Ney; the fourth was an Army of Observation, under Prince Eugène; the fifth consisted of Poles under Prince Poniatovski; the sixth, in which the Bavarians were included, under Saint-Cyr; the seventh, made up of the troops from Saxony, under Reynier; the eighth, of Westphalians under Vandamme, to be succeeded by Junot; the ninth was given to Victor, the tenth to Macdonald. An eleventh Army Corps under Augereau was afterwards created, largely augmented from the ninth. There were also the Austrians commanded by Prince Schwarzenberg, the Imperial Guard, and four divisions of Cavalry under Murat and Latour-Maubourg.

To oppose such a formidable host the Czar finally mustered some 400,000 troops. At the opening of the campaign he had considerably fewer men at his disposal than Napoleon. They were divided into three main armies. The first Army of the West, under Barclay de Tolly, numbered 136,000; the second Army of the West, commanded by Prince Bagration, totalled 39,000; the third, or reserve, under General Tormassoff, reached some 40,000. Other troops, drawn from various places, swelled the initial number to perhaps 250,000. As there is considerable discrepancy in the figures given by the most reliable authorities probably the exact military strength of the two nations will never be known.

CHAPTER XXVIII
THE RUSSIAN CAMPAIGN (1812)

POLAND was the point of concentration, and thither the Grand Army was marching. On the 11th June 1812, the Emperor arrived at Dantzig, which had been turned into a vast military depôt, and on the following morning proceeded to Königsberg, where further supplies were stored. He spent the whole day and night dictating despatches. Having twice communicated with the Czar to no effect, he was now irrevocably committed to the campaign. At Vilkowyski Napoleon took the opportunity to issue a bulletin to his troops couched in the old style which had proved so effectual in former campaigns. It is as follows:

"Soldiers! The second Polish war is begun. The first terminated at Friedland and at Tilsit. At Tilsit, Russia vowed an eternal alliance with France, and war with England. She now breaks her vows, and refuses to give any explanation of her strange conduct until the French eagles have repassed the Rhine and left our allies at her mercy.

"Fate drags her on—let her destinies be fulfilled. Does she imagine we are degenerated? Are we no longer the soldiers who fought at Austerlitz? We are placed between dishonour and war; our choice cannot be doubtful. Let us then march forward. Let us cross the Niemen, and carry the war into her own territory. This second Polish war will be as glorious for the French arms as the first; but the peace we shall conclude will carry with it its own guarantee, and will terminate the fatal influence which Russia, for fifty years past, has exercised in the affairs of Europe."

Alexander's proclamation to his troops, while less forceful than Napoleon's, is more dignified and restrained. It was issued from his headquarters at Vilna, the capital of Lithuania, on the 25th June 1812, two days later than the one given above.

The Retreat from Moscow

By V. Werestchagin

By permission of the Berlin Photographic Co., London, W

"We had long observed," it runs, "on the part of the Emperor of the French, the most hostile proceedings towards Russia; but we always hoped to avert them by conciliatory and pacific measures. At length, experiencing a continued renewal of direct and evident aggression, notwithstanding our earnest desire to maintain peace, we were compelled to complete and to assemble our armies. But even then, we flattered ourselves that a reconciliation might take place while we remained on the frontiers of our empire, and, without violating one principle of peace, were prepared only to act in our own defence.... The Emperor of the French, by suddenly attacking our army at Kovno, has been the first to declare war. As nothing, therefore, can inspire him with those friendly sentiments which possessed our bosoms, we have no choice but to oppose our forces to those of the enemy, invoking the aid of the Almighty, the Witness and Defender of the truth. It is unnecessary for me to remind the generals, officers, and soldiers of their duty, to excite their valour; the blood of the brave Slavonians flows in their veins. Warriors! you defend your religion, your country, and your liberty. I am with you: God is against the aggressor." Alexander promised the Governor of St Petersburg that he would not sheath his sword "so long as a single enemy remains in Russian territory."

Practically the whole of the Grand Army—an effective force at the beginning of the campaign of 400,000 troops—crossed the river Niemen at different points, the troops with the Emperor near Kovno, those of Eugène and King Jerome at Pilony and Grodno respectively, the remainder under Macdonald at Tilsit. Prince Schwarzenberg with the Austrians crossed by the River Bug. Davout's corps secured the honour of being first to enter Russian territory, and without much trouble they secured possession of the little town of Kovno, the point of concentration, reference to which is made in the Czar's proclamation.

Alison has painted the scene for us in glowing colours. "The tent of the Emperor," he writes, "was placed on an eminence three hundred paces from the bank, and as the sun rose he beheld the resplendent mass slowly descending to the bridges. The world had never seen so magnificent an array as lay before him; horse, foot, and cannon in the finest order, and in the highest state of equipment, incessantly issued from the forest, and wound down the paths which led to the river: the glittering of the arms, the splendour of the dress, the loud shouts of the men as they passed the Imperial station, inspired universal enthusiasm and seemed to afford a certain presage of success. The burning impatience of the conscripts; the calm assurance of the veteran soldiers; the confident ardour of the younger officers; the dubious presentiments of the older generals, filled every breast with thrilling emotion. The former were impatient for the campaign as the commencement of glory and fortune; the latter dreaded it as the termination of ease and opulence. None entered on it without anxiety and interest. No sinister presentiments were now visible on the countenance of the Emperor; the joy which he felt at the recommencement of war communicated a universal degree of animation. Two hundred thousand men, including forty thousand horse, of whom twelve thousand were cuirassiers, cased in glittering steel, passed the river that day in presence of the Emperor. Could the eye of prophecy have foreseen the thin and shattered remains of this immense host, which a few months afterwards were alone destined to regain the shore of the Niemen, the change would have appeared too dreadful for any human powers of destruction to have accomplished."

The passage of the fourth Army Corps was not made under such happy auspices, but the men were cheered by the news that on the 28th June Napoleon had entered Vilna. This enabled them to shake off to some extent the depressing effects of the wet weather, and the presence of Eugène, Viceroy of Italy, and the dauntless Junot, both of whom personally superintended the construction of the bridge, did much to inspire enthusiasm. There was no enemy to contest them, and the crossing was effected in good order.

"Scarcely had we reached the opposite shore," says Captain Eugène Labaume, who was with the expedition, "when we seemed to breathe a new air. However, the roads were dreadfully bad, the forests gloomy, and the villages completely deserted; but imagination, inflamed by a spirit of conquest, was enchanted with everything, and cherished illusions which were but too soon destroyed.

"In fact, our short stay at Pilony, in the midst of a tempestuous rain, was marked by such extraordinary disasters, that any man, without being superstitious, would have regarded them as the presage of future misfortunes. In this wretched village, the Viceroy himself had no house to shelter him; and we were heaped upon one another under wretched sheds, or else exposed to all the inclemencies of the weather. An extreme scarcity made us anticipate the horrors of famine. The rain fell in torrents, and overwhelmed both men and horses; the former escaped, but the badness of the roads completed the destruction of the latter. They were seen dropping by hundreds in the environs of Pilony; the road was covered with dead horses, overturned waggons and scattered baggage. It was in the month of July that we suffered thus from cold, and rain, and hunger. So many calamities excited within us sad forebodings of the future, and everyone began to dread the event of an enterprise, the commencement of which was so disastrous; but the sun reappeared on the horizon, the clouds dispersed, our fears were scattered with them, and at that moment we thought that the fine season would last for ever."

The captain's narrative is replete with similar instances, showing the almost complete failure of the commissariat on which so much care and anxiety had been bestowed, the treacherous nature of the weather, and the impossibility in so barren a country of putting into effect Napoleon's maxim that war should support itself. Indeed, the truth was shown of another of the Emperor's principles, that "an army marches on its stomach." In the paragraph immediately following the one quoted above, Labaume says that on entering Kroni the soldiers again found the houses deserted, "which convinced us that the enemy, in order to ruin the country through which we were to pass, and deprive us of all the means of subsistence, had carried along with them the inhabitants and the cattle." In a march of fifty miles no fewer than 10,000 horses succumbed.

But a greater difficulty than those we have enumerated soon presented itself. The Russian army, like a will-o'-the-wisp, enticed the French further and further from their base by a series of retreats which made it impossible for Napoleon to fall on the enemy with the fierce rapidity characteristic of his method of warfare. Alexander was playing a waiting game. When the ranks of the enemy were thinned by death, sickness, and desertion, when want and privation stalked hand in hand with the French armies as they painfully made their way along the snow-covered ruts—then would be the time to strike. The Czar could afford to wait, his antagonist could not; one was on the defensive, the other on the offensive, and many hundreds of miles from the capital of his unwieldy Empire. There was little or no opportunity for the soldiers to pay unwelcome attentions to the inhabitants of the villages through which they passed. The peasants had forsaken their wretched wooden shanties, the furniture of the houses of many of the nobles had been removed, making the places almost as cheerless as the frowning forests where their former owners had sought refuge.

At Vilna, which the Russians had evacuated, Napoleon experienced none of these troubles. The Poles, longing to restore the independence of their beloved country, regarded him as their potential liberator, delivering to him the keys of the town, donning their national costumes, and indulging in merry-making. The ancient capital of Lithuania awoke from her long sleep. Deputation after deputation waited on the Emperor, hungering to hear the words which would give them back their lost freedom. They were never uttered; he dare not break faith with his allies at this juncture. He made vague promises in order to stimulate their enthusiasm, set up a provisional government, and began to reorganise the provinces with his usual insight, but further than this he would not go. The Poles repaid him well by immediately ordering some 12,000 men to be placed at the Emperor's disposal, and from first to last they furnished no fewer than 85,000 troops. To the Diet (Parliament) of Warsaw he admitted that he could sanction no movement which might endanger the peaceable possession of Austria's Polish provinces, but he issued a fiery proclamation to those who were serving with the Russian colours. It runs:

"Poles! You are under Russian banners. It was permitted you to serve that Power while you had no longer a country of your own; but all that is now changed; Poland is created anew. You must fight for her complete re-establishment, and compel the Russians to acknowledge those rights of which you have been despoiled by injustice and usurpation. The General Confederation of Poland and Lithuania recalls every Pole from the Russian service. Generals of Poland, officers and soldiers, listen to the voice of your country; abandon the standard of your oppressors; hasten to range yourselves under the eagles of the Jagellons, the Casimirs, and the Sobieskis![4] Your country requires it of you; honour and religion equally command it."

---

[4] Former Kings of Poland.

Note the subtle phrase, "Poland is created anew." It is delightfully vague, meaning little, yet conveying much, and probably understood by many to promise the longed-for restoration.

Napoleon did not leave Vilna, where he had stopped much too long, until the 16th July, but the troops under King Jerome and Davout had been busy in an endeavour to cut off Prince Bagration from the main army under Barclay de Tolly. This measure was far from successful. Jerome was too slow in his movements, two combats ensued in which the Russians were successful, and Bagration made good his retreat to Bobruisk, Barclay falling back on Drissa, where a strongly entrenched camp was in course of construction, and later to Vitebsk. Napoleon was furious at his brother's failure, saying, "It is impossible to manœuvre worse than he has done," and superseding him by the more energetic Davout. With the intention of fighting Barclay, Napoleon pushed on to Glubokoie, only to find that the enemy had proceeded to Vitebsk, which in turn had been evacuated for Smolensk, where Bagration joined hands with Barclay on the 2nd August. Some advantages had been gained by Murat, Macdonald, and Oudinot, but the great opportunity of defeating the two armies separately had been lost, and the combined forces now numbered some 120,000 troops. The Emperor had again wasted time from various causes at Vitebsk, which centre several of his officers wished to make the winter-quarters of the army. He had already lost 100,000 men without accomplishing anything of importance, and as he himself admitted, "Russia is too powerful to yield without fighting: Alexander will not treat till a great battle has been fought." The Emperor was for pushing on, and would brook no interference. "Why should we remain here eight months," he asked his generals when the subject was under discussion, "when twenty days are sufficient to accomplish our purpose? Let us anticipate Winter and its reflections. We must strike soon and strongly, or we shall be in danger. We must be in Moscow in a month, or we shall never be there. Peace awaits us under its walls. Should Alexander still persist, I will treat with his nobles: Moscow hates St Petersburg; the effects of that jealousy are incalculable."

Spurred on by the defeat of the advanced guard under Murat, the Emperor now decided to attack Smolensk with practically his entire army. According to Chambray this was now reduced, excluding various detachments, to some 194,000 men. On the 16th August Ney, with all his old fire and vigour, attempted to storm the citadel and was repulsed. Following their former plan, and fearing to be cut off from Moscow, part of the Russian army under Bagration began to retreat in the early hours of the following morning, Barclay remaining to defend the town with about 30,000 troops. After much heavy fighting the Emperor was in possession of the suburbs, but the losses on either side had been severe. Very soon the dense masses of smoke which arose from the walled city made it evident that to the terrors of shot and shell had been added that of fire. Flames burst out in all directions, the wooden roofs of the smaller houses quickly fell in, larger buildings caught alight and blazed away, fanned by the breeze. Within a few hours Smolensk was little more than a smouldering charnel-house. The conclusion of this dreadful incident is best told by an eye-witness, an officer in the French army.

"At one o'clock the ruins of the town were abandoned," he says. "Our first grenadiers prepared to mount the breach at two o'clock in the morning, when, approaching without opposition, they discovered that the place was entirely evacuated. We took possession of it, and found on the walls many pieces of cannon, which the enemy could not take away.

"Never," the narrator adds, "can you form an adequate idea of the dreadful scene which the interior of Smolensk presented to my view, and never during the whole course of my life can I forget it. Every street, every square, was covered with the bodies of the Russians, dead and dying, while the flames shed over them a horrible glare."

Labaume thus continues the dreadful story begun by his friend:—

"The next day (August 19th) we entered Smolensk by the suburb built along the river. In every direction we marched over scattered ruins and dead bodies. Palaces yet burning offered to our sight only walls half destroyed by the flames, and, thick among the fragments were the blackened carcases of the wretched inhabitants whom the fire had consumed. The few houses that remained were completely filled by the soldiery, while at the doors stood the miserable proprietors without an asylum, deploring the death of their children, and the loss of their property. The churches alone afforded some consolation to the unhappy victims who had no other shelter. The cathedral, celebrated through Europe, and held in great veneration by the Russians, became the refuge of the unfortunate beings who had escaped the flames. In this church and round its altars, were to be seen whole families extended on the ground; in one place was an old man just expiring, and casting a look on the image of the saint whom he had all his life invoked; in another an infant whose feeble cry the mother, worn down with grief, was endeavouring to hush.... In the midst of this desolation, the passage of the army into the interior of the town formed a striking contrast. On one side was seen the abject submission of the conquered—on the other, the pride attendant upon victory; the former had lost their all—the latter, rich with spoil, and ignorant of defeat, marched proudly to the sound of warlike music, inspiring the unhappy remains of a vanquished population with mingled fear and admiration."

Again the Emperor pondered, apparently undecided as to his next movement. Should he take up his winter quarters at Smolensk, as he had originally intended, or push on to Moscow? A great battle had been fought and yet the situation remained unchanged. He had merely taken a ruined city! Ney, Grouchy, and Murat, who had followed the retreating Russians, had but sorry tales to tell on the 19th, and the action near Valutino on that day was indecisive largely owing to the hesitation of Junot in coming to the aid of Ney. Defeat and disaster alone seemed to attend the efforts of the Grand Army. Still Napoleon hesitated. How could he, the virtual Master of Europe, the Conqueror who never failed, quietly lay aside his sword and by so doing tacitly admit failure? No, ten thousand times no; he would push towards Moscow though the heavens fall!

CHAPTER XXIX
THE TRIUMPHAL ENTRY INTO MOSCOW—AND AFTER (1812)

GRUMBLING was not confined to the French army in the campaign of 1812. The Russian troops said hard things of their generals which were not always justifiable, and the patriotic sentiments of the nobles suffered somewhat by the continued retreats, which were taken as evidence of weakness. As a concession to public opinion the much maligned Barclay was superseded by Kutusov, the Russian Commander-in-chief at Austerlitz, an old man approaching seventy years of age who had but recently returned from the war which his country had been waging with Turkey. He was to have an opportunity of showing his prowess within a few days of his joining the army, which now comprised nearly 104,000 men to the 125,000 or so of Napoleon. Severe fighting occurred on the 5th September, a redoubt near the village of Shevardino being taken and retaken three times by the advance guard before the Russians finally withdrew. So great was the bloodshed that when the Emperor afterwards asked where a certain battalion was, he received the reply, "In the redoubt, sire," every individual having lost his life in the desperate assault. Over 1000 men on either side perished in defending or storming this position.

The enemy had fallen back on Borodino, a name which will be always associated with one of the most terrible battles ever fought on European soil. As the sun rose on the 7th September Napoleon exclaimed, "It is the sun of Austerlitz!" and shortly afterwards issued the following proclamation, which aroused some of the old enthusiasm amongst his troops but failed to invoke the plaudits of all. It is short and shows that the Emperor attached more importance to the battles of Vitebsk and Smolensk than the facts warranted:

"Soldiers! The battle is at hand which you have so long desired. Henceforth the victory depends on yourselves. It has become necessary, and will give you abundance; good winter quarters, and a speedy return to your country! Conduct yourselves as you did at Austerlitz, Friedland, Vitebsk, and Smolensk. Let the remotest posterity recount your actions on this day. Let your countrymen say of you all, 'He was in that great battle under the walls of Moscow!'"

Firing began at six o'clock, and continued for twelve anxious hours. The contestants disputed the ground with such determination, each carrying and losing positions again and again, that at times it was difficult to say which army had the advantage. According to Labaume thirty of the Emperor's generals were wounded, including Davout and Rapp, the former by being thrown from his horse as it fell dead, the latter by a ball which struck him on the hip. General Augustus de Caulaincourt, brother of the more celebrated Armand de Caulaincourt, Duke of Vicenza, after performing prodigies of valour in the Russian entrenchments, where the hardest fighting was done, was killed, as was General Montbrun but a little time before, while leading a similar attack. Prince Bagration afterwards died of the injuries he received, and many other Russian generals were more or less seriously wounded.

The key of the position, the Russian entrenched battery, with its terrible heap of dead and dying, was at last captured by the French. The officer commanding it was about to throw himself on his sword rather than surrender, but was prevented in the nick of time by the victors, who took him prisoner.

As Napoleon and his staff were surveying the field after the battle his horse stepped on a wounded man, whose groans attracted the rider's attention. "It is only a Russian," one of his attendants said, probably to allay Napoleon's feelings rather than from want of sympathy. "After victory," the Emperor retorted, "there are no enemies, but only men." He was neither callous nor did he love war for its own sake. It was the result that pleased him, the humbling of the enemy, the addition of territory to the Empire, the driving of one more nail in England's coffin. The maimed were ever his first care after battle. His besetting sin was an abnormal, and consequently unhealthy, ambition—the vice at which he had railed so much in his early days.

Napoleon failed to use his 20,000 Guards at Borodino, why is still a matter of conjecture. Some writers maintain that it would have been foolish for him to use up his last reserves, others hold that had he flung them into the battle he might have annihilated the Russian army and saved himself the agonies which followed. The reason he gave was, "At 800 leagues from Paris one must not risk one's last reserve."

Mr Hereford B. George, one of our greatest authorities on the invasion of Russia in 1812, states that Borodino was a butchery which cost the contestants not less than 70,000 men in killed and wounded. "No battle of modern times," he says in summing up, "no encounter since the days before gunpowder, when the beaten side could be cut down *ad libitum* by the victors and quarter was seldom given, has witnessed such awful slaughter.... Whether it can be fairly called useless may be doubted, except to the nominal conqueror. Napoleon certainly deserves that title: the enemy had been dislodged from their position, and, as it proved, left the way open to Moscow. So much he might have attained by manœuvring; more he could not attain unless the courage of his enemies gave way. Without the brave men who fell at Borodino Napoleon could not possibly attempt any further offensive movement, when his occupation of Moscow led to no overtures for peace. Without them, he was substantially inferior in force when at length the inevitable retreat began. The Russian Te Deums, chanted for the victory that Kutusoff falsely claimed, were in truth only premature."

Holy Moscow was to be the city of abundance, its entry the herald of a happier order of things. On the 14th September, as Napoleon rode forward with his troops, its domes and minarets burst upon his view. Ségur says that the soldiers shouted "Moscow! Moscow!" with the eagerness of sailors on sighting land after a long and tedious voyage. The city looked more like a mirage than the home of a quarter of a million people, more like the deserted city of an extinct race than a hive of humanity. General Sebastiani, who led the vanguard, knew the secret, and so did Murat. The Russians had arranged a hasty armistice in order to evacuate the place, leaving behind them only the riff-raff, the wounded, the aged, and the aliens.

After Moscow: "Advance or Retreat?"

By V. Werestchagin

By permission of the Berlin Photographic Co., London, W

No clang of bells greeted the Conqueror as he made his triumphal entry, no crowds of men and women craned their necks to get a glimpse of the mighty Emperor. Only undesirables welcomed him, the unrepentant prodigal son and the convict, released from prison by the governor before the last inhabitants fled in the wake of the retreating Russian army. There stood the mammoth Kremlin, the Acropolis of the ancient capital, surrounded by its massive walls; the gorgeous Cathedral of the Assumption in which the Czars were crowned; the Great Palace begun but six years before, and churches innumerable. Ikons but no worshippers, palaces but no courtiers! The Emperor took up his quarters in the Kremlin, appointing Mortier governor with strict instructions to prevent the troops from plundering. We shall see how the orders were obeyed later. Suddenly tongues of flame shot up from different quarters of the city, to be extinguished by the troops with great difficulty. Then a large public building was discovered to be alight. The flames began to spread with alarming and all-devouring rapidity. Soon a portion of the Kremlin itself was in imminent danger, and as there was much gunpowder stored in the fortress-palace the Emperor was forced to retire to a château some distance away, to return two days later when the work of destruction had somewhat abated. Labaume witnessed many terrible scenes, which he thus records with his usual vivacity:

"As I advanced towards the fire, the avenues were more obstructed by soldiers and beggars carrying off goods of every kind. The less precious articles were despised, and soon thrown away, and the streets were covered with merchandise of every description. I penetrated at length into the interior of the Exchange; but, alas! it was no more the building so renowned for its magnificence; it was rather a vast furnace, from every side of which the burning rafters were continually falling, and threatening us with instant destruction. I could still, however, proceed with some degree of safety under piazzas lined with warehouses which the soldiers had broken open; every chest was rifled, and the spoil exceeded their most sanguine expectations. No cry, no tumult was heard in this scene of horror; everyone found enough to satisfy his most ardent thirst for plunder. Nothing was heard but the crackling of flames, the noise of doors that were broken open, and occasionally a dreadful crash caused by the falling in of some vault. Cottons, muslins, and all the most costly productions of Europe and of Asia, were a prey to the flames. The cellars were filled with sugar, oil, and vitriol; these burning all at once in the subterraneous warehouses, sent forth torrents of flame through thick iron grates, and presented a dreadful spectacle. It was terrible and affecting; even the most hardened minds acknowledged the conviction that so great a calamity would, on some future day, call forth the vengeance of the Almighty upon the authors of such crimes."

The fire began on the 14th September, and on the 16th it was raging worse than ever. "The most heart-rending scene which my imagination had ever conceived," adds the narrator, "now presented itself to my eyes. A great part of the population of Moscow, terrified at our arrival, had concealed themselves in cellars or secret recesses of their houses. As the fire spread around, we saw them rushing in despair from their various asylums. They uttered no imprecation, they breathed no complaint; fear had rendered them dumb: and hastily snatching up their precious effects, they fled before the flames. Others, of greater sensibility, and actuated by the genuine feelings of nature, saved only their parents, or their infants, who were closely clasped in their arms. They were followed by their other children, running as fast as their little strength would permit, and with all the wildness of childish terror, vociferating the beloved name of mother. The old people, borne down by grief more than by age, had not sufficient power to follow their families, but expired near the houses in which they were born. The streets, the public places, and the churches were filled with these unhappy people, who, lying on the remains of their property, suffered even without a murmur. No cry, no complaint was heard. Both the conqueror and the conquered were equally hardened; the one by excess of fortune, the other by excess of misery."

Many contemporary writers, including Labaume, assert that the conflagration was the deliberate work of patriotic citizens headed by Count Rostopchin, governor of Moscow. The latter certainly spoke of such a project, and according to the twenty-fifth bulletin of the Grand Army three hundred incendiaries provided with appliances for setting fire to the wooden houses were arrested and shot. As the Count afterwards denied the story it is difficult to say whether he actually carried into practice what he preached; it is quite possible that some of those who were left behind had actually more to do with the affair than the supposed prime mover. Professor Eugen Stschepkin, of the Imperial University of Odessa, says that "Moscow was burnt neither by Napoleon nor by Count Rostopchin. Probably, the fire was in part accidental, and due to plunderers, both Russian and French; in part the deliberate work of patriotically-minded inhabitants." The conclusions of Mr Hereford B. George are: "On the face of the undoubted facts there is no adequate evidence that the burning of Moscow was deliberate, though there is of course no evidence that it was not."

Napoleon now hoped that Alexander would negotiate with him for peace. The unexpected happened; the Czar showed the most determined resolution. He realised that the entry into Moscow would have smaller effects upon the final results of the campaign than the twin evils of winter and famine which must necessarily follow unless what remained of the Grand Army beat a speedy retreat. As for his own troops, they were constantly reinforced, and had the additional advantage of being hardened to the severe climate and the peculiar nature of the country. Moreover many of the peasants, following the example of the Tyrolese and the Spaniards, waged a savage guerrilla warfare whenever they had an opportunity.

CHAPTER XXX
THE MARCH OF HUMILIATION
(1812)

FOR several weeks the Emperor remained in Moscow anxiously awaiting what he hoped would be a favourable answer to his proposals to Alexander. "I am blamed," he said, according to Ségur, "for not retreating; but those who censure me do not consider that it requires a month to reorganise the army and evacuate the hospitals; that, if we abandon the wounded, the Cossacks will daily triumph over the sick and the isolated men. A retreat will appear a flight; and Europe will re-echo with the news. What a frightful course of perilous wars will date from my first retrograde step! I knew well that Moscow, as a military position, is worth nothing; but as a political point its preservation is of inestimable value. The world regards me only as a general, forgetting that I am an Emperor. In politics, you must never retrace your steps: if you have committed a fault, you must never show that you are conscious of it; error, steadily adhered to, becomes a virtue in the eyes of posterity."

The Czar refusing to treat with the enemy at Moscow, Napoleon offered in his desperation to withdraw his opposition to Russian plans regarding Constantinople, hitherto the cause of so much bitterness—all to no purpose. Alexander remained as adamant, and having previously told Sir Robert Wilson, the British commissioner, that he would sooner dig potatoes in Siberia than negotiate while a French soldier remained in Russian territory, neither went back on his word nor regretted it. European affairs were far too unsettled for Napoleon to take up winter quarters. There was no alternative but to order a retreat, to "pocket his pride," as schoolboys say. So the march which he knew must humiliate him in the sight of both his allies and his enemies was begun with what speed was possible in the circumstances.

Gallant and gay they marched along,
Fair Russia to subdue.
Sneaking and sad they back return,
While brave Cossacks pursue.

Cossacks in clouds, and crows and kites,
Surround them as they go,
And when they fall and sink in death,
Their winding sheet is snow.

Thus run two stanzas of a poem written in the manner of the famous "John Gilpin" and published in London. If it is not particularly good poetry it is true history. At first Napoleon hoped by marching southward to find territory less devastated and poverty-stricken than that through which he had passed. In this he was frustrated by a conflict which took place between Eugène's corps and the army under Kutusoff. The Viceroy of Italy captured Malojaroslavetz only to find that he had won a barren victory at extreme cost, leaving the Russians posted securely on the hills at the back of the ruined town. The Emperor had wished to push on; the enemy's position prevented it. Had he known that Kutusoff had previously arranged to retreat if he were attacked, Napoleon would not have hesitated. He weighed the matter in his own mind and discussed it with his Marshals, finally coming to the conclusion that his army must of necessity retire by the road along which it had advanced, or in the expressive terms of Labaume, via "the desert which we ourselves had made."

Werestchagin's picture of the retreat conveys some idea of the tragedy. There is the stern and unbending Emperor wearing the crown of fir cones which he wore at this time, and followed by his dejected staff and the empty carriage. We can almost hear the crunch of the snow as it powders under foot, catch the low murmurings of the disillusioned men as they trudge along the uneven roadway, and feel the icy grip and stinging smart of the cruel wind. And yet the artist's conception, vivid beyond question, cannot bring home to us a tithe of the terrors and misery of that awful march. Horses stumbled and perished, men fell by the wayside and died of hunger and cold, some flung away their arms in sheer despair, others tramped on like machines, cognisant only of the bitter blast which froze their moustaches and whistled through their tattered garments.

According to Labaume, the first snow fell on the 6th November, when the army was tramping towards Smolensk comforted by the thought that in three days they would reach their destination and secure some kind of rude shelter, "when suddenly the atmosphere, which had hitherto been brilliant, was clouded by cold and dense vapours. The sun, enveloped by the thickest mists, disappeared from our sight, and the snow falling in large flakes, in an instant obscured the day, and confounded the earth with the sky. The wind, furiously blowing, howled dreadfully through the forests, and overwhelmed the firs already bent down with the ice; while the country around, as far as the eye could reach, presented unbroken one white and savage appearance.

"The soldiers, vainly struggling with the snow and the wind, that rushed upon them with tempestuous violence, could no longer distinguish the road; and falling into the ditches which bordered it, there found a grave. Others pressed on their journey, though scarcely able to drag themselves along. They were badly mounted, badly clothed, with nothing to eat, nothing to drink, shivering with cold, and groaning with pain. Becoming selfish through despair, they afforded neither succour nor even one glance of pity to those who, exhausted by fatigue and disease, expired around them. On that dreadful day, how many unfortunate beings, perishing by cold and famine, struggled hard with the agonies of death! We heard some of them faintly bidding adieu to their friends and comrades. Others, as they drew their last breath, pronounced the name of their mothers, their wives, their native country, which they were never more to see; the rigour of the frost seized on their benumbed limbs, and penetrated through their whole frame. Stretched on the road, we could distinguish only the heaps of snow that covered them, and which, at almost every step, formed little undulations, like so many graves. At the same time vast flights of ravens, abandoning the plain to take refuge in the neighbouring forests, croaked ominously as they passed over our heads; and troops of dogs, which had followed us from Moscow, and lived solely on our mangled remains, howled around us, as if they would hasten the period when we were to become their prey.

"From that day the army lost its courage and its military attitude. The soldier no longer obeyed his officer; the officer separated himself from his general; the disbanded regiments marched in disorder; searching for food, they spread themselves over the plain, pillaging whatever fell in their way. No sooner had the soldiers separated from the ranks, than they were assailed by a population eager to avenge the horrors of which it had been the victim. The Cossacks came to the succour of the peasants, and drove back to the great road, already filled with the dying and the dead, those of the followers who escaped from the carnage made among them."

Marshal Ney defending the Rearguard

By Adolphe Yvon

By permission of Braun, Clément & Co., Dornach (Alsace)

At the little town of Dorogobuï, previously burnt by the Emperor's orders, practically no comfort could be obtained. "The few houses that remained," says Labaume, "were occupied exclusively by a small number of generals and staff-officers. The soldiers who yet dared to face the enemy, had little shelter from the rigours of the season, while the others, who had wandered from their proper corps, were repulsed on every side, and found no asylum in any part of the camp. How deplorable was then the situation of these poor wretches! Tormented by hunger, we saw them run after every horse the moment it fell. They devoured it raw, like dogs, and fought among themselves for the mangled limbs. Worn out by want of sleep and long marches, they saw nothing around them but snow; not one spot appeared on which they could sit or lie. Penetrated with the cold, they wandered on every side to find wood, but the snow had caused it entirely to disappear; if perchance they found a little, they knew not where to light it. Did they discover a spot less exposed than others, it afforded them but a momentary shelter, for scarcely had their fire kindled, when the violence of the wind extinguished it, and deprived them of the only consolation which remained in their extreme distress. We saw crowds of them huddled together like beasts at the root of a beech or pine, or under a waggon. Others were employed in tearing huge branches from the trees, or pulling down by main force, and burning the houses at which the officers lodged. Although they were exhausted by fatigue, they stood erect; they wandered like spectres through the livelong night, or stood immovable around some enormous fire."

Smolensk was reached on the 9th November. During the few days that were spent there the soldiers lost all idea of discipline and pillaged the rations, with the result that while some had plenty others starved. After having made his way to Krasnoi, largely owing to the slow advance of the enemy, Napoleon was joined by Eugène and Davout, and on the 19th the ice-bound Dnieper was crossed. Ney and the rear-guard, unable to come up with the Emperor in time, sustained a heavy loss. But they fought on, and when they rejoined the main army the corps had dwindled to such an extent that it numbered but 900 men.

Marching towards the Beresina river, Napoleon gave orders for bridges to be hastily constructed. Although there were frequent delays owing to breakdowns, many of the troops and some of the artillery passed over in safety. Consequently, when the Russians appeared they found the French on both banks. Victor, Oudinot, and Ney, recognising the extremely serious predicament in which they were placed, fought so determinedly that the remaining troops, excepting only Victor's rear-guard and some thousands of undesirable camp-followers, were enabled to cross the river. The undertaking was attended by a frightful loss of life, variously estimated at from 20,000 to 25,000 men. At Smorgoni the Emperor, filled with anxiety for the future of his throne and of France, took leave of his Marshals after telling them that he would raise another powerful army, entered his travelling-carriage and was whirled away to Paris as fast as the horses could draw the lumbering vehicle. Twice he narrowly escaped assassination, and the knowledge of a conspiracy engineered by Malet to shatter the Napoleonic dynasty, as well as of continued disasters in the Peninsula, did not tend to sooth his overwrought nerves. The mighty edifice he had erected seemed to be crumbling away at the very moment when he had hoped to complete it.

The remnants of the Grand Army dragged their flagging footsteps to Vilna, commanded, if that word may properly be used, by Murat. Disaster still dogged them, their strength grew feebler and feebler. Only 100,000 troops, chiefly consisting of those under Schwarzenberg and Macdonald, returned to their native land. Doubtless the survivors thought sadly of the fate of half a million comrades, some of whom still lived as prisoners or wanderers, while the majority lay stiff and gaunt on the plains and in the forests of victorious Russia, their winding-sheet the snow. At least 150,000 of the enemy kept them company in death. No priest gave them holy sepulture, but the crows cawed a funeral requiem.

CHAPTER XXXI
THE BEGINNING OF THE END—
THE LEIPZIG CAMPAIGN (1813)

"THE Colossus," said the Abbé Juda to Wellesley, "has feet of clay. Attack it with vigour and resolution, and it will fall to pieces more readily than you expect."

In the early days of 1813 the Iron Duke's opportunity for following the advice of the far-seeing Abbé was not yet come. Prussia, little down-trodden and despised Prussia, with a population of scarcely more than four and a half millions, was to pave the way for the liberation of Europe. When Napoleon had humbled the kingdom by the creation of the Confederation of the Rhine and fixed the Prussian army at the absurdly low number of 40,000 men—a mere handful compared with his own immense armament—he expected no further trouble from King Frederick William III. The Emperor understood the character of the monarch well enough, and he knew sufficient of Stein's patriotic ideals to insist on his dismissal from office. But such a spirit as Stein's was not to be easily curbed. Napoleon, instead of pouring water on the former Minister's zeal had simply added fuel to the flames. Stein, free from the exacting cares of State, proved to be more dangerous than before. He and Sir Robert Wilson had fortified the failing courage of Alexander when Napoleon awaited the Czar's peace overtures in the Kremlin; he and others now came to the aid of their own king, and like Aaron and Hur who held up the feeble arms of Moses at the battle of Rephidim, gave strength to the wavering faith of Frederick William III. There is much truth in Treitschke's statement that "Every step which has been taken in this (the 19th) century towards German unity, has been the realisation of some thought of Stein's."

The conditions of life in Prussia had improved immensely since Jena. Before that decisive defeat it was a land of castes, just as India is to-day, and the agricultural classes serfs, as were the peasants of France before the Revolution. Civilised slavery was now abolished; there was a revival of learning; most important of all, for practical purposes at the moment, there was a revival of patriotism.

Public opinion in Prussia was against Napoleon, but moral force alone could not prove his undoing. Fortunately the country possessed a military genius in Scharnhorst, who had caused thousands of men to pass through the army while it still retained the normal strength allowed by the Emperor of the French. Recruits took the place of the efficient, and after necessary training, made way for others. This is the secret of the 150,000 trained men whom the King of Prussia had at his call.

An incident which did much to bring on the crisis which was felt to be imminent on all sides was the desertion to the Russians of the Prussian corps under General York. In the retreat from Russia, York was in command of Macdonald's rear-guard. The Marshal, leading the centre, duly arrived at Tilsit, opened communications with Königsberg, and waited for York. At first Macdonald thought that the Prussian General had met with misfortune on the road, then rumour whispered of treachery, and finally an officer who had been testing the ice on the river informed him that he had seen the Prussians rapidly re-cross the Niemen. "Good Heavens!" Macdonald exclaimed as the full force of the blow became apparent to him, "we are betrayed—perhaps given up; but we will sell our lives dearly." His feeble forces, however, made their way through the dense forest of Bömwald, and after a sharp skirmish at Labiau, reached Königsberg. From thence they marched to Elbing, crossed the frozen Vistula, and were soon within sight of the fortress of Danzig. Here Macdonald handed over his command to General Rapp, the Governor, and shortly afterwards was recalled to Paris to assist in the organisation of new army corps. During an interview the Emperor frankly admitted that he had been misled as to Prussia's policy, and that the campaign they were about to undertake would be "the last." "He added," says Macdonald, "that he put implicit trust in his father-in-law, the Emperor of Austria. 'Beware!' I answered. 'Do not trust the clever policy of that Cabinet.'" There was considerable justification for this remark; the Austrian contingents had played but a half-hearted part in the Russian campaign.

What York had done was to take matters into his own hands and come to terms with the Russians because he feared for the safety of his troops. Diebitsch, the commander who suggested a conference, really played a very good game of bluff. He had told York that he was intercepted, whereas the Prussian forces were over seven times as strong as his own! However, they arranged that the district around Memel and Tilsit should be neutral territory until the Prussian monarch's decision should be received. "Strictly considered," says Dr J. Holland Rose, "this Convention was a grave breach of international law and an act of treachery towards Napoleon. The King at first viewed it in that light; but to all his subjects it seemed a noble and patriotic action. To continue the war with Russia for the benefit of Napoleon would have been an act of political suicide."

By a treaty ably engineered by the sleepless Stein and signed on the 27th February 1813, Prussia finally decided to throw down the gauntlet and join Russia against Napoleon. In the following June Prussia promised to raise 80,000 men for a subsidy of £700,000 from Great Britain, Russia supplying double the number of troops for £1,400,000. Even Sweden deserted the Emperor in March by agreeing to bring 30,000 men into the field in return for a subsidy of £1,000,000 per annum from England and the cession of Guadaloupe. Austria, while still pretending to be friendly to the French cause, came to a secret understanding with Russia in January 1813 for the cessation of hostilities. Afterwards overtures for peace were made to Napoleon by a Congress held at Prague in July.5 "Napoleon," says Mignet, "would not consent to diminished grandeur; Europe would not consent to remain subject to him."

---

5 See also p. 299.

When Napoleon heard of the defection of Prussia he muttered, "It is better to have a declared enemy than a doubtful ally"; as he left St Cloud at dawn on the 15th April for the headquarters of the army after having appointed the Empress regent during his absence, he said, according to Caulaincourt, "I envy the lot of the meanest peasant of my Empire. At my age he has discharged his debt to his country, and he may remain at home, enjoying the society of his wife and children; while I—I must fly to the camp and engage in the strife of war. Such is the mandate of my inexplicable Destiny."

While the French were growing tired of the ceaseless struggle, they had nobly supported the Emperor in his appeal for soldiers to fill the gaps in the ranks caused by the campaign of 1812. No fewer than 350,000 conscripts were voted, cities gave liberally and equipped volunteer regiments, the people still seemed to be fascinated by his genius and afraid of incurring his displeasure. But the army for the first Saxon campaign was unlike the old army. There were too many youths in it, fellows brave enough no doubt but unused to the rough life of field and camp. Fortunately for the Emperor the best of his officers had survived, and although Murat called his brother-in-law a madman, they still believed in his sanity and ability. Had the King of Naples termed Napoleon imprudent there would have been more justification in his remark, for his constant warfare tended to become an obsession. "I grew up in the field," he told Metternich, "and a man like me troubles himself little about the lives of a million of men." This was not the Napoleon of the Italian campaign, but a gambler, a man who put his trust in material forces rather than in carefully-chosen strategic positions, and swift, decisive strokes. De Fezensac had noted Napoleon's lack of care in the Polish campaign. "The order," he says, "must be executed without waiting for the means.... This habit of attempting everything with the most feeble instruments, this wish to overlook impossibilities, this unbounded assurance of success, which at first helped to win us advantages, in the end became our destruction."

At the opening of the campaign Russia and Prussia bore all the fighting for the allies, their forces numbering 133,000. Kutusoff, until his death in the early stages of the war, took command of the combined forces; the right wing being under Wittgenstein, who succeeded him; the left wing under Blücher. In point of numbers Napoleon was far ahead, having some 200,000 troops at his disposal, divided into the Army of the Elbe of 60,000, the Army of the Main of about 105,000, and 40,000 Italians and Bavarians. The Emperor's first step was to occupy Leipzig, not a difficult movement seeing that he had 145,000 men, while the Allies had only 80,000 to bring to bear on any one point. The headquarters of the latter were at Dresden. On the 3rd May 1813, two days after an action at Weissenfels in which Marshal Bessières was killed by a cannon-ball, the battle of Gross-Görschen (sometimes called Lützen) was fought, the Russian and Prussian soldiers selling their lives dearly for the cause they had so much at heart, indeed they lost considerably less in killed and wounded than the enemy. There was a disposition on the part of some of the French conscripts to run away at the first taste of real warfare, but when Napoleon approached and said, "Young men, I reckoned on you to save the Empire, and you fly!" they took heart and fought as valiantly as the veterans. Both the Emperor of Russia and the King of Prussia watched from an adjacent hill the great sea of men contest the cluster of villages around which the battle centred. It was not until Napoleon brought up reinforcements that the fate of the day was decided in his favour, no fewer than four of the five villages having fallen into the hands of the Allies, who now retreated towards Dresden. Even then the fiery old Blücher—he was over seventy—could not resist a cavalry charge within an hour of midnight.

Sir Charles Stewart, the British Minister at the headquarters of Frederick William III., thus records this desperately contested battle, the prelude to what is usually called the first Saxon Campaign:

"A very brisk cannonade commenced the action on both sides. The villages of Gross and Klein Görschen were soon set on fire, and taken by the Allied troops, but not without loss. Heavy bodies of cavalry were sent to the left to prevent the enemy from turning that flank; and the Allied troops were frequently drawn within the enemy's fire without producing the effect their exertions merited. The villages alluded to, when taken, afforded no solid advantages, as the enemy were equally strongly posted, barricaded, and entrenched in adjoining ones.

"The cavalry of the Allies[6] (more especially the Prussians) advanced often so rapidly upon the French infantry that they could not get back to the strong villages from whence they had debouched, and they consequently received the charges of the enemy in squares. Great slaughter ensued, and the Prussian cavalry inspired their allies the Russians with the greatest confidence and admiration. The action continued in a struggle for the different villages of Lützen, the Görschens, and Geras, which were taken and retaken several times, the Görschens remaining, however, always in the hands of the Allies. Towards the close of the day, however, a very strong column arrived from Leipzig, belonging to Beauharnais' corps, which threatened the right of the Allies, and prevented their making further progress. They remained on the ground they had so gallantly fought over, masters of the field of battle. The Emperor of Russia, the King of Prussia, the Princes of Prussia were present, animating the troops by the greatest display of personal exertions and bravery.

6 Napoleon's cavalry was very weak in this campaign owing to the dearth of horses due to losses in the Russian campaign.

"The result of the battle was the capture of sixteen pieces of cannon, some standards, and some hundreds of prisoners. The battle lasted from ten o'clock in the morning till dark. It is very difficult to obtain any correct information as to the loss of the enemy. That of the Allies may be estimated at about 12,000 Prussians and 3,000 Russians *hors de combat*. The main efforts in the action fell upon General Blücher's corps, who was himself wounded, as well as the chief of the Prussian *État Major*, General Scharnhorst,[7] the latter severely. Many most distinguished officers were killed and wounded, among the former the Prince of Hesse-Homburg."

7 He died shortly afterwards, on the 28th June.

As a sequel to this battle Dresden was restored to the King of Saxony, now only too glad to come to terms with his former friend after having abandoned him. Napoleon soon followed up the advantage he had gained by winning a second battle at Bautzen on the 20th and 21st May. The enemy was forced to retire into Silesia, but they did so in good order notwithstanding the severe fighting which continued, during which Duroc was mortally wounded. "Farewell, my friend," the Emperor said to the dying general, "we shall see each other again, it may be ere long!" He was so affected by the distressing scene that he refused to transact any further military business that day. "Everything to-morrow," was the only answer he would vouchsafe to his astonished aides-de-camp.

An armistice was now arranged, Austria making further overtures for peace which it would have been wise for the Emperor to have accepted, especially as they were by no means so preposterous as he made them out to be. Briefly stated, the principal conditions were that the boundaries of the Empire should be fixed at the Rhine, that Germany should be evacuated and the title of Protector of the Confederation of the Rhine given up, the handing over of Hamburg, Lübeck, and Bremen, and the partition of unfortunate Poland once again between Austria, Prussia, and Russia. Napoleon was scarcely civil to Metternich, the Austrian Minister who was charged with the delicate mission. "But I know what you desire in secret," he said in his abrupt manner. "You Austrians desire to get Italy entirely to yourselves; your friends the Russians desire Poland; the Prussians are set on Saxony; the English on Belgium and Holland. And if I yield to-day, you will to-morrow demand of me those the objects of your most ardent desires. But before you get them, prepare to raise millions of men, to shed the blood of many generations, and to come to treat at the foot of Montmartre. Oh, Metternich, how much has England given you to propose such terms to me?"

"You persist then," the Emperor concluded after a fierce war of words, "in bidding me defiance; you will give the law to me? Be it so! Let it be war, and the field of combat Vienna."

As a result of the armistice Austria threw in her lot with Russia, Prussia, and Sweden, whose combined forces consequently outnumbered those marching with the French colours. Now began a long series of engagements in quick succession, the most important being the battle of Dresden between the troops under Napoleon and Schwarzenberg on the 27th August, which ended in the retreat of the Allies, and the defeat of the French at Kulm, where 10,000 prisoners were taken. After Dresden the Emperor ordered the pursuit of the dejected Russo-Prussian columns, but it was not carried out with sufficient energy to achieve decisive results.

Napoleon suddenly decided to return to Dresden, for what reason is unknown; some authorities aver that he was taken ill. It seemed as though the French had lost their prowess; Macdonald met with disaster, Ney failed at Dennewitz when victory seemed in his grasp, Reynier was forced to retreat, Bertrand to abandon Wartenburg. Everything was going from bad to worse, but it was not Napoleon himself who met these rebuffs it must be remembered. The Allies were still afraid of him.

The Emperor now concentrated some 190,000 troops on Leipzig, the enemy having at their command a possible 300,000, all of whom, however, were not available at the beginning of the now famous "Battle of the Nations." This lasted from the 16th October till the 19th, and ended in the defeat of Napoleon. During the four days no fewer than 120,000 men were killed or wounded, eloquent proof of the awful nature of the desperate conflict. Deserted by the Saxons, Würtembergers and Bavarians, Napoleon fought his way to the Rhine, crossed the river, and leaving his army, now reduced to about 70,000 men, arrived in Paris on the 9th November. "The close of the campaign," said Mignet, "was as disastrous as that of the preceding one. France was threatened in its own limits, as it had been in 1799; but the enthusiasm of independence no longer existed, and the man who deprived it of its rights found it, at this great crisis, incapable of sustaining him or defending itself. The servitude of nations is, sooner or later, ever avenged." The concluding sentence sums up the whole philosophy of history.

CHAPTER XXXII
THE CONQUEST OF THE CONQUEROR (1814–1821)

THE Allies now had the upper hand beyond the shadow of a doubt. Napoleon the Conqueror—for he has surely as much right to that title as William of Normandy—who had used the greater part of Europe as a parade ground for his matchless legions, who had overturned thrones and founded a dynasty in the modern nineteenth century, had been defeated in two great campaigns. It is difficult to realise that he was now only forty-four years of age, in the prime of life, but "One grows old quickly on battlefields," as he once remarked. His astounding energy, physically if not mentally, was wearing out. Superactivity is a consuming fire.

1814

By J. L. E. Meissonier

By permission of Messrs. Goupil & Co.

Although the Allies had brought the Emperor to his knees, or almost so, there was considerable difference of opinion among them as to their next step. He had lost much; the Confederacy of the Rhine was shattered, the greater part of Germany was unshackled, disasters had occurred in Italy, the British were masters of the Peninsula, yet his enemies wanted more. The Czar and England were the most determined; Prussia, Sweden and Austria were lukewarm. They eventually agreed to give the Emperor another chance, to offer terms humiliating without doubt, but affording him an opportunity of restoring peace to Europe, a blessing long desired but now absolutely necessary. The boundaries of France were to be the Rhine, the Pyrenees, and the Alps. He could accept them or choose the only alternative—war. The proud nature of the man, the memory of former conquests, more especially of the time when Alexander and Frederick William III. had been as so much clay in his hands, made a negative answer practically certain, and accordingly the terms of the Allies were refused.

France was all but exhausted; Napoleon could raise not more than 200,000 troops against the 620,000 men who were with the Allies. Still, he argued, it was worth the risk. The brilliant, dashing days when he could take the offensive were gone, and in its turn Paris was the objective of the enemy. On the 29th January 1814, four days after he had left the capital, Napoleon attacked and defeated Blücher at Brienne; at La Rothière on the 1st February, Blücher having received reinforcements, the reverse was the case, the Emperor losing several thousand men. There was again an offer of peace, more humiliating than before, which met with no more favourable response. On the 10th February the Emperor was victorious at Braye, on the 11th at Montmirail, on the 12th at Château-Thierry, on the 13th at Vauchamp. It was but the final glory of the sun as it sinks below the horizon. In the middle of the following month Wellington, having compelled the French to retire from the Peninsula, after an extremely arduous campaign, crossed the Pyrenees and occupied Bordeaux, while Napoleon fought desperately at Craonne and Laon without decisive result, Marmont's corps sustaining heavy losses. The Emperor now turned his attention to the main army under Schwarzenberg, but was obliged to fall back upon St Dizier. Meanwhile Marmont and Mortier were taking measures for the defence of Paris, upon which the Allies were marching. The Marshals did their best but were overwhelmed, and eventually, acting on the advice of Napoleon's brothers, Joseph and Jerome, arranged an armistice. Paris, the scene of so much splendour and glory under the Imperial *régime*, capitulated. The Emperor, marching to the relief of the capital when it was too late, heard the awful news from some straggling soldiers at a post-house while his carriage-horses were being changed. "These men are mad!" cried the Emperor, "the thing is impossible." When he found that the announcement was only too true, large beads of perspiration stood out on his forehead. "He turned to Caulaincourt," writes Macdonald, "and said, 'Do you hear that?' with a fixed gaze that made him shudder."

Napoleon retired to Fontainebleau and discussed the terrible situation with Oudinot, Maret, Caulaincourt, Ney, Macdonald, Berthier, Lefebvre and others. He asked Macdonald what opinions were held by his soldiers as to the surrender of Paris, and whether they would be willing to make an attempt to regain the city.

"They share our grief," the Marshal replied, "and I come now to declare to you that they will not expose Paris to the fate of Moscow. We think we have done enough, have given sufficient proof of our earnest desire to save France from the calamities that are now crowding upon her, without risking an attempt which would be more than unequal, and which can only end in losing everything. The troops are dying of hunger in the midst of their own country, reduced in number though they are by the disastrous events of the campaign, by privation, sickness, and, I must add, by discouragement. Since the occupation of the capital a large number of soldiers have retired to their own homes, and the remainder cannot find enough to live upon in the forest of Fontainebleau. If they advance they will find themselves in an open plain; our cavalry is weakened and exhausted; our horses can go no farther; we have not enough ammunition for one skirmish, and no means of procuring more. If we fail, moreover, as we most probably shall, what remains of us will be destroyed, and the whole of France will be at the mercy of the enemy. We can still impose upon them; let us retain our attitude. Our mind is made up; whatever decision is arrived at, we are determined to have no more to do with it. For my own part, I declare to you that my sword shall never be drawn against Frenchmen, nor dyed with French blood. Whatever may be decided upon, we have had enough of this unlucky war without kindling civil war."

The Emperor was quite calm; he met his defeat with less apparent concern than in the old days when a minor error had instantly provoked a violent outburst of temper. Taking up a pen he wrote an offer of abdication on behalf of his son. Again and again he endeavoured to win his old comrades-in-arms to his side ere he realised that the game was up. On the 11th April 1814, he signed his own dismissal, making no conditions, surrendering everything.

"The Allied Powers," he wrote, "having declared that the Emperor was the sole obstacle to the re-establishment of peace in Europe, the Emperor, faithful to his oaths, declares that he renounces, for himself and his heirs, the thrones of France and Italy, and that there is no sacrifice, not even that of life, which he is not ready to make for the interest of France."

With mock generosity the Allies gave the former Emperor of the West the tiny island of Elba as his future kingdom, an army of 400 men, and an income of 2,000,000 francs a year—which was never paid. The Empress and her son were granted the duchies of Parma, Placentia and Guastalla and an ample subsidy, and the remaining members of the Bonaparte family had no reason to complain of their treatment.

Napoleon's activity in his miniature possession, which is 17½ miles wide and 12 miles from North to South, has been likened to a bluebottle under a glass tumbler. He certainly imported considerable energy into his administration, erected fortifications, built roads, created a make-believe navy, and annexed the adjacent island of Palmaiola. It was all useful dust to throw into the eyes of those who watched. On the 29th April 1814, Napoleon had set sail for Elba in the *Undaunted*, a British vessel commanded by Captain Ussher; less than a year later, on the 26th February 1815, he stepped on board the French brig *Inconstant* for his last desperate adventure. With 1050 troops he had decided to invade France, to "reach Paris without firing a shot."

He had chosen a favourable time for putting into action the scheme on which he had been secretly brooding. The Allies still quarrelled amongst themselves, the Czar in particular showing a disposition towards the others more warlike than pacific; some 300,000 troops had been released from German fortresses, Spanish prisons, and British hulks, and might rally around him; the Bourbons, who had been replaced in power, were anything but popular, and people were beginning to talk about "the good old times" when the insatiable French appetite for glory had been appeased. On the first day of March the Commander and his little army landed near Cannes and pushed on to Grenoble as quickly as possible. The garrison did not seem particularly anxious to listen to his overtures. Unbuttoning his coat he declaimed to the soldiers, "Here is your Emperor; if any one would kill him, let him fire!" This dramatic appeal was irresistible. The detachment instantly joined him, followed by many others as he marched in the direction of Paris. Peasants who would have heard with unfeigned delight of his assassination ten months before, now saluted and cheered him as he rode at the head of his rapidly increasing army, which included Ney and the 6000 soldiers who had been sent to capture him. The new king deemed it advisable to leave Paris; on the following day Napoleon entered it and was again in the Tuileries. Without losing a moment he began to reconstruct the Government. Great Britain, Russia, Austria, and Prussia, declared him an outlaw, a step less serious than their agreement to keep 600,000 troops under arms "till Bonaparte should have been rendered absolutely incapable of stirring up further troubles." At the commencement of hostilities the Emperor had 125,000 men, the Allies 210,000.

Of Napoleon's campaign in Belgium little need be said. It was short and it was decisive. On the 16th June 1815, he won his last victory at Ligny, where he defeated the Prussians under Blücher, Wellington gaining the battle of Quatre Bras against Ney. Two days later Wellington and

Blücher routed the French on the field of Waterloo. The Iron Duke afterwards told Thomas Creevey that it was "the nearest run thing you ever saw in your life."

The Flight from Waterloo

By A. C. Gow, R.A.

By permission of the Berlin Photographic Co., London, W.

"On the morning of the 18th," relates Sir Hussey Vivian, who led a British brigade, "about eleven o'clock, our advanced posts were driven in, and we saw the enemy's column advancing to attack us.

"The firing soon began, and about one o'clock one of the most desperate attacks I ever witnessed was made on the centre and left centre of our line; this was defeated, and repeated twice, the armies constantly mixed actually with each other, and the French always covering each attack by the most tremendous cannonade you can possibly imagine. With respect to the particular situation in which my brigade was placed, it did not suffer much until towards the last attack; the ground on the left did not admit of the cavalry advancing, and I, being on the left of all, consequently suffered only from the cannonade. About six o'clock, however, I learnt that the cavalry in the centre had suffered dreadfully, and the Prussians about that time having formed to my left, I took upon myself to move off from our left, and halted directly to the centre of our line, where I arrived most opportunely at the instant that Bonaparte was making his last and most desperate effort. And never did I witness anything so terrific: the ground actually covered with dead and dying, cannon shot and shells flying thicker than I ever heard musquetry.

"In this state of affairs I wheeled my brigade into line close (within ten yards) in the rear of our infantry, and prepared to charge the instant they had retreated through my intervals (the three squadron officers were wounded at this instant). This, however, gave them confidence, and the brigades that were literally running away halted on our cheering them and again began fighting. The enemy on their part began to waver. The Duke observed it, and ordered the infantry to advance. I immediately wheeled the brigade by half-squadrons to the right and in column over the dead and dying, trotted round the right of our infantry, passed the French infantry, and formed lines of regiments on the first half-squadrons. With the 10th I charged a body of French Cuirassiers and Lancers infinitely superior to them, and completely routed them. I then went to the 18th, and charged a second body that was supporting a square of Imperial Guards, and the 18th not only defeated them, but took fourteen pieces of cannon that had been firing grape at us during our movement. I then, with the 10th, having reformed them, charged a square of infantry, Imperial Guards, the men of which we cut down in the ranks, and here the last shot was fired—from this moment all was deroute.... I never saw such a day, nor any one else."

In confirmation of the last statement Sir Harry Smith, who also fought under Wellington in this campaign, says "I had never seen anything to be compared with what I saw," excepting only "one spot at New Orleans, and the breach of Badajos." He adds a description of the field as he observed it on the following day:

"At Waterloo," he writes, "the whole field from right to left was a mass of dead bodies. In one spot, to the right of La Haye Sainte, the French Cuirassiers were literally piled on each other; many soldiers not wounded lying under their horses; others, fearfully wounded, occasionally with their horses struggling upon their wounded bodies. The sight was sickening, and I had no means or power to assist them. Imperative duty compelled me to the field of my comrades, where I had plenty to do to assist many who had been left out all night; some had been believed to be dead, but the spark of life had returned. All over the field you saw officers, and as many soldiers as were permitted to leave the ranks, leaning and weeping over some dead or dying brother or comrade. The battle was fought on a Sunday, the 18th June, and I repeated to myself a verse from the Psalms of that day—91st Psalm, 7th verse: 'A thousand shall fall at thy side, and ten thousand at thy right hand, but it shall not come nigh thee.' I blessed Almighty God our Duke was spared, and galloped to my General, whom I found with some breakfast awaiting my arrival." In Sir Harry's opinion "Napoleon fought the battle badly, his attacks were not simultaneous, but partial and isolated, and enabled the Duke to repel each by a concentration."

A fleeting glimpse of the fallen Colossus as he rushes towards Paris is afforded us by Alexandre Dumas, then staying with his mother at the posting-house of Villers-Cotterets, about fifty-five miles from the capital. The novelist had seen the Emperor pass through the little town before the crushing conflict. He had then been accompanied by General Letort and Jerome Bonaparte. Says Dumas:

"At seven o'clock a courier arrived; he was covered with mud, his horse shook from head to foot, and was ready to drop with fatigue. He ordered four horses to be ready for a carriage which was following him, then he leapt on his horse and set off on his journey again.

"It was in vain we questioned him; he either knew nothing or would not say anything.

"The four horses were taken out of the stables and harnessed in readiness for the carriage: a rapidly approaching heavy rumble announced it was coming, soon we saw it appear round the corner of the street and draw up at the door.

"The master of the post came forward and stood stupefied. I took hold of his coat tails and asked: 'It is he? the Emperor?'

"'Yes.'

"It was indeed the Emperor, just in the same place and carriage, with one aide-de-camp near him and one opposite him, as I had seen him before. But his companions were neither Jerome nor Letort. Letort was killed, and Jerome was commissioned to rally the army by Laon.

"It was just the same man, it was just the same pale, sickly, impassive face, but his head was bent a little more forward on his chest.

"Was it merely from fatigue, or from grief at having staked the world and lost it?

"As on the first occasion, he raised his head when he felt the carriage pull up, and threw exactly vague look around him which became so penetrating when he fixed it upon a person or scanned the horizon, those two unknown elements behind which danger might always lurk.

"'Where are we?' he asked.

"'At Villers-Cotterets, sire.'

"'Good! eighteen leagues from Paris?'

"'Yes, sire.'

"'Go on.'"

In his second abdication, signed on the 22nd June, the Emperor declared that his public life was finished, and proclaimed his son as Napoleon II., Emperor of the French. But the child for whom his father had anticipated so glorious a career in 1811, who had been born with the mighty title of King of Rome, was never destined to wear the crown of France. That insignia of royal rank was donned once more by Louis XVIII.

The mighty conqueror had run his course. He threw himself on the mercy of the nation to which he had shown no mercy, and which he had hated with exceeding hatred. Great Britain consigned him to the island rock of St Helena, far away on the broad bosom of the Atlantic, and in the well-known picture by the late Sir W. Q. Orchardson, "Napoleon on the 'Bellerophon,'" we see Napoleon taking his final farewell of France. He stands alone, bearing, in place of the weight of Empire, the almost insupportable burden of shattered hopes. Gone dynasty and throne and kindred, everything that was worth while in his complex life, but the Imperial Dignity will never be discarded. He remains Napoleon the Great. The rigidity of the mouth and the stern and unbending demeanour tell you that the will is still unconquered.

Napoleon on Board the "Bellerophon"

By Sir W. Q. Orchardson, R.A.

By permission of the Berlin Photographic Co., London, W.

His "star" had led him far from insignificant Ajaccio and was now leading him still further. Unknown lad, cadet, lieutenant, general, emperor, statesman, constructor, destructor, he had been all, and more. Destiny had now set him a far more difficult task, namely, to reign over himself. In this he was perhaps less successful than myriads who have gone down to the grave in silence, and whose names find no place in the printed page or the scrolls of history. In lonely St Helena, isolated from other human habitation, spied on by soldiers of the army which had done so much to bring about his downfall, but surrounded by a little band of men who refused to desert him in his last days of trial and despair, he spent the remainder of a life which had been lived to the full.

Sometimes his old enthusiasm would revive as he reviewed the history of a campaign, at others he would show the capriciousness of a spoilt child at the over-conscientious sense of duty displayed by Sir Hudson Lowe, the Governor of the island. It is perhaps a more dramatic ending to so marvellous a story than if he had fallen in battle. Many men have met their death in that way, but there has been but one Imperial prisoner at St Helena, the exiled monarch whose soul took its flight on the stormy night of the 5th May 1821.

"The glories of our blood and state
Are shadows, not substantial things;
There is no armour against fate;
Death lays his icy hand on kings;
Sceptre and crown
Must tumble down,
And in the dust be equal made
With the poor crooked scythe and spade."

"I desire that my ashes may repose on the banks of the Seine, in the midst of the French people I have loved so well," wrote Napoleon in his will, and the nation responded with emotion to the wish of its great Son. They forgot that he had lavished French treasure and resources as a spendthrift, that his insane ambitions had brought them financial and political ruin; they forgave him that he had led the youth of France to the shambles and had bereaved their homes of fathers, of husbands, of brothers, of sons. They remembered only that he had glorified France, and in the midst of beautiful Paris they raised the most noble Tomb that the genius of modern times has conceived. It is a sacred place of pilgrimage to every son and daughter of France, and men and women of other nations pass, a continual stream, before the massive sarcophagus which—oh, irony of fate!—was hewn out of a Russian quarry, the memorial tribute of Czar Nicholas I. to his brother's mighty antagonist. None who enters that quiet place fails to bow the head before those ashes, and we, too, perhaps from afar, may reflect one moment upon the vanity of human glory and ponder the eternal truth:

"Only the actions of the just
Smell sweet, and blossom in their dust."

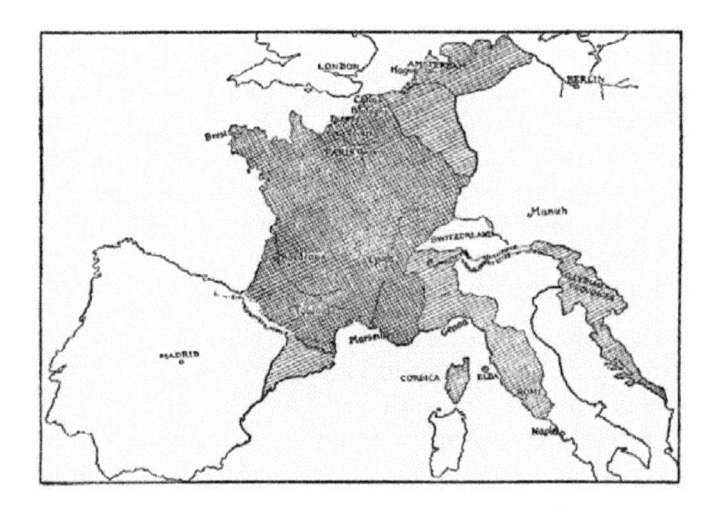

The less deeply shaded portion shows the extent of the French Empire at the height of Napoleon's power. The darker part shows its diminished size after 1815.

Milton Keynes UK
Ingram Content Group UK Ltd.
UKHW030904151124
451262UK00006B/1030